STEAM CLASSIC GUIDE

GREAT WESTERN EXPRESS PASSENGER LOCOMOTIVES

THIS ONE'S FOR MICKY.

I've told her before that I can't write a book on needlework
because I don't know a thing about it. I fail to see why
God's Wonderful Railway doesn't have the same appeal for her.

STEAM CLASSIC GUIDE

GREAT WESTERN
EXPRESS PASSENGER LOCOMOTIVES

MARTIN SMITH

ARGUS BOOKS

Argus Books
Argus House
Boundary Way
Hemel Hempstead
Herts HP2 7ST
England

First published by Argus Books 1992

ISBN 1 85486 078 X

Publisher's Note

Although some of the older timetable extracts are not of the best quality they have been included for their historical interest.

Phototypesetting by The Studio, Exeter
Printed and bound in Great Britain by Clays Ltd., St. Ives plc, Bungay

Contents

Introduction

The Great Western Railway was, arguably, the most individual of Britain's railway companies. Never one to follow the herd, the GWR, when it started constructing its lines, plumped for a gauge of 7ft 0 ¼ in despite the fact that the fledgling railways elsewhere in Britain were using a gauge of 4ft 8 ½ in.

For passenger services, the broad gauge was undoubtedly the superior of the two, but the standard gauge lobby was both vociferous and well-supported. One of the strongest opponents of the broad gauge was Robert Stephenson, who relished his reputation as the grandfather of the country's railways, and he was decidedly unwilling to let the southern upstart steal his glory. As the history books show, the Stephenson campaign was the eventual winner but the legacies of the broad gauge included wide trackbeds and comparatively gentle curves and gradients which were ideally suited to fast running.

The GWR also showed its individuality in the motive power stakes and, rather than hire a star name to look after its locomotive department, it recruited Daniel Gooch who, at the time of his appointment, was still looking forward to his twenty-first birthday. Gooch went on to design some remarkable locomotives, not just in broad gauge days but also when the standard gauge had been forced on the West Country. During the nineteenth century, the GWR established a tradition of continuity in the locomotive department and this was to continue for the rest of the company's existence. Gooch's eventual successor was his principal assistant Joseph Armstrong and, from then on, all out-going superintendents were succeeded by their deputies. This tradition ensured that, when a new incumbent took over at the reins, there would not be wholesale changes just so that an ego could be massaged.

The succession of GWR-trained personnel meant, of course, continuity of locomotive development and, by the turn of the century, most of the basic foundations had been laid for the future. When G.J. Churchward took over the top job in 1902, he finished off the foundations. By the time of Churchward's retirement twenty-one years later, standardisation in the locomotive department had reached such a degree that his successors had little more to do than update and enlarge his designs to keep pace with contemporary needs.

Although traffic requirements placed a variety of demands on the locomotive department, it was the express passenger services which took the limelight and, while the GWR usually kept ahead of its rivals, the folks at Swindon did not ignore the competition. The main line between Paddington and Bristol was not the subject of any rivalry but traffic to Plymouth was fought for by the London & South Western Railway. The ocean liner trains were not only profitable but they also had high prestige value, and so the GWR and the L&SWR were often at each other's corporate throats to grab the maximum income and publicity from these services. It was, therefore, the Plymouth services and not the Bristol ones which tended to act as the catalyst for the design of faster and more powerful classes of express locomotives.

The GWR's individuality did not disappear with Churchward's arrival. In the first decade of the new century, Swindon turned out the first express passenger 4-6-0s in England and, as if that weren't enough, Churchward put together Britain's very first 4-6-2. The 4-6-0s started the ball rolling for a long line of superb express passenger engines which was to include the Stars, the Castles and, ultimately, the Kings. The 4-6-2, by contrast, remained a one-off and its story is a good example of the GWR's attitude to its express passenger locomotives. The machine was constructed purely as a public relations exercise, as the company's 4-6-0s were perfectly capable of handling all that was thrown at them. In the 1920s, when other companies started to develop 4-6-2s and milk every possible drop of publicity from them, the GWR calmly rebuilt its own example as a 4-6-0.

The continuity of the development of express passenger locomotives is best illustrated by the members of the Castle class. The first Castle emerged from Swindon in 1923 and, apart from the logical updating of certain components, the design was largely unaltered when the last member of the class was completed twenty-seven years later. The forerunners of the Castles were the Stars and several members of the Star class, including some which were around twenty years-old, were rebuilt as Castles. Wearing their new hats, a number of the rebuilds had an extra quarter century added to their lives.

Whenever the word 'standardisation' is used as a criticism of locomotive design, it is often the GWR which is selected to face judge and jury. That accusation, however, is totally unjustified, particularly when aimed at the GWR's express passenger locomotives. They were very stylish machines and, despite being physically dwarfed by some of their counterparts on other railways, the Swindon designs proved more successful than many other ostentatious creations which were allowed to escape from other company's workshops.

Martin Smith
Coleford
Somerset

CHAPTER 1

The Nineteenth Century

The Great Western Railway was unique. While the other early railway companies in Britain standardised to a gauge of 4ft 8½in, the GWR's chief engineer, Isambard Kingdom Brunel, chose to construct his railway to the gauge of 7ft 0¼in. Supporters of the broad gauge pointed out that, as the centre of gravity of the rolling stock would be lower than on the standard gauge, the speeds, stability and all-round comfort would be far superior. Brunel was, of course, aware that a

The Star class 2-2-2s were designed and built by R. Stephenson & Co. They were intended for the 5ft 6in guage New Orleans Railway in the United States but, when the order was cancelled, the GWR was more than happy to purchase them provided, of course, that they were converted to Brunel's 7ft gauge. *North Star* was the class leader and it was delivered to the GWR in November 1837; although not the first engine on the GWR's books, it became the most celebrated of the early GWR locomotives after hauling the company's first passenger train on 31 May 1838. The locomotive was retired in 1871 and was preserved at Swindon until 1906. For the Stockton & Darlington Centenary Exhibition in 1925, the GWR constructed a replica of the engine using some of the parts of the original and, after the Exhibition, the replica was displayed at Swindon works. It now lives at the Great Western Railway Museum in Swindon.

Photo: Rail Archive Stephenson

different gauge would isolate the GWR from the rest of Britain's embryonic railway network but, modest to the last, he assumed that all of the other railways in the country would adopt his reasoning and, eventually, convert to the broad gauge.

As the history books show, Brunel was a little adrift with his assumption, but the broad gauge did not become totally extinct until 23 May 1892. The GWR was not, however, the only railway company to use the broad gauge. In the West Country, several other companies started life as broad gauge concerns but their reasons for doing so were, in the main, twofold. Firstly, they were engineered by a certain Mr. Brunel and, secondly, there were periods during which they relied on the GWR to provide locomotives to work their lines.

While the GWR's civil engineering was in the capable hands of Brunel, the locomotive department was entrusted to Daniel Gooch a protégé of the Stephenson school. Gooch took up his post with the GWR a few days before his twenty-first birthday and, within three years of his appointment, was designing his own locomotives for the GWR. Prior to the emergence of Gooch's own designs, the GWR's locomotives were supplied by an assortment of outside builders and this policy enabled Brunel and Gooch to analyse the various machines.

The first GWR passenger locomotives were, to be kind, a rather mixed bunch. Between 1837 and 1840, eight different builders delivered a total of forty-nine broad gauge machines and, although a surprising total of ten of these were still in service in the 1870s, eight others did not see the end of 1840. Two of those which had brief lives were constructed by R.&W. Hawthorn to a patent design of T.E. Harrison, and both incorporated the feature of separate frames for boiler and engine. These

TABLE 1.1: ORIGINAL DIMENSIONS OF EARLY BROAD GAUGE 2-2-2 LOCOMOTIVES

	STAR CLASS	FIREFLY CLASS
BUILT:	1837–41	1840–42
WORKS NOS (Stephensons):	149/50/265–74	
(Sharp Roberts):		82/84/85/88/92/95/96/102/104/112
(Jones, Turner & Evans):		18–23
(Fenton, Murray & Jackson):		25–34/41–50
(Stothert & Slaughter):		(a)
(G&J Rennie):		113/36
(Longridge & Co):		11–16
(Nasmyth, Gaskell):		25–32/35–42
WEIGHTS FULL (locomotive):	23 tons 7 cwt	24 tons 4 cwt
(tender):	12 tons 0 cwt	
TENDER CAPACITY (water):	1,000 gallons	
(coke):	1½ tons	
WHEELBASE (locomotive):	10ft 6in	13ft 2in
WHEEL DIAMETER (carrying):	4ft 0in	4ft 0in
(driving):	7ft 0in	7ft 0in
CYLINDERS:	(2) 16in × 16in	(2) 15in × 18in
BOILER PRESSURE:	60 lb/psi	50 lb/psi
HEATING SURFACES (tubes):	655 sq ft	602 sq ft
(firebox):	70 sq ft	97 sq ft
GRATE AREA:	13.6 sq ft	13.5 sq ft

N.B. Several members of each class had detail differences when new.
(a) Stothert & Slaughter did not introduce works numbers until 1860.

TABLE 1.2: NAMES OF FIREFLY CLASS BROAD GAUGE 2-2-2s

1) BUILT BY JONES, TURNER & EVANS (Total 6):

Fireball	*Fire Fly* (*)	*Fire King*	*Spit Fire*	*Wild Fire*
Fire Brand				

2) BUILT BY SHARP, ROBERTS (Total 10):

Falcon	*Hawk*	*Lynx*	*Panther*	*Tiger*
Greyhound	*Leopard*	*Ostrich*	*Stag*	*Vulture*

3) BUILT BY FENTON, MURRAY & JACKSON (Total 20):

Acheron	*Cyclops*	*Harpy*	*Lethe*	*Phlegethon*
Argus	*Erebus*	*Hecate*	*Medea*	*Pluto*
Cerberus	*Ganymede*	*Hyra*	*Medusa*	*Prosperine*
Charon	*Gorgon*	*Ixion*	*Minos*	*Vesta*

4) BUILT BY G.&J. RENNIE (Total 2):

Arab	*Mazeppa*

5) BUILT BY R.B. LONGRIDGE (Total 6):

Jupiter	*Mars*	*Mercury*	*Saturn*	*Venus*
Lucifer				

6) BUILT BY NASMYTH, GASKELL (Total 16):

Achilles	*Centaur*	*Hector*	*Orion*	*Pollux*
Actaeon	*Damon*	*Mentor*	*Pegasus*	*Priam*
Bellona	*Electra*	*Milo*	*Phoenix*	*Stentor*
Castor				

7) BUILT BY STOTHERT & SLAUGHTER (Total 2):

Arrow	*Dart*

(*)The first to be delivered, hence the class name.

TABLE 1.3: STAR CLASS BROAD GAUGE 2-2-2s

NAME	DELIVERED	WITHDRAWN	NAME	DELIVERED	WITHDRAWN
North Star	11/1837	1/1871	*Lode Star*	1/1841	7/1870
Morning Star	1/1839	11/1869	*Rising Star*	3/1841	4/1871
Evening Star	7/1839	6/1871	*Bright Star*	4/1841	4/1864
Dog Star	9/1839	3/1869	*Shooting Star*	8/1841	9/1871
Polar Star	7/1840	7/1870	*Western Star*	11/1841	10/1866
Red Star	8/1840	2/1865	*Royal Star*	11/1841	6/1871

articulated locomotives were delivered to the GWR in 1838. One was an 0-4-0 named *Thunderer* and the other a 2-2-2 named *Hurricane* which had ten-foot diameter driving wheels. The 2-2-2 might not have had the longest of lives but, in 1839, it set a remarkable precedent in that it was recorded as covering the twenty-two and a half miles from Paddington to Taplow in a mere sixteen minutes.

It did not take the GWR long to realise the benefits of standardisation. The oddball locomotives had provided useful lessons in engineering, but the ones which proved to be the most consistent were the twelve Star class 2-2-2s which had been designed and built by Stephensons. Before the last of the Stars was delivered, the first of Gooch's Firefly class 2-2-2s was completed and, by the end of 1842, sixty-two of the Fireflies were in service. On 17 March 1840, the class leader *Firefly* hauled a Director's Special over the thirty-one miles from Twyford to Paddington in just thirty-seven minutes.

Although the Stars had worked at many of the GWR's earliest inaugural ceremonies, the Fireflies notched up a string of notable duties. Queen Victoria's first railway journey was from Slough to Paddington on 13 June 1842 and the locomotive which she ticked off in her Combined Volume was *Phlegethon*. Before the Royal excursion, the first GWR trains from Bristol to Bath and to Bridgwater were both hauled by *Fireball* while *Actaeon* officiated on the first Paddington to Exeter service. The Exeter run of 194 miles each way was made on 1 May 1844 and the locomotive was driven by Daniel Gooch. The outward trip took five hours and, after the invited entourage had indulged in the customary spa water and sticky buns, the return was completed in four hours and forty minutes.

The services south of Bristol were over the tracks of the Bristol & Exeter Railway which, in its formative years, had opted for the GWR to provide the motive power and rolling stock. The broad gauge had, therefore, been laid as a necessity. The GWR also worked the broad gauge Cheltenham & Great Western Union Railway between Swindon and Cheltenham and, for passenger duties west of Swindon, the Firefly class locomotives were augmented by twenty-two Sun class 2-2-2s.

While the Great Western and several other West Country railways pursued the broad gauge, companies in the rest of Britain seemed not to have paid attention to Brunel's prediction that his gauge would become the accepted one throughout the country. The inconvenience of breaks of gauge became the favourite topic of both public debate and letters to *The Times*, and so the Government established a Gauge Commission to look into matters. Comparison tests were instigated between locomotives and trains of the rival gauges and, in every department, the broad gauge Firefly class 2-2-2s won hands-down. This was not the outcome which the Commissioner would have preferred. The standard (4ft 8 ½ in) gauge network that had spread over much of Britain was, by then, so vast that it would have been totally unrealistic, not to mention hazardous, to suggest that it should all be converted to the broad gauge. Perching themselves firmly mid-fence in the best traditions of government commissioners, the officials decreed that, apart from lines which were under construction or already authorised, no further broad gauge lines should be built.

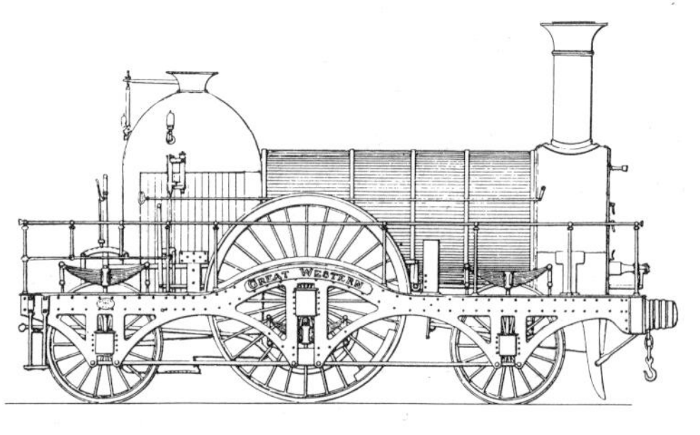

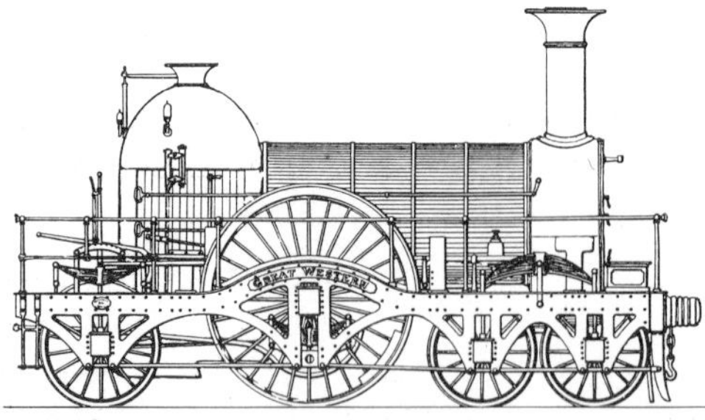

The first locomotive to be constructed at Swindon Works was Gooch's broad gauge 2-2-2 *Great Western*. It was completed in April 1846 but, within a few months, its weight distribution resulted in a fracture of the leading axle and, consequently, the engine was rebuilt as a 4-2-2. In its new guise, it worked express passenger trains until its retirement in December 1870, by which time it had covered over 370,000 miles.

Courtesy: Bill Ling

The Commissioners' report was made in 1846 and, as the broad gauge did not finally expire until 1892, it is obvious that government reports were taken no more seriously in the 1840s than they are in the 1990s. The reaction of Messrs. Brunel and Gooch was the construction of the broad gauge 2-2-2 *Great Western*. The locomotive was the first to be built at the GWR's brand new premises at Swindon and it emerged from the works in April 1846. It had been designed to show what really could be achieved on the broad gauge and, on 1 June 1846, it ran the 194 miles from Paddington to Exeter in 208 minutes. A few months later, six Prince class 2-2-2s were built at Swindon; they were smaller versions of the *Great Western* and were used, initially, on West of England expresses and, later, on fast services to Birmingham.

Between April 1847 and July 1855, twenty-nine 4-2-2s were constructed to Gooch's design and these featured the same eight-foot diameter driving wheels as those used to such effect on *Great Western*. The 4-2-2s were named after the class leader, *Iron Duke*, and they soon became acknowledged as the crack passenger locomotives of the day but, despite this, the class was not without its miscreants. On 30 September 1852, the Directors' Special, which preceded the public opening of the broad gauge line to Birmingham, ran into the rear of another 'pre-

TABLE 1.4: ORIGINAL DIMENSIONS OF BROAD GAUGE SINGLES BUILT AT SWINDON*

	GREAT WESTERN	PRINCE	IRON DUKE
BUILT:	1846	1846/47	1847–55
FRAMES:	Outside	Inside	Outside
WEIGHTS FULL (locomotive):	29 tons 0 cwt	26 tons 2 cwt	35 tons 10 cwt
(tender):			17 tons 4 cwt
TENDER CAPACITY (water):	1400 gallons	1400 gallons	1760 gallons
(coke):			1½ tons
WHEELBASE (locomotive):	16ft 0in	14ft 10in	19ft 6in
WHEEL DIAMETER (carrying):	4ft 6in	4ft 0in	4ft 6in
(driving):	8ft 0in	7ft 0in	8ft 0in
CYLINDERS:	(2) 18in × 24in	(2) 16in × 24in	(2) 18in × 24in
BOILER PRESSURE:	100 lb/psi	80 lb/psi	100 lb/psi
HEATING SURFACES (tubes):	1582.2 sq ft	876.3 sq ft	1797.1 sq ft
(firebox):	151 sq ft	105.9 sq ft	147.9 sq ft
GRATE AREA:	22.6 sq ft	13.7 sq ft	21.7 sq ft

N.B. Some members of each class had detail differences when new.
* Seven Iron Duke class locomotives built by Rothwell & Co.

TABLE 1.5: IRON DUKE CLASS BROAD GAUGE 4-2-2s

Alma (a)	*Emperor*	*Iron Duke* (*)	*Prometheus*	*Timour*
Amazon	*Estaffete*	*Kertch* (a)	*Rougemont*	*Tartar*
Balaklava (a)	*Eupatoria* (a)	*Lightning*	*Rover*	*Tornado*
Courier	*Great Britain*	*Lord of the Isles*	*Sebastopol* (a)	*Warlock*
Crimea (a)	*Hirondelle*	*Pasha*	*Sultan*	*Wizard*
Dragon	*Inkerman* (a)	*Perseus*	*Swallow*	

(*) The first to be delivered, hence the class name.
(a) Built by Rothwell & Co.

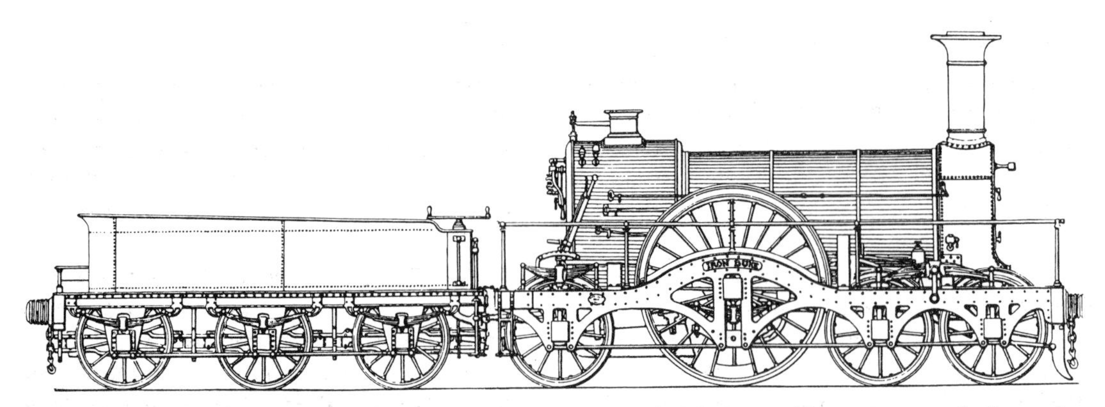

Gooch's Iron Duke 8ft singles were, in their day, the star locomotives on the broad gauge. They were among the first engines to be built at Swindon works and the class leader, *Iron Duke*, was completed in April 1847. The class worked the main express from Paddington to Bristol and Birmingham and one representative, *Lord of the Isles*, was preserved at Swindon until 1906.
Courtesy: Bill Ling

opening' special at Aynho. Fortunately, there were no fatalities and the locomotive *Lord of the Isles*, was repaired and went on to perform a further thirty-two years' service before being preserved at Swindon. *Lord of the Isles* had originally been named *Charles Russell*, but that nameplate was solely for use during display at the Great Exhibition of 1851 and was not used in service. Another member of the class, *Perseus*, was in the news in 1862 when its boiler exploded at Westbourne Park shed; after extensive rebuilding, the locomotive was returned to service and continued its duties until 1880.

It took many years before the GWR had another class of broad gauge express passenger locomotives as celebrated as the Iron Dukes and, fittingly, the engines which took the accolades were renewals of the original 4-2-2s. Between 1871 and 1888, twenty-four 4-2-2s were constructed at Swindon under the category of 'renewals' but, although the first three contained some parts of the locomotives which they replaced, the other twenty-one were brand spanking new. The first of the 1871 renewals to be completed was *Rover* and this engine gave the official name to the class but, when *Iron Duke* itself was renewed in 1873, the old class name was revived, albeit unofficially. The renewal of the 4-2-2s was the last broad gauge construction work undertaken by the GWR and this, itself, was the first such job since 1866. By the time the last of the renewals was completed, the end of the broad gauge was less than four years away.

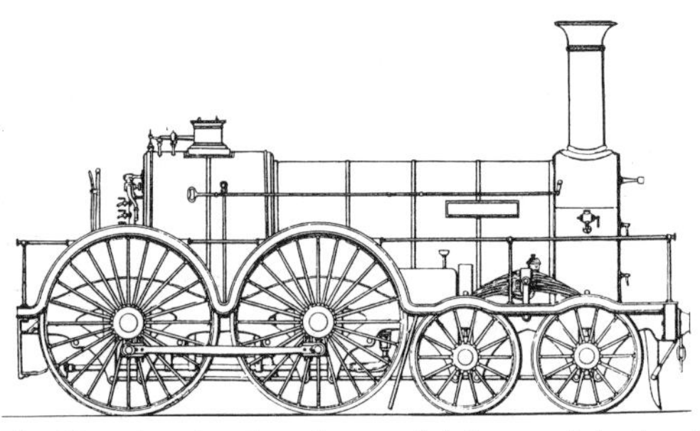

The Waverley class broad gauge 4-4-0s were introduced in 1855 for passenger duties from Swindon to Bristol, Gloucester and South Wales. Designed by Gooch and built by Stephensons, all ten members of the class were put to sleep between 1872 and 1876.
Courtesy: Bill Ling

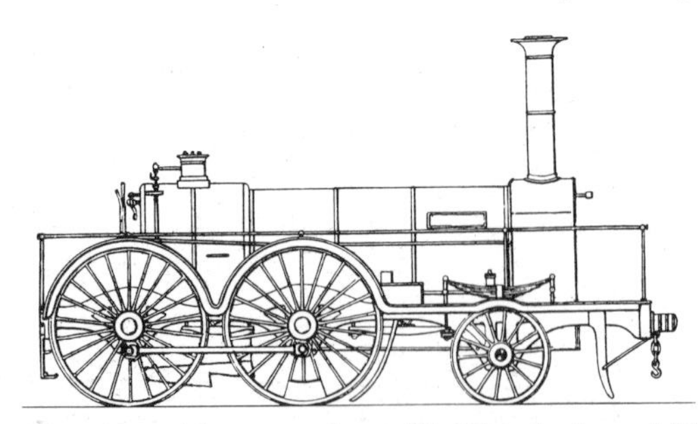

There were eighteen members of the Victoria class; eight were built in 1856 and the rest in 1863/64. They were regarded as lighter versions of the successful Waverley class and, although intended for secondary duties, they had their share of express workings, particularly on the line to Weymouth. One of the class, *Brunel* had the distinction of 'mopping up' after the official extinction of the broad gauge in South Wales in May 1872. As a class, they were all retired between 1876 and 1880.
Courtesy: Bill Ling

The first of the 'new' Iron Duke locomotives emerged from Swindon under the administration of Joseph Armstrong, Daniel Gooch having retired from the hot seat in 1864. Prior to moving to Swindon, Armstrong had been the locomotive superintendent at Stafford Road works in Wolverhampton which was the centre of the locomotive department of the Shrewsbury & Chester Railway when that company had been absorbed by the GWR in 1854; Wolverhampton works and Armstrong himself had been included in the deal. By August 1863, three other standard gauge companies — the Shrewsbury & Birmingham, the Birkenhead and the West Midland Railways — had also been absorbed by the GWR to give Armstrong some more engines to play with.

Armstrong had had to look after more than two hundred absorbed locomotives, and he had also shouldered the responsibility for the design and construction of standard gauge replacements at Wolverhampton. Five of his nine engines had been 2-2-2s which incorporated Gooch-style domeless boilers but, unlike Swindon products, four of Armstrong's 2-2-2s had utilised inside bearings for the driving wheels. After Joseph Armstrong's departure for Swindon, the locomotive department at Wolverhampton was placed in the tender loving care of his brother George and, although locomotive construction continued at the works until 1908, only goods or mixed traffic engines were constructed there.

The GWR's need for standard gauge locomotives was not only to replace those which had been absorbed from smaller companies in the Midlands. Many of the GWR's main lines elsewhere were being laid with a third rail so that they could be used by trains of either gauge and, by the mid-1870s, even the old broad gauge bastion, the run between Paddington and Bristol, was mixed gauge throughout.

In the early years of the GWR's flirtation with the standard gauge, most of the goods locomotives had been constructed at Swindon but the passenger engines had been ordered from outside builders. As early as 1855, Daniel Gooch had ordered four standard gauge 2-2-2 passenger engines from Beyer Peacock and one of these was the very first locomotive to be constructed by the company. Wearing,

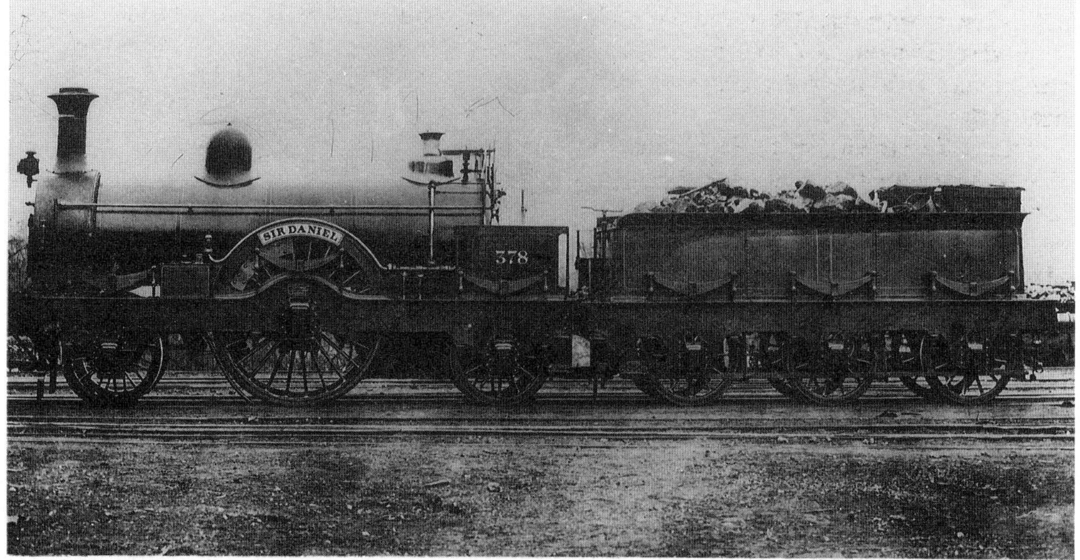

Armstrong's standard gauge 378 class 2-2-2s were built between 1866 and 1869. However, when the class leader, No 378, was named *Sir Daniel* after the recently retired Daniel Gooch, the entire class became known as 'Sir Daniels'. Here, No 378 is seen in its original condition with its number painted on the cabside and only a weatherboard to protect the crew from the elements. There were thirty members of the class and all but seven were eventually rebuilt as 0-6-0s. No 378 was one of those which saw out its days as a single but, in 1898, it claimed the unfortunate distinction of being the first of the class to be retired.

Photo: Rail Archive Stephenson

logically, works No 1, it was delivered on 21 July 1855 and, as the GWR had adopted a numbering system for its standard gauge acquisitions, it was given GWR No 69. Four similar 2-2-2s with 6ft 6in driving wheels were delivered from Beyer Peacock the following year and, as a class, they were drafted on to express services between Paddington and Wolverhampton as soon as the mixed gauge was laid throughout.

The Beyer Peacock 2-2-2s were all renewed between 1872 and 1875 and again between 1895 and 1897; the second bout of major surgery converted them to mixed traffic 2-4-0s. Sharp Stewart supplied ten 2-2-2s in 1862 which, apart from having 7ft 0in driving wheels, were basically similar to the earlier 2-2-2s. These newcomers were also put to work on express services between Paddington and Wolverhampton but, in contrast to

TABLE 1.6: ORIGINAL DIMENSIONS OF EARLY STANDARD GAUGE 2-2-2s

	69 CLASS	157 CLASS
BUILT:	1855/56	1862
MAKERS:	Beyer, Peacock	Sharp, Stewart
WORKS NOS:	1–4/15–18	1329–34/65–68
WEIGHTS FULL (locomotive):	30 tons 6 cwt	29 tons 8 cwt
(tender):		
TENDER CAPACITY (water):	1,800 gallons	1,800 gallons
(coke):		
WHEELBASE (locomotive):	15ft 6in	16ft 0in
WHEEL DIAMETER (carrying):	4ft 0in	4ft 0in
(driving):	6ft 6in	7ft 0in
CYLINDERS:	(2) 15½in × 22in	(2) 16in × 24in
BOILER PRESSURE:		130 lb/psi
HEATING SURFACES (tubes):	1002 sq ft	1121.3 sq ft
(firebox):	109.8 sq ft	119.6 sq ft
GRATE AREA:	13.6 sq ft	14.6 sq ft
TRACTIVE EFFORT (at 85% boiler pressure):		8,082 lb

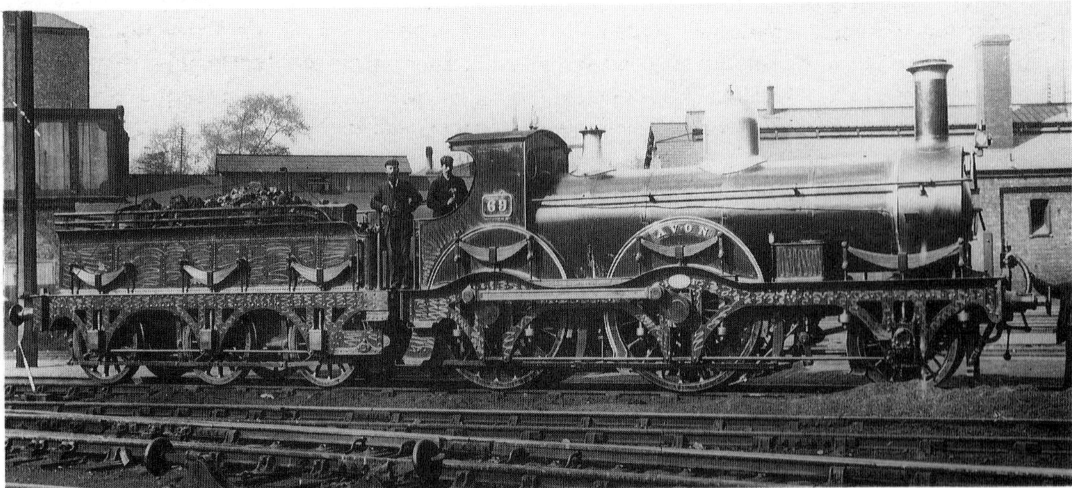

William Dean's River class 2-4-0s were renewals of old Gooch singles. No 69 was renewed in 1896 and was named *Avon*; although intended for secondary work, No 69 and its chums often performed on express duties, particularly in the Bristol Division. This picture was taken just after the locomotive's reboilering of 1902 but withdrawal ensued five years later.
Photo: Rail Archive Stephenson

During the incumbency of William Dean, the Sir Daniel 2-2-2s were modified. In this picture, No 478 proudly displays its brass numberplates and, to the delight of the crews, it also had the luxury of a cab. Unlike most of its classmates, this locomotive was not rebuilt as an 0-6-0 and, when withdrawn in 1903, it was less than thirty-four years old.
Photo: Rail Archive Stephenson

their predecessors, they were extinct by 1881. The first standard gauge 2-4-0 express locomotives built for the GWR were the eight members of the Chancellor class, Nos 149–56, which were constructed by George England & Company in 1862. They were initially put to work on fast trains northwards from Wolverhampton but, in their later years, saw service at Bristol, Hereford and Oxford. The last survivor was No 155 which was retired in 1920 with over one million miles on the clock.

The first express passenger locomotives to be built at Swindon under Armstrong's incumbency were the ten 2-2-2s of the Sir Daniel class which were completed in 1866. The class was boosted by twenty in 1869 and, of the total contingent, four were named. Nos 380/381/471 were christened *North Star*, *Morning Star*, and *Sir Watkin* respectively, all of those names having been used previously by broad gauge locomotives, while the class leader, No 378, was named *Sir Daniel* after the recently knighted Daniel Gooch who had taken a directorship of the GWR. As the mixed gauge reached new territories, so did the Sir Daniels. At first, they had been used on Wolverhampton expresses but they later appeared on fast services to Devon and to South Wales. The doyen, *Sir Daniel*, was withdrawn in 1898 and was the only one not to see the new century. Six others were scrapped between 1900 and 1904 but, remarkably, the remaining ones were converted to 0-6-0s between 1900 and 1902. As such, No 474 went on to become the senior member and lasted until 1920.

Never let it be said that the GWR was a presumptuous company but, in 1873, it named a new locomotive *Queen* so that it would be suitable for future royal duties. Logically, however, the GWR did operate to places such as Windsor and so the company could be assured of royal patronage on a far more regular basis than, say, the South Wales Mineral Railway. The regally-named engine was No 55, a 2-2-2 which was, basically, a larger edition of the Sir Daniels; it was constructed at Swindon in 1873 and twenty similar machines were built two years later. The new members of the class took Nos 999/1000/1116–33 and, eventually, nine were named. Their duties were on express services from London and their destinations were usually Swindon, Gloucester or Wolverhampton but, despite their impressive performances and regal connections, they were eventually rendered obsolete by 4-2-2s and, later, 4-4-0s. All but two of the class were retired between 1904 and 1907 but the survivors, Nos 1124 and 1128, continued to operate from Oxford shed until 1912 and 1914 respectively.

The Queen class 2-2-2s were the last new type of locomotive to be designed by Joseph Armstrong before his death in 1877. It was suggested that he

In September 1873, 2-2-2 No 55 *Queen* emerged from Swindon works and, between March and July 1875, twenty similar engines were built. Somewhat predictably, they became known as the Queen class and the last was to survive until 1914. No 55 itself was treated to several modifications through its career and this photograph shows its condition in 1885, just prior to reboilering.

Photo: H. C. Casserley Collection

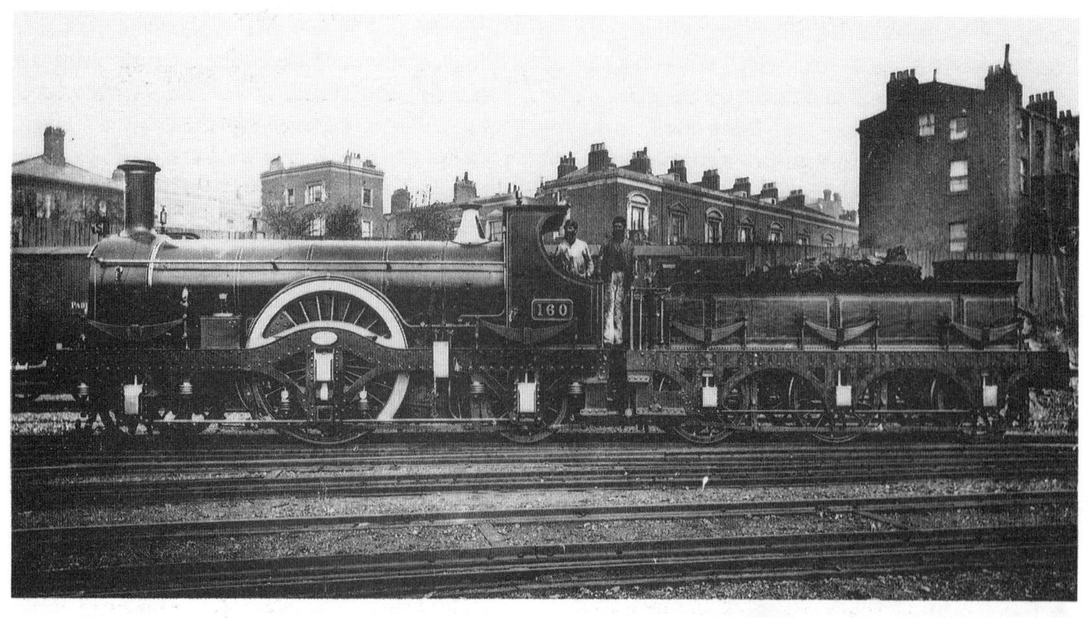

During 1878 and 1879, the ten members of the 157 class of 2-2-s were renewed. This picture shows No 160 during the early 1880s; it received enclosed splashers simultaneously with its first reboilering in 1886. No 160 spent its life as a Wolverhampton engine and worked regularly to London on smartly-timed expresses.

Photo: Rail Archive Stephenson

TABLE 1.7: ORIGINAL DIMENSIONS OF STANDARD GAUGE 2-2-2s

	378 CLASS	QUEEN CLASS	157 CLASS
ALTERNATIVE CLASS NAMES:	Sir Daniel		Sharpie
BUILT:	1866/69	1873/75	1878/79
SWINDON WORKS NOS:	69–78/175–94	482/583–602	814–23
WEIGHTS FULL (locomotive):	29 tons 13 cwt	33 tons 10 cwt	34 tons 14 cwt
(tender):	24 tons 0 cwt		32 tons 10 cwt
TENDER CAPACITY (water):			3000 gallons
(coal):			
WHEELBASE (locomotive):	16ft 0in	17ft 6in	17ft 8in
WHEEL DIAMETER (carrying):	4ft 0in	4ft 1in	4ft 0in
(driving):	7ft 0in	7ft 0in	7ft 0in
CYLINDERS:	(2) 17in × 24in	(2) 18in × 24in	(2) 18in × 24in
BOILER PRESSURE:	140 lb/psi	140 lb/psi	140 lb/psi
HEATING SURFACES (tubes):	1105 sq ft	1155 sq ft	1099.3 sq ft
(firebox):	98 sq ft	128 sq ft	115 sq ft
GRATE AREA:	16.6 sq ft	18.8 sq ft	19.3 sq ft
TRACTIVE EFFORT (at 85% boiler pressure):	9,624 lb	11,016 lb	11,016 lb
**SWINDON WORKS DIAGRAMS:		2-2-2 A/D	2-2-2 B

**This categorisation was not introduced until the early 1900s and was applied in accordance with contemporary dimensions.

TABLE 1.8: QUEEN CLASS 2-2-2s WHICH CARRIED NAMES

NO	NAME	NAME GIVEN	NAME REMOVED
55	*Queen*	9/1873 (*)	6/1905 (*)
999	*Sir Alexander*	3/1875 (*)	10/1904 (*)
1118	*Prince Christian*	3/1875 (*)	7/1905 (*)
1119	*Princess of Wales*	1896	8/1906 (*)
1122	*Beaconsfield*	4/1875 (*)	4/1904 (*)
1123	*Salisbury*	5/1875 (*)	7/1906 (*)
1128	*Duke of York*	6/1893	1897
1129	*Princess May*	6/1893	1898
1130	*Gooch*	1884	1894
1132	*Prince of Wales*	1896	9/1905

(*) Names carried at delivery and/or withdrawal.

had died of exhaustion as, in his thirteen years in charge, he had reorganised operations at Swindon so that the works could cope with the inevitable total transition from broad gauge to standard gauge. The GWR had a policy of continuity of staff and so the man who had been Armstrong's principal assistant, William Dean, was assured of taking over the top job.

The first express passenger locomotives which William Dean designed were ten 2-2-2s with 7ft 0in drivers and they were nicknamed 'Sharpies' as they had originally been intended as renewals of the

1862 Sharp Stewart engines. They were given Nos 157–66 and, for many years, shared the working of almost all the expresses from London to Wolverhampton and Swindon with Armstrong's Queen class singles. The Sharpies were delivered in 1878/79 but, although No 165 survived until 1914, the rest had been withdrawn by 1906.

For express duties north of Wolverhampton and in South Wales, Dean introduced the 806 class 2-4-0s , Nos 806–25, in 1873. Eight years later, the class was augmented by Nos 2201–20 but these tended to be used on secondary services. In 1892/93, the last completely new 2-4-0s were constructed at Swindon and these were, basically, updated versions of the 2201s of 1881 but were intended for express duties. They were given Nos 3232–51 and were used on fast trains to South Wales and between Swindon and Weymouth and, although they were eventually ousted from express turns by 4-4-0s, the class did not become extinct until No 3251 was retired from Oswestry in 1930.

Among Dean's experimental engines were Nos 9 and 10 which appeared in 1881 and 1886 respectively. The former was a 4-2-4T with 7ft 8in driving wheels, which was similar to a batch of Bristol & Exeter Railway express locomotives, but it did not exactly set the engineering world alight and was rebuilt as a 2-2-2 tender engine. This fared little better and was rebuilt again, this time with 7ft 0in drivers, in 1890. When No 10 was constructed, it was similar to the first rebuild of No 9 and, like its predecessor, it was fitted with 7ft 0in drivers in 1890. After the final rebuildings, Nos 9 and 10 were named *Victoria* and *Royal Albert* respectively; the former was put to work on Wolverhampton expresses and the latter retained its original duties on the Swindon run. Both survived until the early years of the next century.

Early in 1876, the GWR's stock list was boosted by over two hundred locomotives and the vast majority were broad gauge machines. This had not, however, been a direct result of Joseph Armstrong's

Dean's 2201 class 2-4-0s of 1881/82 represented a continuation of Armstrong's 806 class of 1873. This photograph was taken at Southall shed and it shows the last of the class to have been built, No 2220, after receiving its Belpaire firebox in 1916. By then, a number of the 2201s had been retired and the survivors had been ousted from express turns by modern 4-4-0s; No 2220 itself was withdrawn in September 1921.

Photo: H. C. Casserley Collection

TABLE 1.9: ORIGINAL DIMENSIONS OF EXPRESS PASSENGER 2-4-0s

	CHANCELLOR	806 CLASS	3232
BUILT:	1862	1873/81–82	1892/93
MAKERS:	George England	GWR	GWR
WORKS NOS:	185–92	462–81 866–85	1341–50 1381–90
WEIGHTS FULL (locomotive):	30 tons 19¾ cwt	32 tons 8 cwt	38 tons 6 cwt
(tender):	22 tons 7 cwt		25 tons 0 cwt
TENDER CAPACITY (water):	1800 gallons	1800 gallons	2500 gallons
(coal):			4½ tons
WHEELBASE (locomotive):	16ft 0in	16ft 9in	16ft 6in
WHEEL DIAMETER (leading):	4ft 0in	4ft 0½in	4ft 1in
(driving):	6ft 6in	6ft 6½in	6ft 7in
CYLINDERS:	(2) 16in × 24in	(2) 17in × 24in	(2) 17½in × 24in
BOILER PRESSURE:	130 lb/psi	140 lb/psi	150 lb/psi
HEATING SURFACES (tubes):	1121.3 sq ft	1216.5 sq ft	1264.9 sq ft
(firebox):	119.6 sq ft	98 sq ft	102.7 sq ft
GRATE AREA:	14.6 sq ft	16.3 sq ft	17.2 sq ft
TRACTIVE EFFORT (at 85% boiler pressure):	8,704 lb	10,298 lb	11,852 lb
**SWINDON WORKS DIAGRAM:	2-4-0 L	2-4-0 D/S	G/Q/A6/A10
**ROUTE AVAILABILITY:	Yellow	Yellow	Yellow
**POWER CLASSIFICATION:		Ungrouped	Ungrouped

**These categorisations were not introduced until the early 1900s and were applied in accordance with contemporary dimensions.

TABLE 1.10: WITHDRAWAL AND FINAL ALLOCATIONS OF 3232 CLASS 2-4-0s

NO	1921 SHED	WDN	LAST SHED	NO	1921 SHED	WDN	LAST SHED
3232	Southall	8/29	Llanidloes	3242	Reading	10/26	Reading
3233	Reading	10/25	Didcot	3243		8/18	Bristol
3234	Wellington	12/26	Wellington	3244	Wolverhampton	9/26	Wellington
3235	Oxford	3/26	Bristol	3245	Didcot	9/26	Winchester
3236	Reading	10/26	Reading	3246	Wolverhampton	9/26	Crewe
3237	Wolverhampton	3/28	Crewe	3247	Slough	10/25	Fairford
3238	Bristol	5/28	Slough	3248	Didcot	9/23	Didcot
3239	Didcot	3/25	Machynlleth	3249	Winchester	2/25	Didcot
3240	Wellington	11/28	Wellington	3250	Reading	2/25	Reading
3241	Didcot	4/27	Winchester	3251	Reading	4/30	Whitchurch

N.B. The allocations reflect that, by 1921, the locomotives had lost their express passenger status.

During the late 1800s, locomotive designers throughout the country became well aware of the success of compound cylinder operation in marine engines. Consequently, experiments with compound railway locomotives became all the rage and, of course, the GWR was not to be left out. In typical Swindon fashion, however, William Dean did not follow the herd blindly. Instead, he opted for a tandem arrangment for the siting of his locomotive's cylinders instead of the in-line arrangement favoured by others. Dean's experimental compound locomotive was No 7 and, after its completion in February 1886, it was based at Swindon for duties to Bristol and Newport. In theory, the tandem arrangement had distinct advantages over the other systems but, in practice, routine maintenance proved laborious as access to those important little places was far from easy. No 7 was withdrawn in 1887 but was renewed as a non-compound 4-4-0 seven years later.

Photo: GWR Museum, Swindon

policies. The windfall was a consequence of the GWR's absorption of the Bristol & Exeter Railway on 1 January and both the South Devon Railway and the West Cornwall Railway one month later. On 1 May 1849, the B&E had started working its own services but, at the outset of its total independence, its locomotive stock comprised just twenty-nine machines, all but one to standard Gooch designs. The return to the Swindon fold must have been quite painful for the B&E, not only because of injured pride after almost twenty-seven years of complete independence, but also because the B&E had been, in its heyday, as great a proponent of the broad gauge as the GWR. It had been with the greatest reluctance that the B&E had laid the third rail between Bristol and Taunton but the company's admission that the standard gauge was taking over was shown by the twenty-five standard gauge locomotives on its books at the time of the GWR takeover.

The Bristol & Exeter's stock of express passenger locomotives at the time of absorption included eight 4-2-2s which were smaller versions of Gooch's Iron Dukes and four 4-2-4Ts which were renewals of older locomotives. The original 4-2-4Ts were coke-burners and had driving wheels of nine feet in diameter. They handled the crack expresses between the company's two outposts and were regarded as some of the fastest engines in the country at the time, one of the class being credited with an 81.8 mph dash on Wellington Bank.

The 4-2-4Ts were designed by the company's locomotive superintendent, James Pearson, but were built by Rothwell & Co. as the Bristol & Exeter's own construction shop in Bristol was not functional until 1854. Prior to his appointment on the B&E, Pearson had held the position of atmospheric superintendent on the South Devon Railway, a post paralleled in later years by the captaincy of the *Titanic*. The original B&E livery was a smartly lined green but this did not meet with the approval of Pearson, who was a devout Quaker. As soon as he was able, he introduced a severe unadorned black for all of the company's locomotives.

In contrast to the Bristol & Exeter's grudging acceptance of the standard gauge, the South Devon Railway's assets at the time of its absorption were 123¼ *miles* of broad gauge track, 600 *yards* of mixed gauge and not one single inch of exclusively-standard gauge line. The South Devon worked the passenger services of the West Cornwall Railway and its contribution to the GWR's stock list in 1876 was eighty-five locomotives, all broad gauge.

The South Devon Railway had problems very early on in its existence when its much-publicised atmospheric system of traction proved to be about as useful as a lifeboat station in Birmingham. The South Devon had to hire locomotives from the GWR in order to extricate itself from the guano but, by 1851, it had started to take delivery of its own machines. Main line passenger services on the South Devon were entrusted to 4-4-0STs and the last of these to be delivered were designed to be easily converted to the standard gauge if, heaven forbid, that should be required. The idea of convertible locomotives was not wasted on Swindon and a total of 111 such machines was constructed by the GWR.

The vast majority of the Swindon convertibles were designed for either freight or branch duties and only sixteen were specifically intended for express passenger work. Five of these, Nos 3501/02/05/07/08, started their lives as 2-4-0Ts in 1885 but were altered to tender engines in 1890 and 1891 to work the newly-inaugurated Cornishman non-stop between Exeter and Plymouth. Of the remaining express convertibles, three were experimental 2-4-0s; one, No 8, was a compound and the others, Nos 14/16, were simples. The compound was a troublesome little beast and was eventually rebuilt as a standard gauge 4-4-0 but, although Nos 14 and 16 behaved themselves, they too were transformed to 4-4-0s in the 1890s. The only really successful express convertibles were Nos 3021–28 which were double-framed 2-2-2s with 7ft 8½in driving wheels; their cylinders of 20in × 24in were the largest ever used on any singles anywhere. They were built in the summer of 1891, very late in the

Daniel Gooch designed locomotives for companies other than the GWR but, admittedly, the railways concerned were either physically or corporately linked to the Swindon empire. The broad gauge Bristol & Exeter Railway was, at first, worked by the GWR but, in 1849, it decided to go it alone. The B&E's first express passenger engines were 4-2-2s which were, basically, smaller versions of Gooch's famous Iron Dukes and twenty were delivered during 1849. The B&E gave them Nos 1 – 20 and, when the GWR absorbed the B&E in 1876, eight were still in service. One of these was B&E No 9 which became GWR No 2008; it was withdrawn in 1889, just three years before the extinction of the broad gauge.

Photo: Rail Archive Stephenson

LINE.														Week Days.
	N.G.		B.G.		N.G.		N.G.		N.G.		N.G.			
	151		152		153		154		155		156		157	
STATIONS.	Portishead Passenger.		Paddington and Plymouth Fast Passenger.		Weston and Highbridge Ordinary Passenger.		Portishead Passenger.		Bristol and Taunton Conditional **Goods.**		Paddington and Weston Passenger.			
	arr.	dep.	arr.	dep.	arr.	dep.	arr.	dep.	arr.	dep.	arr.	dep.		
	P.M.	P.M.	P.M.	P.M.	P.M.	P.M.	P.M.	P.M.	P.M.	P.M.	P.M.	P.M.		
Paddington	....	....	....	5 0	....	....	....	....	....	....	....	6 20	....	....
Swindon ..	..	..	6 50	7 0	..	..	..	..	R	R	8 7	8 17	..	..
N. Somerset J.	....	....	—	—	....	....	....	....	....	....	—	—	....	....
Bristol ..	..	7 20	8 5	8 15	..	8 25	..	8 30	..	..	9 15	9 25	..	..
Pylle Hill	—	—	—	—	—	—	—	—	....	*8 40*	—	—	....	....
Bedminster	7 24	7 25	—	—	—	—	—	8 35	—	—	9 29	9 30	..	..
Malago Siding	—	—	—	—	—	—	—	—	—	—	—	—	....	....
Portishead Jn.	7 30		—	—	—	—	8 40		—	—	—	—	..	..
S. Liberty Sg.			—	—	—	—			—	—	—	—	....	....
Bourton ..	..	..	—	—	—	—	..	..	—	—	9 37	9 38	..	..
Nailsea	....	....	—	—	—	—	....	....	—	—	9 43	9 45	....	....
Yatton ..	..	..	—	—	8 43	8 45	..	..	—	—	9 53	9 55	..	..
Puxton	....	....	—	—	—	—	....	....	—	—	10 1	10 3	....	....
Worle Junc.	..	..	—	—	8 55		..	..	9 14		—	—	..	..
Loop Line { Worle	....	....	—	—	—	—	....	....	—	—	10 7	10 9	....	....
Loop Line { **W-s-M.**	..	....	—	—	9 0	9 3	..	..	*9 20*	*9 50*	10 15	....	..	..
Uphill Junct.	..	..	8 44		9 6		..	..	9 55		..	..	..	..
Bleadon&Up'il	....	....	—	—	—	—	....	....	—	—	....	....	....	....
Brent Knoll	..	..	—	—	—	—	..	..	—	—	..	..	..	..
Highbridge	....	....	8 52	8 53	9 18	....	....	....	—	—	....	....	....	....
Pottery Siding	..	..	—	—			..	..	—	—	..	..	..	..
Dunball	....	....	—	—	....	....	....	....	—	—	....	....	....	....
Bridgwater	..	..	9 3	9 7	..	..	..	..	*10 25*	*10 35*	..	..	..	..
Durston	....	....	—	—	....	....	....	....	*10 50*	*11 0*	....	....	....	....
Chard Junction	..	..	—	—	..	..	..	..	—	—	..	..	..	..
Taunton	....	....	9 24	9 28	....	....	....	....	*11 15*	....	....	....	....	....
Norton Ftzwrn	..	..	—	—	..	..	..	..	..	..	..	..	..	..
Victory Siding	....	....	—	—	....	....	....	....	....	....	....	....	....	....
Poole Siding	..	..	—	—	..	..	..	..	..	..	..	..	..	..
Wellington	....	....	—	—	....	....	....	....	....	....	....	....	....	....
Whiteball Sidg	..	..	—	—	..	..	..	..	..	..	..	..	..	..
Burlescombe	....	....	—	—	....	....	....	....	....	....	....	....	....	....
Sampford Sidg	..	..	—	—	..	..	..	..	..	..	..	..	..	..
Tiverton Junct	....	....	9 55	9 59	....	....	....	....	....	....	....	....	....	....
Cullompton	..	..	—	—	..	..	..	..	..	..	..	..	..	..
Kensham Sidg	....	....	—	—	....	....	....	....	....	....	....	....	....	....
Hele& Bradnch	..	..	—	—	..	..	..	..	..	..	..	..	..	..
Silverton	....	....	—	—	....	....	....	....	....	....	....	....	....	....
Stoke Canon	..	..	—	—	..	..	..	..	..	..	..	..	..	..
StokeCanon Jn	....	....	—	—	....	....	....	....	....	....	....	....	....	....
CowleyBdgJnc	..	..	—	—	..	..	..	..	..	..	..	..	..	..
ExeterTktPfm	....	....	—	—	....	....	....	....	....	....	....	....	....	....
Exeter	..	..	10 20	10 25	..	..	..	..	..	..	..	..	..	..
St. Thomas	....	....	10 27		....	....	....	....	....	....	....	....	....	....
Newton Abbot	..	..	11 3	11 8	..	..	..	..	..	..	..	..	..	..
Plymouth	....	....	12 15	....	....	....	....	....	....	....	....	....	....	....
Penzance	..	..			..	..	..	..	..	..	..	..	..	..

This extract from the GWR's working timetable of October 1886 shows the distinction between the broad gauge and narrow (standard) gauge workings. The 'fast' passenger service from Paddington to Plymouth was timed for 7¼ hours while the 'ordinary' passenger train from Paddington to Weston was scheduled for almost four hours.

The most magnificent single-drivers to appear on the GWR were, undoubtedly, Dean's Achilles class 4-2-2s. Their heritage dated back to 1891 when a class of ten broad gauge convertible 2-2-2s was constructed and these were followed by twenty standard gauge versions in 1892. In 1894, all thirty 2-2-2s were rebuilt as 4-2-2s and the transformation proved so successful that fifty more 4-2-2s were built before the end of the decade. Throughout Britain, single-drivers had previously fallen out of favour as four-coupled designs were found to give better adhesion but, with the development of reliable steam sanding gear in the early 1890s, single-drivers were given a new lease of life on several major railway companies. This picture shows No 3067 *Duchess of Teck* in its full splendour; it was built in December 1897 but withdrawn in December 1914.
Photo: H. C. Casserley Collection

day in view of the impending extinction of the broad gauge, but the number of broad gauge locomotives had been reduced at a greater rate than the route mileage and so the Iron Duke renewals were about the only other engines available for the surviving broad gauge services.

Nos 3021–28 were duly converted to the standard gauge in the summer of 1892, by which time twenty-two standard gauge versions of the same 2-2-2 design had been constructed at Swindon. These took Nos 3001–20/29/30 and had all received names by early 1893. Because of the 7ft 8½in diameter of the driving wheels, the boilers of the 2-2-2s were restricted to a maximum diameter of 4ft 3in and so, in order to generate adequate power, the boilers were elongated. The theory of this might have been sound but, in practice, this additional weight at the front ends made the engines prone to unsteadiness at speed. No 3021 *Wigmore Castle* demonstrated this trait admirably in September 1893 when it became derailed in Box Tunnel. The solution to the problem came in the form of a front bogie and, between March and December 1894, all thirty were converted to 4-2-2s.

The conversion to bogie singles transformed the locomotives into what was acknowledged as one of the most striking designs on any British railway. The prestige value of the 4-2-2s showed as they were always kept in first-class condition and, whether by accident or design, their abundance of brasswork was ready-made for enthusiastic engine cleaners. In the same month as the first was converted from a 2-2-2, the forerunner of an additional fifty 4-2-2s was built and delivery of the entire batch was completed by March 1899. Although the class leader, No 3001, was named *Amazon*, the engines became known as the Achilles class after the name carried by No 3031, the first to be purpose-built as a 4-2-2. The locomotives dominated the fast express services between Paddington and the West Country and, apart from occasional forays into South Wales, the Achilles' were rarely seen elsewhere on the GWR system. The main reason for their initial exclusion from the Midlands was a lack of suitable turntables but, when Stafford Road shed, Wolverhampton, was equipped with a larger turntable in 1900, it enabled the class to be used on Birmingham expresses as well.

Single-driver designs had been synonymous with express passenger haulage since the earliest days of the railways. Their numerous advantages included smoothness of running, coal economy and simplicity of maintenance but the constant increases in the weights of passenger trains had, by the turn of the century, placed severe limitations on their usefulness. The 4-4-0 design had become finely tuned by the end of the nineteenth century and the year 1899 saw the advent of the passenger 4-6-0; with the superior haulage power of four- and six-coupled locomotives, the heyday of the singles was over. The last singles to be constructed for a British railway were the eleven Ivatt 4-2-2s which were built for the Great Northern in 1900 and 1901, while the last to undertake main line passenger duties were the Johnson 4-2-2s of the Midland Railway, two of which survived until 1928.

The GWR's Achilles class 4-2-2s may have been magnificent-looking machines but they were ousted from their express duties with irreverent haste by equally fine-looking and, more crucially, stronger types of locomotives. In February 1908, just nine years after the last of the class had been built, No 3005 *Britannia* and No 3020 *Sultan* were withdrawn and, when No 3050 *Royal Sovereign* and No 3074 were retired in December 1915, the single-wheeler became extinct on the GWR. To add insult to injury, the nameplates from No 3074, which bore the title *Princess Helena*, had been removed in April 1914 so that they could be set aside for the Star class 4-6-0 No 4051.

TABLE 1.11: ORIGINAL DIMENSIONS OF ACHILLES CLASS LOCOMOTIVES

	2-2-2 AS BUILT	4-2-2 AS BUILT
BUILT:	1891/92	1894–99
SWINDON WORKS NOS:	1221–40/61–70	1391–1420/1612–31
WEIGHTS FULL (locomotive):	44 tons 4 cwt	49 tons 0 cwt
(tender):	32 tons 10 cwt	32 tons 10 cwt
TENDER CAPACITY (water):	3,000 gallons	3,000 gallons
(coal):	5 tons	5 tons
WHEELBASE (locomotive):	18ft 6in	23ft 6in
WHEEL DIAMETER (carrying):	4ft 7in	—
(bogie):	—	4ft 1in
(driving):	7ft 8½in	7ft 8½in
(trailing):	—	4ft 7in
CYLINDERS:	(2) 20in × 24in	(2) 19in × 24in
BOILER PRESSURE:	160 lb/psi	160 lb/psi
HEATING SURFACES (tubes):	1342.9 sq ft	1434.3 sq ft
(firebox):	123.9 sq ft	127.1 sq ft
GRATE AREA:	20.8 sq ft	20.8 sq ft
TRACTIVE EFFORT (at 85% boiler pressure):	14,115 lb	12,738 lb
**SWINDON WORKS DIAGRAMS:		A/B/C/D/E/F

**This categorisation was not introduced until the early 1900s and was applied in accordance with contemporary dimensions.

TABLE 1.12: NAMES OF ACHILLES CLASS 4-2-2s

No.	Name	No.	Name	No.	Name
3001	*Amazon* (a)	3028	*Wellington* (b)	3055	*Trafalgar* **
3002	*Atalanta* (a)	3029	*White Horse* (a)	3056	*Timour* **
3003	*Avalanche* (a)	3030	*Westward Ho* (a)	3057	*Tartar* **
3004	*Black Prince* (a)	3031	*Achilles*	3058	*Ulysses* **
3005	*Britannia* (a)	3032	*Agamemnon*	3059	*Voltigeur* **
3006	*Courier* (a)	3033	*Albatross*	3060	*Warlock* **
3007	*Dragon* (a)	3034	*Behemoth*	3061	*Alexandra* **
3008	*Emperor* (a)	3035	*Bellerophon* **	3062	*Albert Edward*
3009	*Flying Dutchman* (a)	3036	*Crusader*	3063	*Duke of York*
3010	*Fire King* (a)	3037	*Corsair*	3064	*Duke of Edinburgh*
3011	*Greyhound* (a)	3038	*Devonia*	3065	*Duke of Connaught*
3012	*Great Western* (a)	3039	*Dreadnought*	3066	*Duchess of Albany*
3013	*Great Britain* (a)	3040	*Empress of India*	3067	*Duchess of Teck*
3014	*Iron Duke* (a)	3041	*Emlyn* **	3068	*Duke of Cambridge*
3015	*Kennet* (a)	3042	*Frederick Saunders*	3069	*Earl of Chester*
3016	*Lightning* (a)	3043	*Hercules*	3070	*Earl of Warwick*
3017	*Nelson* (a) **	3044	*Hurricane*	3071	*Emlyn*
3018	*Racer* (a) **	3045	*Hirondelle*	3072	*North Star* **
3019	*Rover* (a)	3046	*Lord of the Isles*	3073	*Princess Royal*
3020	*Sultan* (a)	3047	*Lorna Doone*	3074	*Princess Helena* **
3021	*Wigmore Castle* (b)	3048	*Majestic*	3075	*Princess Louise*
3022	*Rougemont* (b) **	3049	*Prometheus* **	3076	*Princess Beatrice*
3023	*Swallow* (b)	3050	*Royal Sovereign*	3077	*Princess May*
3024	*Storm King* (b)	3051	*Stormy Petrel*	3078	*Shooting Star* **
3025	*St George* (b) **	3052	*Sir Walter Raleigh*	3079	*Thunderbolt*
3026	*Tornado* (b)	3053	*Sir Francis Drake*	3080	*Windsor Castle*
3027	*Thames* (b) **	3054	*Sir Richard Grenville*		

(a) Locomotives built as 2-2-2s.
(b) Locomotives built as broad gauge convertibles.
** Locomotives renamed; list follows.

Renaming or removal of names:

3017 renamed *Prometheus* in 1895.
3018 renamed *Glenside* in 1911.
3022 renamed *Bessemer* in 1898.
3025 renamed *Quicksilver* in 1907.
3027 renamed *Worcester* in 1895.
3035 renamed *Beaufort* in 1895.
3041 renamed *The Queen* in 1897 and *James Mason* in 1910.
3049 renamed *Nelson* in 1895.
3055 renamed *Lambert* in 1901.
3056 renamed *Wilkinson* in 1901.
3057 renamed *Walter Robinson* in 1901.
3058 renamed *Grierson* in 1895.
3059 renamed *John W Wilson* in 1908.
3060 renamed *John G Griffiths* in 1909. Name removed 1914.
3061 had name removed 1910. Renamed *George A Wills* in 1911.
3072 had name removed 1906. Renamed *Bulkeley* in 1906.
3074 had name removed 1914.
3078 renamed *Eupatoria* in 1906.

From 1837 right up to the end of the century, the GWR's locomotive development had been in the care of just four different superintendents. Admittedly, the company had had a flying start with the young Daniel Gooch, but his engineering and design capabilities had not been his only legacies. Gooch had prepared the ground for a policy of continuity and this was furthered by the Armstrong brothers and William Dean. Unlike most of Britain's other railway companies, the GWR had started out as a passenger company instead of a freight company, and so the services which reaped the maximum benefit from the developments of the 1800s were the express passenger trains. By the mid-1890s, the GWR's motive power for those services outshone that of most other railway companies in Britain but the best was yet to come.

CHAPTER 2

The Four-Coupled Classes

By the end of the nineteenth century, almost every main line railway company in Britain had discovered that bogie 4-4-0s gave reasonable adhesion and adequate power, while keeping axle weights and wheelbases within the limits of the day. Even at the time of the grouping in 1923, 4-4-0s still vastly outnumbered 4-6-0s and one of Britain's most prominent railway companies, the Midland, went to the grouping with all its express passenger services in the care of nothing grander than 4-4-0s.

Necessity had been the mother of invention. Many independent British locomotive builders supplied engines for foreign railways where, quite often, the gradients and curvature of tracks would have sent British engineers rushing for the valium. It was R.&W. Hawthorn who came up trumps in 1854 with a revolutionary design for a tortuously-laid South American railway; their trendsetter was a 4-4-0 with the leading wheels mounted on a bogie. The following year, the GWR introduced its

William Dean's experimental tandem compound 2-4-0 of 1886 was renewed as a simple 4-4-0 in 1894. Still carrying No 7, it was named, at first, *Charles Saunders* although it was later rechristened *Armstrong*. Three other experimental locomotives, Nos 8/14/16, were similarly rebuilt in 1894 and were classified along with No 7 as the 'Armstrongs'. Mechanically, the design of the rebuilds leant heavily on the celebrated 4-2-2s of the 1890s but, of course, the wheel arrangement provided an easily-identifiable differential for even the most myopic observer. Subsequent modifications resulted in the Armstrongs being almost identical to later 4-4-0s and, consequently, they were renumbered in the conventional sequence.

Photo: H. C. Casserley Collection

broad gauge 4-4-0s but, unlike the Hawthorn exports, Gooch's engines had fixed leading wheels. Although various builders persevered with bogie 4-4-0s for overseas markets, the first to appear on a British railway surfaced in 1860 on, most appropriately, the Stockton and Darlington Railway. From that year on, every self-respecting railway company wanted bogie 4-4-0s to play with.

Despite its reputation for engineering ability and innovation, it took the GWR a long time to 'cotton-on' to the advantages of bogie 4-4-0s. It was not until 1894 that the first standard gauge bogie 4-4-0s emerged from Swindon and these were William Dean rebuilds of older engines; the four locomotives were Nos 7/8/14/16 and all had started life as 2-4-0s. Mechanically, the rebuilds utilised similar types of boilers, bogies and double frames to the 3001 class 4-2-2s while, externally, they were very smart machines which set the trend for the cosmetic appearances of future GWR 4-4-0s. They had driving wheels of 7ft 1in and 20in × 26in cylinders; in full working order and paired with a standard six-wheel, 3,000 gallon tender, each locomotive weighed in at 87 tons 11 cwt.

The four rebuilds became known as the Armstrong class and, during their lives, all were subjected to the usual bouts of reboilering and modifications which included the superheating of three in 1911 and the fourth in 1913. The final major modifications were carried out between 1915 and 1923 and these incorporated the fitting of 6ft 8½in driving wheels and 18in × 26in cylinders, similar to the Flower class engines, and so the Armstrongs were reclassified and renumbered 4169-72. In the late 1890s, the engines' main duties were between Paddington and Bristol but, by 1910, they had been transferred to Wolverhampton from where they worked to Chester and Birkenhead. They were withdrawn between 1928 and 1930, each with over one million miles on the clock, and, in their final year, two had become resident at Bristol, one at Cardiff and the other at Chester.

TABLE 2.1: ORIGINAL DIMENSIONS OF THE ARMSTRONG CLASS

BUILT:	Rebuilt 1894 from 2-4-0s
WORKS NOS (original engines):	1052/1073/1115/1116
WEIGHTS FULL (locomotive):	50 tons 16 cwt
(tender):	36 tons 15 cwt
TENDER CAPACITY (water):	3,000 gallons
(coal):	5 tons
WHEELBASE (locomotive):	23ft 6in
WHEEL DIAMETERS (bogie):	4ft 1in
(coupled):	7ft 1in
CYLINDERS:	(2) 20in × 26in
BOILER PRESSURE:	160 lb/psi
HEATING SURFACES (tubes):	1434.3 sq ft
(firebox):	127.1 sq ft
SUPERHEATERS FITTED:	1911/1913
GRATE AREA:	20.8 sq ft
TRACTIVE EFFORT (at 85% boiler pressure):	16,640 lb
ROUTE AVAILABILITY:	Red
GWR POWER CLASSIFICATION:	A
SWINDON WORKS DIAGRAMS:	A: 7ft 1½in wheels
	T: ditto plus No 2 boiler
	A4: as above plus superheater
	A12: 6ft 8½in wheels, No 2 boiler and superheater
	A12: as above but with new superheater

TABLE 2.2: ARMSTRONG CLASS LOCOMOTIVES REBUILT FROM 2-4-0s

OLD NOS	BUILT	WORKS NOS	ORIGINAL TYPE	NEW NOS	NAMES	WDN	LAST SHED
7	2/1886	1052	SG compound	4171	*Armstrong* (*)	9/1928	Chester
8	5/1886	1073	BG compound	4172	*Gooch*	4/1929	Bristol (SPM†)
14	5/1888	1115	BG simple	4170	*Charles Saunders*	8/1928	Bristol (BR†)
16	6/1888	1116	BG simple	4169	*Brunel*	7/1930	Cardiff

(*) Originally named *Charles Saunders*
(†) St Philip's Marsh/Bath Road.

The Badminton 4-4-0s were the first class on the GWR to be fitted with Belpaire fireboxes from new. They were exceptionally handsome machines and so no excuses are offered for including two pictures of similar engines in their 'as built' condition. No 3294 *Blenheim* and No 3295 *Bessborough* were both constructed in May 1898 and were later renumbered as 4102/03 respectively. After the renumbering, the Badmintons were always readily identifiable as they were the only 4-4-0s in the 41XX series to have curved frames.

Both Photos: Rail Archive Stephenson

The Armstrongs did not set the engineering world alight when they first appeared but they were adequately reliable performers and so William Dean persevered with the concept of bogie 4-4-0s. The Duke and Bulldog classes appeared in 1895 and 1899 respectively and, although locomotives of these two classes were used on fast passenger duties, they were primarily intended for secondary and mixed traffic work. The first 4-4-0s to be built by the GWR specifically for express passenger work were the Badmintons, twenty of which were constructed between December 1897 and January 1899. The new engines were needed as replacements for the 4-2-2s on duties between Paddington and Bristol as the ever-increasing weights of the expresses were getting beyond the capabilities of the singles.

The Badmintons were built with 6ft 8in coupled wheels and 18in × 26in cylinders and were the first GWR locomotives to be fitted with Belpaire fireboxes from new. As they rolled out of Swindon works one by one, the detail differences between individual members of the class became apparent. One had a window cab, some were named, a few had internal feed pipes and one had Ramsbottom safety valves. When G.J. Churchward took over at Swindon in 1902, his attitude was that the good-natured Badmintons wouldn't object to the introduction of a few more differentials. Domeless boilers, flush boilers, twin-windowed cabs and redesigned nameplates all manifested themselves on different members of the class at different times during Churchward's reign but, between 1911 and 1913, a degree of rationalisation crept in when Standard No 2 boilers and superheating became the norm.

One of the more subtle differences among the various Badmintons was seen when No 3297 *Earl Cawdor* and No 3308 *Savernake* were paired with enlarged tenders in 1899. The purpose of this was to enable either locomotive to work the Royal Train non-stop from Windsor to Folkestone as there were no water troughs on the route. The prospect of running dry was not to be entertained, particularly in view of Queen Victoria's reluctance to be amused.

At first, the Badmintons had been numbered 3292-3311, but the final bout of rebuilding had rendered them mechanically similar to locomotives of the later Atbara and Flower classes. Consequently, the Badmintons were renumbered 4100-19 to fit in with the number sequence which was also applied to the other two classes. The Badmintons' heyday

Of the Badminton class 4-4-0s, No 3310 *Waterford* was a one-off. It was built with the prototype Standard No 2 boiler and had a different cab. No 3310 was later renumbered 4100 and survived until 1929.

Photo: H. C. Casserley Collection

Badminton class 4-4-0 No 3297 *Earl Cawdor* was rebuilt in 1903 with a larger, round-top boiler and a double-window cab; the result was a distinctly un-GWR looking creature. The new boiler proved unsuccessful and so it was replaced by a standard one in 1906; the custom cab was replaced at the same time. No 3297 finished its life wearing No 4105 as a conventional member of the class.

Photo: Rail Archive Stephenson

TABLE 2.3: BADMINTON CLASS LOCOMOTIVES

OLD NO	NEW NO	NAME	BUILT	WDN	LAST SHED
3292	4100	*Badminton* (a)	12/1897	9/1929	Tyseley
3293	4101	*Barrington*	4/1898	4/1930	Oxford
3294	4102	*Blenheim*	5/1898	9/1928	Tyseley
3295	4103	*Bessborough*	5/1898	4/1930	Bristol
3296	4104	*Cambria*	5/1898	6/1929	Cardiff
3297	4105	*Earl Cawdor*	5/1898	11/1927	Bristol
3298	4106	*Grosvenor*	6/1898	8/1929	Bristol
3299	4107	*Alexander Hubbard* (b)	6/1898	2/1930	Tyseley
3300	4108	*Hotspur*	7/1898	3/1930	Bristol
3301	4109	*Monarch*	7/1898	3/1931	Bristol
3302	4110	*Charles Mortimer* (c)	7/1898	10/1928	Tyseley
3303	4111	*Marlborough*	7/1898	10/1928	Oxford
3304	4112	*Oxford* (d)	9/1898	9/1929	Tyseley
3305	4113	*Samson*	9/1898	5/1931	Didcot
3306	4114	*Shelburne*	9/1898	7/1927	Goodwick
3307	4115	*Shrewsbury* (d)	11/1898	3/1931	Tyseley
3308	4116	*Savernake*	12/1898	7/1927	Cardiff
3309	4117	*Shakespeare*	12/1898	10/1927	Bristol
3310	4118	*Waterford*	12/1898	7/1927	Bristol (SPM)
3311	4119	*Wynnstay*	1/1899	7/1927	Didcot

(a) Unnamed until April 1898.
(b) Named *Hubbard* until August 1903.
(c) Named *Mortimer* until August 1904.
(d) Names removed in May 1927.

Class leader No 3373 *Atbara* is shown in the condition in which it was built in 1900. Its parallel boiler was replaced by a taper version in 1904 and, six years later, it was fitted with a superheated boiler.

Photo: Rail Archive Stephenson

Atbara class No 3405 *Mauritius* was rebuilt as the prototype of the famous City class. This photograph was taken during the locomotive's twelve-month spell as an Atbara prior to its operation in September 1902.

Photo: Rail Archive Stephenson

as crack express engines was to be short-lived, as the City and the County class 4-4-0s soon superseded them. The Badmintons were subsequently relegated to secondary and mixed traffic duties and were dispersed over most of the GWR system; the last survivor was No 4113 (ex-No 3305) *Samson* which was withdrawn from Didcot in May 1931.

Two of the Badmintons had, by the time of their retirement, lost their nameplates. Nos 4112 and 4115 (ex-Nos 3304 and 3307) had been named *Oxford* and *Shrewsbury* respectively but, in common with many other railway companies, the GWR had found that some members of the public were prone to mistaking a locomotive name for a destination board. Considering that locomotives of the Badmintons' contemporaries, the Atbaras, included the names *Khartoum*, *Aden* and *Colombo*, it must have been very confusing.

The first Atbara class locomotive, No 3373, appeared in April 1900 and, by October 1901, forty had been built. Initially, the Atbaras had similar basic dimensions to the Badmintons and they were

The ungroomed condition of Flower class No 4156 (formerly No 4108) *Gardenia* provides evidence that, when this picture was taken in the late 1920s, the top-link status of the class was a thing of the past.

Photo: Rail Archive Stephenson

Flower class 4-4-0 No 4112 (later No 4160) *Carnation* was photographed in 1912, the year after it was fitted with top feed. The superheater which can be seen was fitted in 1910.

Photo: Rail Archive Stephenson

also intended to take over from the 4-2-2s on express passenger duties. The first bout of re-boilering in the early 1900s divided the Atbaras into two camps. In September 1902, No 3405 *Mauritius* was fitted with a larger No 4 boiler and thus became the prototype for a completely new class, the Cities. Nine other Atbaras were rebuilt as Cities, but the remaining thirty members of the class were modified with coned boilers and strengthened frames. In 1908, twenty Flower class 4-4-0s, Nos 4101-20, were built at Swindon and these were, basically, similar to the reboilered Atbaras.

The GWR was not averse to purloining names from specific locomotives and attaching them to other machines if and when circumstances dictated, and the Atbaras seemed to suffer from these identity crises more than most. For the homecoming of the victorious Horatio Kitchener in July 1902, locomotive No 3377 *Kitchener* was unavailable for hauling the special train and so its nameplates were removed and attached, instead, to No 3374 *Baden Powell*. Although No 3374 was little over two years' old when it ran in disguise for the Boer War hero, it had already carried different nameplates on three separate occasions. On 29 October 1900, No 3374 had been in charge of a City Imperial Volunteer's special and had borrowed the nameplate from No 3389 *Pretoria* for the occasion. Two other specials which operated for the Volunteers on the same day were hauled by Nos 3373 and 3392 which, under normal circumstances, carried the names of *Atbara* and *White* respectively but, for the special duty, masqueraded under the names of *Maine* and *Powerful* which were usually worn by Nos 3381 and 3385.

Twice in May 1902, No 3374 had carried the name *Britannia* when on royal duties. Another royal function involved No 3373 *Atbara* which was given the name *Royal Sovereign* on 2 February 1901 for the purpose of hauling Queen Victoria's funeral train. On 16 September 1907, No 3408 *Ophir* was rostered for the inaugural Paddington to Killarney day excursion and the engine was renamed *Killarney* for the trip but, instead of the intended temporary renaming, No 3408 retained the new nameplates for the rest of its existence. Another change of status among the Atbaras involved No 3394 *Adelaide* which lost its nameplates in 1910 to avoid any possible confusion when a new Star class 4-6-0 was named *Queen Adelaide*.

In the best tradition of Swindon 4-4-0s, the Atbara class locomotives were eye-catchers. This picture shows No 3385 (later No 4131) *Powerful* in its original condition, save for the Westinghouse brake, but complete with the original oval nameplates and numberplates.

Photo: Rail Archive Stephenson

When built, twenty-three members of the Atbara class had the oval nameplates while the others had conventional numberplates and full-segment nameplates. By 1904, however, those locomotives wearing that latter type of nameplate had all received standard plates. Here, No 3412 (later 4148) *Singapore* is seen modelling the full-segment creation in 1902.
Photo: R. M. Casserley Collection

TABLE 2.4: ATBARA CLASS LOCOMOTIVES

OLD NO	NEW NO	NAME	BUILT	WDN	LAST SHED
3373	4120	*Atbara* (a)	4/1900	9/1929	Leamington
3374	4121	*Baden Powell* (b)	4/1900	12/1928	Bristol
3375	4122	*Colonel Edgcumbe* (c)	4/1900	10/1928	Swansea
3376	4123	*Herschell* (d)	4/1900	11/1928	Cardiff
3377	4124	*Kitchener*	5/1900	4/1930	Didcot
3378	4125	*Khartoum*	5/1900	4/1927	Bristol
3379	4126	*Kimberley*	5/1900	10/1927	Tyseley
3380	4127	*Ladysmith*	5/1900	9/1929	Tyseley
3381	4128	*Maine*	5/1900	7/1927	Swindon
3382		*Mafeking*	5/1900	9/1911	Tyseley
3383	4129	*Kekewich*	7/1900	11/1928	Shrewsbury
3384	4130	*Omdurman*	7/1900	4/1930	Didcot
3385	4131	*Powerful*	7/1900	4/1929	Didcot
3386	4132	*Pembroke* (e)	8/1900	4/1931	Tyseley
3387	4133	*Roberts*	8/1900	7/1927	Cardiff
3388	4134	*Sir Redvers*	8/1900	10/1927	Cardiff
3389	4135	*Pretoria* (f)	8/1900	11/1927	Bristol (SPM)

TABLE 2.4 CONT.

OLD NO	NEW NO	NAME	BUILT	WDN	LAST SHED
3390	4136	*Terrible*	8/1900	10/1927	Banbury
3391	4137	*Wolseley*	9/1900	10/1928	Westbury
3392	4138	*White* (g)	9/1900	11/1929	Old Oak
3393	4139	*Auckland*	6/1901	9/1928	Chester
3394	4140	*Adelaide* (h)	6/1901	4/1929	Salisbury
3395	4141	*Aden*	7/1901	2/1930	Salisbury
3396	4142	*Brisbane*	7/1901	10/1928	Swansea
3397	4143	*Cape Town*	8/1901	4/1929	Tyseley
3398	4144	*Colombo*	8/1901	11/1927	Goodwick
3399	4145	*Dunedin*	8/1901	12/1930	Westbury
3400	3700	*Durban*	8/1901	4/1907	(*)
3401	3701	*Gibraltar*	8/1901	2/1907	(*)
3402	3702	*Halifax*	8/1901	12/1908	(*)
3403	3703	*Hobart*	9/1901	2/1909	(*)
3404	3704	*Lyttleton*	9/1901	10/1907	(*)
3405	3705	*Mauritius*	9/1901	9/1902	(*)
3406	3706	*Melbourne*	9/1901	1/1908	(*)
3407	3707	*Malta*	9/1901	11/1908	(*)
3408	3708	*Ophir*	10/1901	5/1907	(*)
3409	3709	*Quebec*	10/1901	11/1907	(*)
3410	4146	*Sydney*	10/1901	10/1927	Salisbury
3411	4147	*St. Johns*	10/1901	7/1927	Tyseley
3412	4148	*Singapore*	10/1901	5/1931	Severn Tunnel

(*) Rebuilt as City class locomotives.
(a) Temporary names carried: *Maine* (29.10.1900); *Royal Sovereign* (2.2.1901).
(b) Temporary names carried: *Pretoria* (29.10.1900); *Britannia* (7.3.1902 and 10.3.1902); *Kitchener* (12.7.1902).
(c) Named *Conqueror* until May 1900 then *Edgcumbe* until May 1903.
(d) Name removed 1914.
(e) Name removed November 1930.
(f) Named *Sir Daniel* until November 1900.
(g) Temporary name carried: *Powerful* (29.10.1900).
(h) Name removed November 1910.

TABLE 2.5: FLOWER CLASS LOCOMOTIVES

OLD NO	NEW NO	NAME	BUILT	WDN	LAST SHED
4101	4149	*Auricula*	5/1908	9/1929	Leamington
4102	4150	*Begonia*	5/1908	4/1931	Didcot
4103	4151	*Calceolaria*	5/1908	11/1927	Pontypool
4104	4152	*Calendula*	5/1908	9/1928	Bristol (SPM)
4105	4153	*Camellia*	5/1908	7/1927	Cardiff
4106	4154	*Campanula*	5/1908	5/1930	Tyseley
4107	4155	*Cineraria*	6/1908	11/1927	Swansea

TABLE 2.5 CONT.

OLD NO	NEW NO	NAME	BUILT	WDN	LAST SHED
4108	4156	*Gardenia*	6/1908	4/1929	Leamington
4109	4157	*Lobelia*	6/1908	10/1928	Leamington
4110	4158	*Petunia*	6/1908	4/1929	Leamington
4111	4159	*Anemone*	6/1908	10/1929	Shrewsbury
4112	4160	*Carnation*	6/1908	7/1927	Swansea
4113	4161	*Hyacinth* (a)	6/1908	4/1929	Salisbury
4114	4162	*Marguerite*	7/1908	8/1929	Salisbury
4115	4163	*Marigold*	7/1908	4/1929	Cardiff
4116	4164	*Mignonette*	7/1908	10/1930	Bristol
4117	4165	*Narcissus*	7/1908	7/1927	Salisbury
4118	4166	*Polyanthus*	7/1908	11/1927	Tyseley
4119	4167	*Primrose*	7/1908	7/1929	Cardiff
4120	4168	*Stephanotis*	7/1908	5/1930	Taunton

(a) Spelt *Hyacinthe* until May 1916.

TABLE 2.6: ORIGINAL DIMENSIONS OF THE BADMINTON, ATBARA AND FLOWER CLASS LOCOMOTIVES

	BADMINTON	ATBARA	FLOWER
BUILT:	1897–1899	1900–1901	1908
WORKS NOS:	1592–1611	1826–65	2330–49
WEIGHTS FULL (locomotive):	52 tons 3 cwt	51 tons 12 cwt	53 tons 6 cwt
(tender):	32 tons 10 cwt	32 tons 10 cwt	40 tons 0 cwt
TENDER CAPACITY (water):	3000 gallons	3000 gallons	3500 gallons
(coal):	5 tons	5 tons	7 tons
WHEELBASE (locomotive):	23ft 3in	22ft 6in	22ft 6in
WHEEL DIAMETER (bogie):	4ft 0in	3ft 8in	3ft 8in
(coupled):	6ft 8in (a)	6ft 8½in	6ft 8½in
CYLINDERS:	(2) 18in × 26in	(2) 18in × 26in	(2) 18in × 26in
BOILER PRESSURE:	180 lb/psi	180 lb/psi	195 lb/psi
HEATING SURFACES (tubes):	1175.3 sq ft (b)	1540.2 sq ft	1396.6 sq ft
(firebox):	121.6 sq ft	124.1 sq ft	121.3 sq ft
SUPERHEATERS FITTED:	1909–13	1910–13	1910–13
GRATE AREA:	18.3 sq ft	21.3 sq ft	20.3 sq ft
TRACTIVE EFFORT (at 85% boiler pressure):	16,010 lb	16,010 lb	17,345 lb
ROUTE AVAILABILITY:	Red	Red	Red
GWR POWER CLASSIFICATION:	A	A	A
SWINDON WORKS DIAGRAMS:	J/K/O/Y/A5 A14/A24	L/A1/A16/A19	R/A16/A19

(a) Thicker tyres increased the diameter to 6ft 8½in.

(b) Badmintons Nos 3292/94–3302 (later 4100/02–10) fitted with Serve tubes which had a heating surface of 830 sq ft.

TABLE 2.7: YEARLY TOTALS OF BADMINTON, ATBARA AND FLOWER CLASSES

Totals taken at 31 December each year.

1897	1	1902	59	1907	54	1912	69	1917	71	1922	71	1927	51
1898	18	1903	59	1908	51	1913	69	1918	71	1923	73	1928	37
1899	20	1904	59	1909	70	1914	69	1919	71	1924	73	1929	18
1900	40	1905	59	1910	70	1915	70	1920	71	1925	73	1930	6
1901	60	1906	59	1911	69	1916	70	1921	71	1926	73	1931	0

N.B.: 1) Ten rebuilt as City class locos.
2) Armstrong class locos incorporated in Atbaras: one in 1915, one in 1917 and two in 1923.

One of the Atbaras, No 3382 *Mafeking*, was damaged beyond repair in an accident at Henley-in-Arden in 1911.

The Atbaras and the Flowers came to be looked on as one and the same class and, subsequently, the Badmintons joined in as well despite the fact the curved frames of the Badmintons were in marked contrast to the straight frames of the other two types. After renumbering, the remaining Atbaras became Nos 4120-48 and the Flowers took Nos 4149-68. The last Atbara to be withdrawn, No 4148 (ex-No 3412) *Singapore*, was retired from Severn Tunnel Junction in May 1931, the same month as the last Badminton was declared redundant.

As already mentioned, No 3405 *Mauritius* unwittingly became the prototype for the famous City class in September 1902 when it was fitted with a larger No 4 boiler. That conversion was instigated by George Jackson Churchward who had taken over the position of locomotive superintendent on 1 June 1902. Churchward was a Devonian who had started his career under the guidance of John Wright, the locomotive superintendent of the South Devon and the Cornwall Railways, and the absorption of those two railways into the GWR empire in 1876 secured Churchward a foothold at Swindon. In 1897, Churchward had been appointed chief assistant to William Dean, a position which ensured that his eventual move to the very top was inevitable. In Dean's final year of office, much of the design work at Swindon was already being undertaken by Churchward and the latter's prototype Saint class 4-6-0 No 100, actually appeared four months before the top job officially changed hands.

In March 1903, Churchward's first purpose-built City class 4-4-0, No 3433 *City of Bath*, was constructed at Swindon and in May, nine more, Nos 3434-42, were completed. The conversion of nine further Atbaras to Cities between 1907 and 1909 brought the class total to twenty, and the numbering sequence was subsequently rationalised as Nos 3700-19. For their day, the Cities were large engines. Their weight in working order was a little over ninety-two tons when paired with standard six-wheel 3,000 gallon tenders, but some of the class were subsequently given larger 3,500 gallon tenders. The basic dimensions of 6ft 8½in coupled wheels and 18in × 26in cylinders were similar to previous classes of 4-4-0s, but the working pressure of the larger boiler was 200 lb and the resultant tractive effort was 17, 790 lb.

The Cities swiftly became established as *the* crack locomotives of the GWR. Several members of the class claimed places in the record books but the most famous performance of the lot was that of No 3440 *City of Truro* which became credited with the first recorded 100 mph in Britain. In 1904, the locomotive was timed at 102.3 mph on Wellington Bank when in charge of a Plymouth to London mail train. The actual speed was not publicised for nearly twenty years as it was felt that it could alarm, not only the authorities, but also some passengers; although the precision of the timing has since been questioned, the clockwatcher was Charles Rous-Marten, to whom the word 'inaccuracy' was foreign. Furthermore, the Bristol & Exeter Railway's broad gauge singles had often been timed at speeds in excess of 80 mph in the 1850s and so the feat of *City of Truro* in 1904 is perfectly feasible.

City class No 3702 *Halifax* started life as No 3402 of the Atbara class but was rebuilt and reclassified in 1908. Here, it is seen in its final condition at Old Oak Common shed in the late 1920s.

Photo: D. K. Jones Collection

It was fitting that *City of Truro*'s record-breaking part of the run was on the Devon border as the Cities made the route between Paddington and Plymouth their own. The south Somerset cut-off route was opened in 1906 to enable West of England trains to miss the bottleneck at Bristol completely and, with the provision of water troughs at Creech Junction near Taunton, the Cities were able to operate between Paddington and Plymouth or Kingswear non-stop.

But even the Cities were not immune to being superseded by 4-6-0s. Despite the addition of superheaters between 1910 and 1912, the engines were gradually drafted away from the West Country on to lower-profile duties — firstly on the Birmingham line and later on the South Wales route — but at least they retained the dignity of hauling the faster trains on those lines. The first of the Cities to be retired was London-based No 3718 (ex-No 3441) *City of Winchester* which went in October 1927, and the slaughter of the others was completed in May 1931 when No 3712 (ex-No 3435) *City of Bristol* was withdrawn from Reading shed. The final mileages for members of the class ranged from 837,000 to 1,160,000.

With due recognition of its record-breaking performance, *City of Truro* was saved after its withdrawal from Shrewsbury shed in March 1931 and dispatched to York Railway Museum. In January 1957, it was loaned to the Western Region of British Railways and was restored to its 1904 condition with No 3440 replacing its final running number, 3717. The purpose of the restoration was to enable the locomotive to be used on special excursion trains but, remarkably, this historic engine spent periods between special duties on ordinary timetabled services from Didcot and Swindon. In May 1961, *City of Truro* was withdrawn for the second time in its life and, this time, restored to its 1920 condition. It went, at first, to Swindon Museum and eventually finished up back at the National Railway Museum at York. Today, *City of Truro* is one of just two ex-GWR 4-4-0s in preservation and, understandably, it is in great demand. During 1991 alone, it has worked on the Severn Valley Railway, the Dean Forest Railway and at gala weekends at Bristol, Hereford and Old Oak Common depot, London.

Although the prototype of the Cities had looked very promising, Churchward was not prepared to pin all his hopes on just one design. He was constantly looking for improvement in all matters of locomotive engineering and, when the de Glehn 4-4-2 compounds of France's Nord Railway became flavour of the month in the engineering world in 1903, Churchward wanted to take a closer look at the machines to see whether the engines had something useful to offer or whether it was merely a

TABLE 2.8: ORIGINAL DIMENSIONS OF THE CITY CLASS LOCOMOTIVES

BUILT:	1902 to 1909 (rebuild); 1903 (new locos)
WORKS NOS:	1853–62 (rebuild); 1993–2002 (new locos)
WEIGHTS FULL (locomotive):	55 tons 6 cwt
(tender):	36 tons 15 cwt
TENDER CAPACITY (water):	3,000 gallons
(coal):	5 tons
WHEELBASE (locomotive):	22ft 6in
WHEEL DIAMETER (bogie):	3ft 8in
(coupled):	6ft 8½in
CYLINDERS:	(2) 18in × 26in
BOILER PRESSURE:	200 lb/psi
HEATING SURFACES (tubes):	1689.8 sq ft
(firebox):	128.3 sq ft
SUPERHEATERS FITTED:	1910–12
GRATE AREA:	20.6 sq ft
TRACTIVE EFFORT (at 85% boiler pressure):	17,790 lb
ROUTE AVAILABILITY:	Red
GWR POWER CLASSIFICATION:	A
SWINDON WORKS DIAGRAMS:	M: as built
	Z: with original superheater
	A17: with later superheater

TABLE 2.9: CITY CLASS LOCOMOTIVES

OLD NO	NEW NO	NAME	BUILT (*)	WDN	LAST SHED
3400	3700	*Durban*	4/1907*	11/1929	Wolverhampton
3401	3701	*Gibraltar*	2/1907*	8/1928	Wolverhampton
3402	3702	*Halifax*	12/1908*	4/1929	Leamington
3403	3703	*Hobart*	2/1909*	8/1929	Banbury
3404	3704	*Lyttelton* (a)	10/1907*	9/1928	Chester
3405	3705	*Mauritius*	9/1902*	9/1928	Oxford
3406	3706	*Melbourne*	1/1908*	6/1929	Banbury
3407	3707	*Malta*	11/1908*	4/1929	Bristol
3408	3708	*Killarney* (b)	5/1907*	10/1929	Shrewsbury
3409	3709	*Quebec*	11/1907*	9/1929	Oxford
3433	3710	*City of Bath*	3/1903	9/1928	Wolverhampton
3434	3711	*City of Birmingham*	5/1903	7/1930	Leamington
3435	3712	*City of Bristol*	5/1903	5/1931	Reading
3436	3713	*City of Chester*	5/1903	12/1929	Chester
3437	3714	*City of Gloucester*	5/1903	11/1929	Oxford
3438	3715	*City of Hereford*	5/1903	10/1929	Chester
3439	3716	*City of London*	5/1903	4/1929	Bristol
3440	3717	*City of Truro*	5/1903	3/1931(P)	Shrewsbury
3441	3718	*City of Winchester*	5/1903	10/1927	Old Oak
3442	3719	*City of Exeter* (c)	5/1903	4/1929	Oxford

(*) Dates are those when the locomotives were rebuilt as City class.

(a) Spelt *Lyttleton* until June 1920.

(b) Named *Ophir* until September 1907.

(c) Originally intended to be *City of Worcester*.

(P) Locomotive preserved.

TABLE 2.10: YEARLY TOTALS OF CITY CLASS LOCOMOTIVES

Totals taken at 31 December each year.

Year	Total	Year	Total	Year	Total	Year	Total	Year	Total	Year	Total	Year	Total
1902	1	1907	16	1911	20	1915	20	1919	20	1923	20	1927	19
1903	11	1908	19	1912	20	1916	20	1920	20	1924	20	1928	15
1904	11	1909	20	1913	20	1917	20	1921	20	1925	20	1929	3
1905	11	1910	20	1914	20	1918	20	1922	20	1926	20	1930	2
1906	11											1931	0

The most famous of all the GWR 4-4-0s is, unquestionably, City class No 3440 (later No 3717) *City of Truro*. Its return to active duty in the BR era provided a most welcome surprise and, in this picture, it is seen at Northam South Junction on a Didcot to Southampton Terminus working on 2 August 1957.

Photo: E. R. Morton

case of hype. While engineers elsewhere frantically adjusted their timetables so that they could visit France to inspect the well-publicised Atlantic compounds, the Swindon hierarchy calmly ordered one of the engines direct from the French builders.

The de Glehn compound was delivered to Swindon in October 1903. Apart from relatively minor modifications to make the locomotive acceptable for the GWR's loading gauge, the fitting of the vacuum brake and the necessary alterations to permit the attachment of a standard GWR tender, the engine was almost identical to the originals right down to

The French-built 4-4-2 No 102 was named *La France* and it underwent several cosmetic and mechanical changes during its twenty-three year life on the GWR. This picture shows it sporting the Standard No1 boiler with which it was fitted in 1916. ***Photo: GWR Museum, Swindon***

the de Glehn bogie. The outside cylinders were the high pressure pair and these drove the trailing coupled axle; the two low pressure cylinders were mounted inside the frames and drove the leading coupled axle. Each pair of cylinders had a separate set of Walschaerts valve gear; a catch on the compound reversing screw could be set to enable the sets of valve gear to work either independently or together. A further option for manual override enabled the locomotive to be worked as a non-compound if required.

The French 4-4-2 had driving wheels which were, coincidentally, to the Swindon standard diameter of 6ft 8½in but the boiler pressure was a decidedly non-standard 227 lb. The tractive effort was an impressive 23,710 lb and, when paired with a 4,000 gallon tender, the working weight of the ensemble was 107 tons 16 cwt. The GWR numbered it 102, named it *La France* and put it through extensive trials before letting it loose on scheduled passenger services in February 1904. No 102 originally ran in a livery of black with red and white lining but was later given the standard Swindon colour scheme of green with Indian Red frames.

No 102 proved to be an excellent performer despite initial concern that its adhesive weight of 33 tons 7 cwt would be too light for work on steep gradients. The doubters were proved wrong in a decisive manner when, on a trial run from Paddington to Exeter, the locomotive and its train had to attack the 1 in 80 Wellington Bank from a standing start. By the time No 102 reached the summit at the entrance of Whiteball Tunnel, it was doing nearly 50 mph. Another adventure featuring No 102 was the hauling of a 350-ton train over the 194 miles from Paddington to Exeter in 198 minutes, and that included an eight-minute stop at Bristol.

Churchward realised that comparison trials involving the French compound could only be fairly evaluated if the opposition was provided by a similar locomotive with non-compound operation. In February 1902, No 171 *Albion*, one of the GWR's prototype two-cylinder 4-6-0s, was completed and was fitted from new with a boiler which worked at 225 lb, almost the same as that of the compound. In order to make the two locomotives as equally matched as possible, No 171 was converted to a 4-4-2 in October 1904. Between February and September 1905, thirteen more two-cylinder 4-4-2s emerged from Swindon and they carried Nos 172/79–90. These were part of an order for nineteen locomotives which were built with gaps in the mainframes so that they could be finished as either 4-4-2s or 4-6-0s as required. The other six, Nos 173–78, were in fact delivered as 4-6-0s. Sir Walter Scott's 'Waverley' novels provided the inspiration for the names of the 4-4-2 versions and No 171 *Albion* was, in fact, renamed *The Pirate* for four months in 1907. The choice of allegiance with Scott was, however, queried by many contemporary observers, as the scribe hardly had the strongest links with the West Country. Identity crises seemed commonplace among the Swindon Atlantics, as seven were subjected to changes of names.

Two more four-cylinder compounds were delivered to the GWR from the Belfort works in France in June 1905. These retained the 6ft 8½ in diameter driving wheels and 227 lb boiler pressure of No 102 but increases in the sizes of the cylinders, grates and heating surfaces made them considerably more powerful than the predecessor. The new arrivals were similar to the locomotives used by the Paris-Orleans Railway; on arrival at Swindon, they were numbered 103/04 and were later named *President* and *Alliance* respectively. Externally, the main differences between Nos 103/04 and the older French compound were that the newcomers had side-window cabs and inside-framed bogies.

With a total of seventeen Atlantics to play with, Churchward was able to compare the compounds with the simples in most spheres of operation. By 1906, Churchward concluded that the economies gained by compounding were so slight that they did not offset the extra time and cost required for maintenance. The only distinct advantage of the compounds was that of smoother running. Although compounding was used successfully in many other countries, the only British railway company which achieved definite advantages with the idea was the Midland Railway.

In their early days of regular service, the French Atlantics tended to be used most frequently on West of England expresses and, for some time, No 102 took turns on the Cornish Riviera Express with a City class 4-4-0 and one of the new 4-6-0s. In 1907, the engines were transferred to duties on Worcester and Wolverhampton expresses. In their later years, they were based at Oxford from where they worked fast passenger trains to Birmingham or Paddington. Nos 102/03/04 were withdrawn in 1926/27/28 res-

All twenty Swindon-built Atlantics were later rebuilt as Saint class 4-6-0s. No 181 was delivered in June 1905, was named *Ivanhoe* in 1907 and succumbed to the transformation to a six-coupled machine in July 1912. That did not, however, mark an end to the changes as it was renumbered 2981 early in 1913. Photographs of the Swindon-built 4-4-2s are rare and this is a pity as it can be clearly seen that they were fine-looking steeds.

Photo: GWR Museum, Swindon

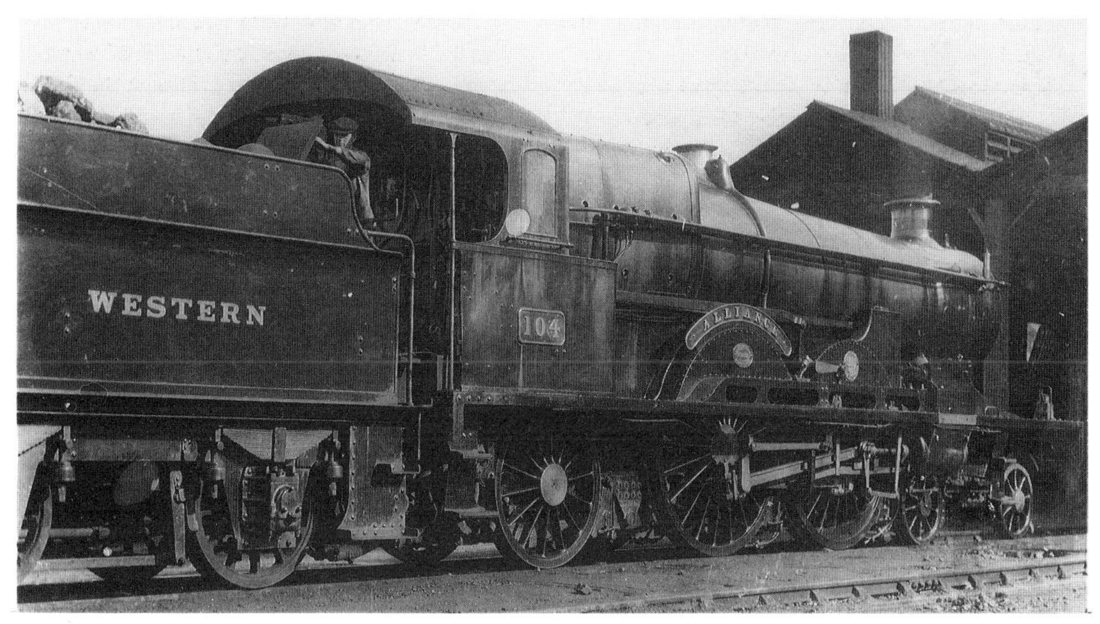

French compound No 104 *Alliance* became gradually Swindonised and this picture shows it in its final condition, complete with taper boiler, on 9 April 1927 at Oxford shed.

Photo: H. C. Casserley

TABLE 2.11: ORIGINAL DIMENSIONS OF FRENCH 4-4-2 LOCOMOTIVES

	NO 102	NOS 103/04
BUILT:	Belfort 1903	Belfort 1905
WORKS NOS:	5409	5601/02
WEIGHTS FULL (locomotive):	64 tons 13 cwt	71 tons 14 cwt
(tender):	43 tons 3 cwt	40 tons 0 cwt
TENDER CAPACITY (water):	4,000 gallons	3,500 gallons
(coal):	7 tons	7 tons
WHEELBASE (locomotive):	27ft 10¾in	28ft 6½in
WHEEL DIAMETER (bogie):	2ft 11⅞in	3ft 2in
(coupled):	6ft 8½in	6ft 8½in
(trailing):	4ft 7⅞in	4ft 8⅜in
CYLINDERS (high pressure):	(2) 13⅜in × 25¼in	(2) 14¼in × 25¼in
(low pressure):	(2) 22⅛in × 25¼in	(2) 23¾in × 25¼in
BOILER PRESSURE:	227 lb/psi	227 lb/psi
HEATING SURFACES (tubes):	2288.8 sq ft	2582.7 sq ft
(firebox):	167 sq ft	174.3 sq ft
SUPERHEATERS FITTED:	1913	1914/15
GRATE AREA:	29.5 sq ft	33.4 sq ft
TRACTIVE EFFORT (at 85% boiler pressure):	23,710 lb	27,174 lb
ROUTE AVAILABILITY:	Blue	Red
GWR POWER CLASSIFICATION:	B	B
SWINDON WORKS DIAGRAMS:	A: as built	C: as built
	G: superheated	E: reboilered
	I: later superheater	H: superheated

pectively and all had covered around three-quarter of a million miles. The Swindon-built versions had shorter lives than their French counterparts and they were all rebuilt as Saint class 4-6-0s between April 1912 and January 1913; renumbering in the mainstream 29XX Saint sequence was completed by December 1912.

Apart from Nos 171/72/79–90, there was one other Swindon-built Atlantic. The comparison trials between the French and the English 4-4-2s persuaded Churchward that a four-cylinder, non-compound Atlantic with a 225 lb boiler would combine most of the advantages of both French and English versions. The prototype, No 40, emerged from Swindon in April 1906 and, five months later, was named *North Star* after one of the earliest GWR locomotives. The 6ft 8½in diameter was used for the driving wheels and the cylinders were 14¼in × 26in; when paired with a 3,500 gallon tender, the full weight of the ensemble in working order was 114½ tons. Of the four cylinders, the outside ones were placed over the rear bogie wheels and drove the trailing coupled axle while the inside cylinders, which were situated much farther forward, drove the leading coupled axle. This enabled both sets of connecting rods to be almost the same length.

At first, No 40 was prone to buckled coupling rods but this problem was soon solved by the fitting of plain rectangular rods instead of the 'I' section type. After overcoming the teething troubles, No 40 went on to prove an excellent locomotive but, when further four-cylinder engines were built in 1907, they were constructed not as 4-4-2s but as 4-6-0s. The prototype of 1906, No 40 *North Star*, had quite unwittingly become the forerunner of all

TABLE 2.12: ORIGINAL DIMENSIONS OF SWINDON 4-4-2 LOCOMOTIVES

	NOS 171/72/79–90	NO 40
BUILT:	1903*/05	1906
WORKS NOS:	2024/2106/13/14/28–37	2168
WEIGHTS FULL (locomotive):	70 tons 10 cwt	74 tons 10 cwt
(tender):	43 tons 3 cwt	40 tons 0 cwt
TENDER CAPACITY (water):	4,000 gallons	3,500 gallons
(coal):	7 tons	7 tons
WHEELBASE (locomotive):	27ft 7in	27ft 9in
WHEEL DIAMETER (bogie):	3ft 2in	3ft 2in
(coupled):	6ft 8½in	6ft 8½in
(trailing):	4ft 1½in	4ft 1½in
CYLINDERS:	(2) 18in × 30in	(4) 14¼in × 26in
BOILER PRESSURE:	225 lb/psi	225 lb/psi
HEATING SURFACES (tubes):	1988.7 sq ft	1988.7 sq ft
(firebox):	154.3 sq ft	154.3 sq ft
SUPERHEATERS FITTED:	1910–12 (a)	(b)
GRATE AREA:	27 sq ft	27.1 sq ft
TRACTIVE EFFORT (at 85% boiler pressure):	23,090 lb	25,090 lb
ROUTE AVAILABILITY:	Red	Red
GWR POWER CLASSIFICATION:	D	D
SWINDON WORKS DIAGRAMS:	B: as built F: superheated	D

* No. 171 rebuilt from 4-6-0 in October 1904
(a) Nos 171/72/79/80/82/84/87 not superheated until after reverting to 4-6-0s.
(b) Not superheated until after rebuilt as a 4-6-0.

TABLE 2.13: YEARLY TOTALS OF ATLANTIC LOCOMOTIVES

Totals taken at 31 December each year.

Year	Total	Year	Total	Year	Total	Year	Total	Year	Total	Year	Total	Year	Total
1903	1	1907	16	1911	16	1915	3	1919	3	1923	3	1927	1
1904	2	1908	16	1912	4	1916	3	1920	3	1924	3	1928	0
1905	17	1909	16	1913	3	1917	3	1921	3	1925	3		
1906	17	1910	16	1914	3	1918	3	1922	3	1926	2		

GWR four-cylinder 4-6-0s and, in November 1909, it was converted to a 4-6-0 and later renumbered 4000 as a member of the famous Star class.

The introduction of the four-cylinder 4-6-0s in 1907 came just three years after the GWR's last new class of express passenger 4-4-0s had emerged. Admittedly, telepathy was one of the few talents which Churchward did not possess and, when the County class 4-4-0s were designed, nobody could have foreseen just how swiftly they would be superseded by more powerful machines. Nevertheless, questions were raised about the necessity for the Counties but not because of any anticipation of four-cylinder 4-6-0s. Other 4-4-0s of both Dean and Churchward designs, in particular the Cities, were doing excellent work and standard two-cylinder 4-6-0s had started to materialise. Churchward had, however, a specific task in mind for the Counties. The London & North Western Railway would not permit the 4-6-0s to use the joint line between Hereford and Shrewsbury, and so the Counties were intended to emphasise the GWR's presence in the battlefield of the borders.

The Counties used the No 4 boilers which had proved so effective on the Cities and both classes shared the same size of 6ft 8½in for their driving wheels, but that was about as far as the exterior similarities went as, unlike any other types of 4-4-0 on the GWR, the Counties had inside frames and outside cylinders. With a 30in cylinder stroke instead of 26in, the Counties produced a tractive effort of 20,530 lb which was greater than any other GWR 4-4-0s but, despite this, the Counties did not turn out to be improved versions of the Cities. One of the problems was that, compared to the smooth riding of the inside-cylindered 4-4-0s, the longer stroke of the Counties' outside cylinders gave much rougher rides and a tendency towards rolling. Crews referred to the Counties as 'Churchward's Roughriders' and, in those days before the advent of 'Quells', such matters were not treated lightly.

The first ten County 4-4-0s were numbered 3473–82 but the next batch, which were all completed between October and December 1906, were numbered 3801–20. The counties after which Nos 3473–82 were named were those in which the GWR operated, but the first ten locomotives of the 1906 batch were named after Irish counties, despite the fact that the GWR had not exhausted the list of 'home' possibilities with the original engines. The remainder of the 1906 batch, and ten additional engines which were built in 1911 and 1912 (Nos 3821–30), all reverted to names of English and Welsh counties but, in a few cases, the geographical links with the GWR's area were, at best, optimistic. To be fair to Nos 3823 *County of Carnarvon*, 3825 *County of Denbigh* and 3826 *County of Flint*, the counties after which they were named were only marginally outside the GWR network but, when it came to Nos 3816 *County of Leicester* and 3821 *County of Bedford*, there must have been a giant hiccup in Swindon's cartographical department.

In October 1909, No 3478 *County of Devon* was superheated and, by the end of 1913, all other members of the 1904 and 1906 batches had been similarly treated. The ten which were delivered in 1911 and 1912 were fitted with superheaters from new. In order to standardise the numbering sequence, the original ten, Nos 3473–82, were renumbered 3800/31–39 in December 1912.

By the early 1920s, the development of 4-6-0s had had the same effect on the Counties as on the other 4-4-0 classes and the Counties had lost almost all of their express duties to the newer, more powerful engines. In 1922, the Counties were scattered over much of the GWR system with nine based at Bristol, eight at Wolverhampton, five at

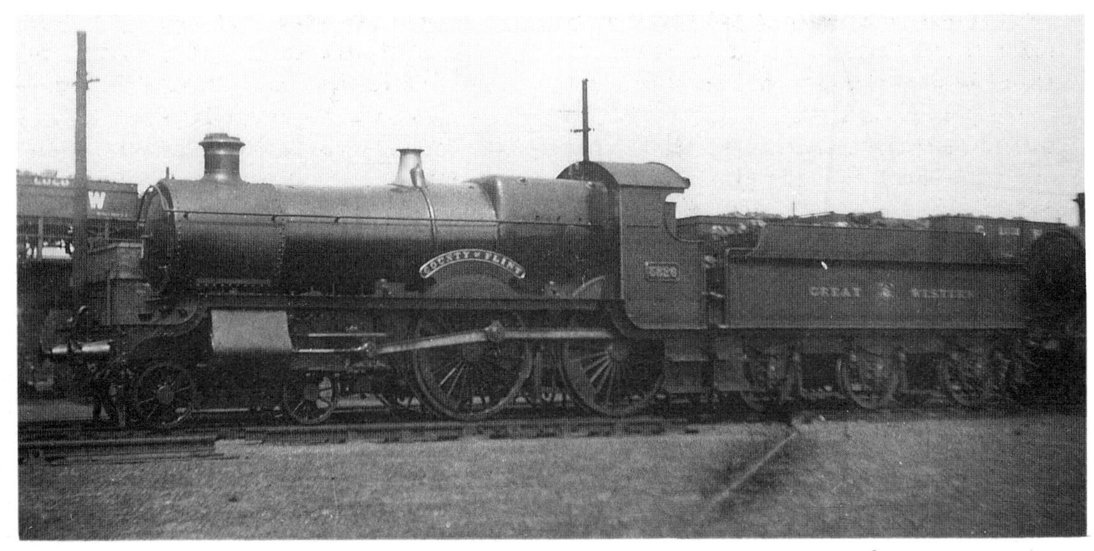

The County class represented the GWR's final development of 4-4-0s and the locomotives were readily distinguishable from other GWR 4-4-0s by being the only ones to have inside frames. However, there was a distinct differential within the class in that the final ten had curved ends to their frames as opposed to the straight ends of their predecessors. One of the curved-frame representatives was No 3826 *County of Flint* which was built in 1912 complete with all mod cons including superheater and top feed. The picture was taken at Old Oak Common shed on 16 May 1925.

Photo: LCGB/Ken Nunn Collection

TABLE 2.14: ORIGINAL DIMENSIONS OF COUNTY CLASS LOCOMOTIVES

BUILT:	1904–12
WORKS NUMBERS:	2056–65/2209–28/2416–25
WEIGHTS FULL (locomotive):	55 tons 6 cwt
(tender):	36 tons 15 cwt *
TENDER CAPACITY (water):	3,000 gallons *
(coal):	5 tons
WHEELBASE (locomotive):	24ft 0in
WHEEL DIAMETER (bogie):	3ft 2in
(coupled): 6ft 8½ in	6ft 8½ in
CYLINDERS:	(2) 18in × 30in
BOILER PRESSURE:	200 lb/psi
HEATING SURFACES (tubes):	1689.8 sq ft
(firebox):	128.3 sq ft
SUPERHEATERS FITTED:	1909–13 *
GRATE AREA:	20.6 sq ft
TRACTIVE EFFORT (at 85% boiler pressure):	20,530 lb
ROUTE AVAILABILITY:	Red
GWR POWER CLASSIFICATION:	C
SWINDON WORKS DIAGRAMS:	N: as built. Q: Reboilering (No 3805 only) X: Superheated. A10: 3821–30. A28: All engines with final superheater.

* From new, Nos 3821–3830 were paired with 3,500 gallon tenders (weight 40 tons) and were superheated.

Swindon and three apiece at Old Oak Common (London) and Shrewsbury. The remainder was divided between nine different sheds including, at one end, Taunton and, at the other, Goodwick. The concentrations at Bristol and Wolverhampton were to service the Bristol to Birmingham route which remained the Counties' last real express stronghold. Until the strengthening of Stonehouse Viaduct in Gloucestershire in 1927, the Counties were the heaviest GWR locomotives permitted over the structure.

The problem of the Counties' instability at speed was never overcome and, in the 1920s, the massive bogie tender from Churchward's experimental Pacific *The Great Bear* was attached firstly to No 3804 *County Dublin*, then to No 3802 *County Clare* and, later, to No 3816 *County of Leicester*. The idea was that such a large tender would act as a counterweight to the rolling which was generated by the locomotive's cylinders but the results of the tests were inconclusive. Even if any positive conclusions had been forthcoming, it is doubtful whether the Counties would have been treated to anything more than minor modifications as, by the late 1920s, it was obvious that the days of the GWR's passenger 4-4-0s were limited. No 3833 *County of Dorset* was the first to succumb when it was retired from Swindon in February 1930 and, when No 3834 *County of Somerset* was withdrawn from Tyseley in November 1933, the class became extinct.

Nine of the Counties had seen out their final days allocated to Swindon while Oxford had been the final resting place of eight others. Of the remainder, the final allocation of five had been Reading, four others had been withdrawn from Leamington while three had been treated to a seaside retirement at Weston-super-Mare. The highest mileage of the class was recorded by No 3836 *County of Warwick* which notched up 1,044,000 miles in its twenty-seven year life.

The GWR's express passenger 4-4-0s benefited from the enviable combination of William Dean and G. J. Churchward. Dean introduced the bogie 4-4-0 to the GWR and Churchward perfected the idea but, ironically, it was the older Dean locomotives which went on to have the longer lives. Apart from engines which were rebuilt as 4-6-0s, all of Churchward's 4-4-0 classes had become extinct by November 1933 but members of Dean's Duke and Bulldog classes lingered on until November 1951, the Dukedog rebuilds doing even better. Dean's 4-4-0s had the versatility of being mixed traffic engines and this helped to lengthen their working lives. By contrast, Churchward's 4-4-0s had been designed for express passenger duties and it was this type of work which demanded the newest and the best machines as soon as they were off the assembly lines.

The replacements for Churchward's 4-4-0s were, invariably, 4-6-0s which had been designed either by Churchward himself or by his successor, Charles Collett. Collett's locomotives, in particular the famous King class 4-6-0s, justifiably received great acclaim but the seeds for most of the designs had been sown by Churchward. As the figurehead of Swindon locomotive development for nineteen years, Churchward did not have the pretentiousness of many of his contemporaries. Instead of feeling jealousy towards the designers of the French compounds, Churchward tried to learn from them. Furthermore, in the same year as the acquisition of the French compounds, one of Churchward's assistants came up with a suggestion for improving the Badminton 4-4-0s and, although the plan was contrary to Churchward's own school of thought, the assistant's idea was given a three-year trial. There could have been very few designers who would have allowed a potentially competitive idea to have such a lengthy trial.

TABLE 2.15: YEARLY TOTALS OF COUNTY CLASS LOCOMOTIVES

Totals taken at 31 December each year.

Year	Total	Year	Total	Year	Total	Year	Total	Year	Total	Year	Total	Year	Total
1904	10	1909	30	1914	40	1918	40	1922	40	1926	40	1930	34
1905	10	1910	30	1915	40	1919	40	1923	40	1927	40	1931	10
1906	30	1911	35	1916	40	1920	40	1924	40	1928	40	1932	5
1907	30	1912	40	1917	40	1921	40	1925	40	1929	40	1933	0
1908	30	1913	40										

TABLE 2.16: COUNTY CLASS LOCOMOTIVES

FINAL NO	FIRST NO	NAME	BUILT	WDN	LAST SHED
3800	3473	*County of Middlesex*	5/1904	3/1931	Weston-s-Mare
3801		*County Carlow*	10/1906	4/1931	Westbury
3802		*County Clare*	10/1906	5/1931	Swindon
3803		*County Cork*	10/1906	1/1932	Oxford
3804		*County Dublin*	10/1906	3/1931	Oxford
3805		*County Kerry*	10/1906	5/1933	Oxford
3806		*County Kildare*	11/1906	2/1931	Tyseley
3807		*County Kilkenny*	11/1906	12/1930	Didcot
3808		*County Limerick*	11/1906	10/1931	Bristol
3809		*County Wexford*	11/1906	9/1931	Leamington
3810		*County Wicklow*	11/1906	3/1931	Swindon
3811		*County of Bucks*	11/1906	1/1931	Oxford
3812		*County of Cardigan*	11/1906	7/1932	Hereford
3813		*County of Carmarthen*	11/1906	11/1931	Didcot
3814		*County of Chester*	11/1906	6/1933	Reading
3815		*County of Hants*	11/1906	1/1932	Leamington
3816		*County of Leicester*	12/1906	9/1931	Swindon
3817		*County of Monmouth*	12/1906	1/1931	Swindon
3818		*County of Radnor*	12/1906	8/1931	Swindon
3819		*County of Salop*	12/1906	5/1931	Weston-s-Mare
3820		*County of Worcester*	12/1906	5/1931	Reading
3821		*County of Bedford*	12/1911	9/1931	Leamington
3822		*County of Brecon*	12/1911	4/1933	Pontypool
3823		*County of Carnarvon*	12/1911	4/1931	Swindon
3824		*County of Cornwall*	12/1911	3/1931	Hereford
3825		*County of Denbigh*	12/1911	3/1931	Reading
3826		*County of Flint*	1/1912	8/1931	Oxford
3827		*County of Gloucester*	1/1912	12/1931	Reading
3828		*County of Hereford*	1/1912	3/1933	Oxford
3829		*County of Merioneth*	1/1912	2/1932	Oxford
3830		*County of Oxford*	2/1912	2/1931	Reading
3831	3474	*County of Berks*	6/1904	11/1930	Tyseley
3832	3475	*County of Wilts*	6/1904	5/1930	Oxford
3833	3476	*County of Dorset*	8/1904	2/1930	Swindon
3834	3477	*County of Somerset*	8/1904	11/1933	Tyseley
3835	3478	*County of Devon*	8/1904	1/1931	Old Oak
3836	3479	*County of Warwick*	10/1904	11/1931	Leamington
3837	3480	*County of Stafford*	10/1904	3/1931	Swindon
3838	3481	*County of Glamorgan*	10/1904	8/1930	Swindon
3839	3482	*County of Pembroke*	10/1904	3/1930	Weston-s-Mare

CHAPTER 3

The Saints

The first 4-6-0 locomotive to be built for service in Britain appeared in September 1894. The owner of such an innovative machine was not one of the high-profile English railway companies but the Highland Railway which operated northwards from Perth across some of the most challenging terrain to be encountered by any of Britain's railways. The Highland's 4-6-0 was the first of a class of fifteen which was designed by David Jones and built by Messrs. Sharp Stewart at their Atlas works in Glasgow. However, contrary to what might have been expected of such new-fangled and powerful machines, David Jones's 4-6-0s were intended for freight work.

By the start of the 1900s, many railway companies on both sides of the border had started to follow the Highland Railway's lead and had turned to 4-6-0s, occasionally for freight duties but usually for express passenger work. In England, the first passenger 4-6-0s were those completed by Wilson Worsdell in June 1899 for the North Eastern Railway but, for freight work, the GWR had introduced 4-6-0 No 36 back in August 1896. Meanwhile, the GWR persevered with 4-4-0s for passenger work, as did most of the other major railway companies in Britain, but it was common knowledge throughout the GWR that changes at Swindon were not far off.

Nominally, William Dean was in charge of the GWR's locomotive department but, by 1901, his health was failing rapidly. During the previous year, most of the GWR's engineering design and development had been, in fact, in the care of Dean's chief assistant, G.J. Churchward, but out of respect to Dean, all innovations were credited to him and not to Churchward. Of the two freight 4-6-0s which had emerged from Swindon in 1896 and 1899, the former had been designed entirely by a fit and healthy William Dean but the latter showed distinct evidence of Churchward's increasing influence. When the GWR's first passenger 4-6-0 was completed at Swindon in February 1902, it was four months before Dean was finally persuaded to take early retirement and so the locomotive's design was officially credited to him, but it was an open secret that the 4-6-0 was virtually pure Churchward.

In 1901, Churchward had discussed the idea of a 4-6-0 for use over the steeply-graded main line west of Exeter, and his idea had been to fit such a locomotive with driving wheels of 5ft 8in for optimum tractive effort. The prototype GWR 4-6-0 which appeared in 1902 had, instead, coupled wheels of the standard diameter of 6ft 8½in. Carrying No 100, the locomotive was at first unnamed but, after William Dean's retirement in June 1902, it was named, simply but respectfully, *Dean*. About this time, various designs were being tried for locomotive nameplates and, in November 1902, a new-style plate was affixed to the front splasher bearing the full name *William Dean*.

The new 4-6-0 was unlike most Swindon products which had gone before. It had inside frames and, in order to simplify the design and facilitate maintenance, the cylinders were worn horizontally on the outside; they had a standard diameter of eighteen inches but the stroke was a massive thirty inches. The parallel boiler of No 100 was an enlarged version of those used successfully on the Atbara 4-4-0s and it was employed in conjunction with a raised Belpaire firebox. The overall visual effect was a stark-looking locomotive and it was not compared favourably with traditional Swindon products which, usually, had sleek, eye-catching lines. Contemporary observers were unanimous that the locomotive looked more American than British and the most regular comment was 'where's the cowcatcher?'.

No 100 was the first GWR locomotive to be fitted with a vacuum brake acting on all wheels of both engine and tender. Previously, the steam brake was commonly used but this was most effective when applied twice in quick succession. In emergency conditions, it was not always possible to apply, disengage and then reapply the brakes and this had been demonstrated at Slough in 1900 when 4-2-2 No 3015 had been forced to perform an emergency stop. In six hundred yards of level road, a single application of the steam brake had reduced the speed of the engine only from 60 mph to 25 mph and that had not been enough to prevent a collision with a stationary train. With the constant increase in the speeds and weights of passenger trains, the decision to fit vacuum brakes to No 100 and all further large express engines was very sensible.

The axle weight of No 100 was eighteen tons and, at first, this caused a few palpitations among the GWR's civil engineering staff, as the strength of the viaduct which crossed Uxbridge Road, between Hanwell and Southall stations was considered questionable. Subsequent tests gave the all-clear for the 4-6-0 to cross the viaduct but, as if to display ingratitude, the locomotive undertook most of its early work between Bristol and Newton Abbot. It was not until 1904, when No 100 regularly worked the newly-introduced, non-stop Cornish Riviera Express between Paddington and Plymouth, that the engine became a common sight in London. In the early days of the Cornish Riviera, the loading was often no more than seven or eight coaches but, until the opening of the Somerset cut-off route in 1906, the trains had to run via Bristol. This made for a distance of almost 247 miles and so the run was far from the proverbial picnic. The scheduled time between Paddington and Plymouth in 1904 was 265 minutes, but No 100 was known to have completed the run on more than one occasion with almost ten minutes to spare.

Despite the success of No 100, it did not signal the start of the mass-construction of 4-6-0s. It was March 1903 before another 4-6-0 crept out of Swindon works and this solitary locomotive, which was the first official Churchward 4-6-0, incorporated several new features. Wearing No 98, the new arrival had a Standard No 1 boiler with a tapered firebox and, although No 100 had been accused of looking American, the idea for the tapered firebox of No 98 had been 'borrowed' from the Illinois Central Railroad. The new 4-6-0 had a redesigned front end which incorporated the raising of the cylinders above the axle centres in order to prevent fouling the lower part of the GWR's loading gauge. The greatest claim to fame of No 98, however, was that it was one of the first products of Churchward's quest for standardisation.

In later years, it was often suggested that Churchward must have been a dab hand at jigsaw puzzles. Given a range of four types of boilers, three sizes of driving wheels, two diameters of carrying wheels and a choice of two cylinder blocks, he could select a permutation to construct almost any type of locomotive for any type of work. The brand new 4-6-0, No 98, was constructed simultaneously with No 97, a 2-8-0 heavy freight engine; apart from the fact that the 4-6-0 had 6ft 8½in coupled wheels and the 2-8-0 had 4ft 7½in drivers, both locomotives had identical boilers, carrying wheels and cylinder blocks. The 2-8-0 was later renumbered 2800 as the leader of a class of 167 excellent engines. The 4-6-0 became the forerunner of the highly acclaimed Saint class express passenger locomotives and was renumbered, eventually, No 2998. Those two early examples of Churchward's standardisation policy proved to be superb recommendations for continuation.

Impatience certainly wasn't a Swindon characteristic. While the very first 4-6-0, No 100, had appeared in February 1902 and the second, No 98, in March 1903, the third 4-6-0 to emerge from the works did not take its bow until December 1903. With an apparent aversion to sequential numbering, the new arrival carried No 171 and, apart from an increase in boiler pressure to 225 lb, it was almost identical to No 98. The GWR's Public Relations Department was not unaware of the external similarities between the two engines and the official publicity pictures of No 171 were, in fact, of No 98

In 1905, Swindon turned out out a batch of nineteen two-cylinder engines which, although sharing many similar features, fell distinctly into one of two categories: twelve of the engines were built as 4-4-2s while the other six appeared as 4-6-0s. Numbered 173 – 78, the 4-6-0s were eventually treated as members of the Saint class and, from the end of 1912, were renumbered in the conventional Saint sequence. As a result of their comparatively short 'out-of-sequence' lives, photographs of them wearing their original three-digit numbers are relatively scarce. This picture shows No 174 *Lord Barrymore* which later became No 2974; interestingly, the engine spent the first two months of its life wearing the shorter name of *Barrymore*.

Photo: Rail Archive Stephenson

Saint class No 2971 *Albion* spent three of its early years as a 4-4-2; in that guise, it had worn No 171 but was renumbered in 1913. Here, it is seen with superheater and top feed. Similar to the picture of *Lord Barrymore*, this locomotive is seen with straight front ends to its frames.

Photo: Rail Archive Stephenson

TABLE 3.1: ORIGINAL DIMENSIONS OF THE THREE PROTOTYPES

	NO 100	NO 98	NO 171
BUILT:	1902	1903	1903
WORKS NOS:	1928	1990	2024
WEIGHTS FULL (locomotive):	67 tons 16 cwt	68 tons 6 cwt	70 tons 4 cwt (a)
(tender):	43 tons 3 cwt	43 tons 3 cwt	43 tons 3 cwt
TENDER CAPACITY (water):	4000 gallons	4000 gallons	4000 gallons (a)
(coal):	7 tons	7 tons	7 tons
WHEELBASE (locomotive):	27ft 2in	27ft 1in	27ft 1in
WHEEL DIAMETER (bogie):	3ft 2in	3ft 2in	3ft 2in
(coupled):	6ft 8½in	6ft 8½in	6ft 8½in
CYLINDERS:	(2) 18in × 30in	(2) 18in × 30in	(2) 18in × 30in
BOILER PRESSURE:	200 lb/psi	200 lb/psi	225 lb/psi
HEATING SURFACES (tubes):	2252.4 sq ft	1988.7 sq ft	1988.7 sq ft
(firebox):	157.9 sq ft	154.4 sq ft	154.3 sq ft
SUPERHEATERS FITTED:	1910	1911	1910
GRATE AREA:	27.7 sq ft	27.2 sq ft	27.1 sq ft
TRACTIVE EFFORT (at 85% boiler pressure):	20,530 lb	20,530 lb	23,090 lb
ROUTE AVAILABILITY:	Red	Red	Red
GWR POWER CLASSIFICATION:	C	C	C
SWINDON WORKS DIAGRAM:	C (1903–10) P (1910–32)	D	E

(a) When Nos 173–78 were built, the different dimensions from No 171 were:
WEIGHT FULL (locomotive): 71 tons 14 cwt;
TENDER CAPACITY (water): 3,500 gallons.

with cunningly retouched numberplates. The reason for increasing the boiler pressure of No 171 from 200 lb to 225 lb was so that the engine could more equally be compared to the French compound 4-4-2 No 102 *La France* which worked at 227 lb. In February 1904, No 171 was named *Albion* to provide a bit of patriotic spice in anticipation of the contest with *La France* and, in October the same year, No 171 was converted to a 4-4-2 in order to provide a fairer comparison with its Continental adversary.

In 1905, nineteen engines with similar mechanical dimensions to No 171 were built at Swindon but thirteen were finished as 4-4-2s and only six as 4-6-0s. The 4-6-0s were given Nos 173–78 and they were put to work between Paddington and Bristol so that the 4-4-2s could be drafted on to the Plymouth run. Comparison trials were not restricted to England versus France, as the Swindon 4-4-2s and 4-6-0s were often pitted against each other with the heavily graded and curving line between Exeter and Plymouth being the most popular battleground. Predictably, the 4-6-0s showed greater adhesion but, apart from that, there was little to choose between the two types. Only three of the 4-6-0s, Nos 173/74/78, were named from new, the others having to wait until 1907 before being rescued from anonymity; the 4-4-2s had names taken from Sir Walter Scott's 'Waverley' novels but the 4-6-0s were named after directors of the GWR.

By the spring of 1906, work was well under way with the construction of the Somerset cut-off route between Castle Cary and Taunton; this would shorten the distance between Paddington and Taunton by some twenty miles and would also avoid the bottleneck at Bristol. The new line would give the GWR an edge in its long-standing battle with the London & South Western for ocean liner traffic to Plymouth but the seventeen 4-4-2s and the eight 4-6-0s were the only suitable passenger engines the GWR had other than 4-4-0s. The decision had to be made whether to pursue 4-4-2s or 4-6-0s for express services via the new line, and bets were taken that the GWR would opt for Atlantics. There was a reason behind the speculation.

TABLE 3.2: THE DIRECTORS AND THE WAVERLEYS

FIRST NO	FINAL NO	ORIGINAL NAME	BUILT	TYPE	REBUILT AS 4-6-0	FIRST SHED
171	2971	*Albion* (a)	12/03	4-6-0 (*)	7/07	Paddington
172	2972	*Quicksilver* (b)	2/05	4-4-2	4/12	Plymouth
173	2973	*Robins Bolitho*	3/05	4-6-0		Paddington
174	2974	*Barrymore* (c)	3/05	4-6-0		Bristol
175	2975	*Viscount Churchill* (d)	3/05	4-6-0		Bristol
176	2976	*Winterstoke* (e)	4/05	4-6-0		Bristol
177	2977	*Robertson* (e)	4/05	4-6-0		Paddington
178	2978	*Kirkland* (f)	4/05	4-6-0		Bristol
179	2979	*Magnet* (g)	4/05	4-4-2	8/12	Bristol
180	2980	*Coeur De Lion* (e)	5/05	4-4-2	1/13	Paddington
181	2981	*Ivanhoe* (e)	6/05	4-4-2	7/12	Ntn. Abbot
182	2982	*Lalla Rookh* (n)	6/05	4-4-2	11/12	Plymouth
183	2983	*Red Gauntlet* (h)	7/05	4-4-2	4/12	Paddington
184	2984	*Churchill* (j)	7/05	4-4-2	8/12	Paddington
185	2985	*Winterstoke* (k)	7/05	4-4-2	5/12	Paddington
186	2986	*Robin Hood* (n)	7/05	4-4-2	5/12	Paddington
187	2987	*Robertson* (m)	8/05	4-4-2	6/12	Exeter
188	2988	*Rob Roy* (e)	8/05	4-4-2	5/12	Ntn. Abbot
189	2989	*Talisman* (n)	9/05	4-4-2	10/12	Bristol
190	2990	*Waverley* (n)	9/05	4-4-2	11/12	Plymouth

NOTES:
(*) Converted to 4-4-2 in October 1904.
(a) Unnamed until Feb 1904. Carried the name *The Pirate* from March to July 1907.
(b) Renamed *The Abbot* in March 1907.
(c) Renamed *Lord Barrymore* in May 1905.
(d) Unnamed until 1907. Renamed *Sir Ernest Palmer* in Feb 1924 and *Lord Palmer* in Oct 1933.
(e) Unnamed until 1907.
(f) Renamed *Charles J Hambro* in May 1935.
(g) Renamed *Quentin Durward* in March 1907.
(h) Renamed *Redgauntlet* in June 1915.
(j) Renamed *Viscount Churchill* in 1906 and *Guy Mannering* in 1907.
(k) Unnamed until Feb 1906. Renamed *Peveril of the Peak* in April 1907.
(m) Unnamed until Nov 1905. Renamed *Bride of Lammermoor* in April 1907.
(n) Unnamed until 1906.
N.B. The allocation of London-based locomotives is given as Paddington, which was the commonly-used name for Westbourne Park shed. That shed was not superseded until March 1906 when the new depot at Old Oak Common was opened.

TABLE 3.2A: WITHDRAWAL AND DISTRIBUTION OF THE DIRECTORS AND THE WAVERLEYS

NO	WDN	1922 SHED	LAST SHED	NO	WDN	1922 SHED	LAST SHED
2971	1/46	Old Oak	Swindon	2981	3/51	Exeter	Banbury
2972	3/35	Bristol	Cardiff	2982	6/54	Bristol	Newport
2973	7/33	Exeter	Chester	2983	3/46	Bristol	Tyseley
2974	8/33	Old Oak	Pontypool	2984	5/33	Old Oak	Bristol
2975	11/44	Swindon	Banbury	2985	8/31	Old Oak	Swansea
2976	1/34	Cardiff	Wolverht'n	2986	11/32	Old Oak	Swindon
2977	2/35	Cardiff	Westbury	2987	10/49	Exeter	Hereford
2978	8/46	Ntn. Abbot	Swindon	2988	5/48	Worcester	Tyseley
2979	1/51	Old Oak	Swindon	2989	9/48	Old Oak	Chester
2980	5/48	Bristol	Newport	2990	1/39	Wolverht'n	Cardiff

Although this picture shows No 2980 *Coeur de Lion* as a fully paid-up member of the Saint class, the engine had started life in 1905 as a 4-4-2. It was not rebuilt as a 4-6-0 until January 1913, thereby just claiming the distinction of being the last Swindon-built Atlantic in traffic.

Photo: Rail Archive Stephenson

One of the very few railway companies in Britain which was able to match the GWR for engineering ability was the North Eastern Railway and, although Worsdell's 4-6-0s had proved successful, the North Eastern had swayed back to 4-4-2s for its express services. Despite the forecasts, the GWR plumped for 4-6-0s for the Plymouth route, mainly because of their superior adhesion but, quite possibly, also because Swindon did not wish to be seen following a lead set by another British company.

Ten new 4-6-0s made their debuts in May 1906 in preparation for duties on the fast line to the South-West. They were numbered 2901–10 and were the first 4-6-0s to be built after the GWR had abandoned the red colour scheme for frames and wheels. These new engines were, basically, similar to No 171 when it had run as a 4-6-0 but, on closer inspection, the new ones were not uniform. Six

By the late 1930s, the Saint class 4-6-0s were often relegated to mixed traffic duties and this is clearly demonstrated by the assortment of rolling stock behind No 2981 *Ivanhoe* in this 1937 photograph. This engine was one of the batch built in 1905 as 4-4-2s; it originally wore No 181 but was renumbered in the Saint sequence after rebuilding.
Photo: Rail Archive Stephenson

Saint class 4-6-0 No 2981 *Ivanhoe* is seen on an unidentified express working at Kensal Green in October 1932.
Photo: Rail Archive Stephenson

TABLE 3.3: THE LADIES

NO	NAME	BUILT	WDN	FIRST SHED	1922 SHED	LAST SHED
2901	*Lady Superior*	5/06	4/33	Bristol	Swindon	Cardiff
2902	*Lady of the Lake*	5/06	8/49	Old Oak	Wolverht'n	Leamington
2903	*Lady of Lyons*	5/06	11/49	Plymouth	Pontypool	Tyseley
2904	*Lady Godiva*	5/06	10/32	Old Oak	Wolverht'n	Shrewsbury
2905	*Lady MacBeth*	5/06	4/48	Ntn. Abbot	Pontypool	Cardiff
2906	*Lady of Lynn*	5/06	8/52	Old Oak	Bristol	Cardiff
2907	*Lady Disdain*	5/06	7/33	Bristol	Bristol	Newport
2908	*Lady of Quality*	5/06	12/50	Old Oak	Ntn. Abbot	Swindon
2909	*Lady of Provence*	5/06	11/31	Old Oak	Ntn. Abbot	Wolverht'n
2910	*Lady of Shalott*	5/06	10/31	Old Oak	Cardiff	Westbury

N.B. No 2901 was unnamed until Oct 1906 and the others until April/May 1907.

had long taper boilers with medium smokeboxes while three had short taper boilers and short smokeboxes. The other one, No 2901, had a short taper boiler but was fitted with a Schmidt firetube heater, thus becoming the first British locomotive with a modern superheater. The boiler pressure of No 2901 was reduced to 200 lb while the cylinders were enlarged to 18⅜in × 30in; the other nine retained 225 lb boiler pressure but had a smaller increase in the size of their cylinders to 18⅛in × 30in.

It was No 2902 which had the privilege of hauling the inaugural express over the new route to the South-West on 2 July 1906 and this heralded the introduction of a three-hour schedule for the 175 mile journey to Plymouth. Four years later, almost to the day, No 2902 was booked for inaugural duties on the two-hour express from Birmingham to London via the Bicester route on 1 July 1910. Before the train's departure from Birmingham, a member of the public threw the lucky charm of a horseshoe onto the footplate of No 2902. The horseshoe missed the driver's forehead by a fraction of an inch and, taking this as suitable endorsement of luck, the fireman later constructed a proper mount for the shoe; it was retained in the cab of No 2902 for the rest of the engine's life. The lucky charm might well have been aimed at the GWR itself, as the opening of the faster route to Birmingham was in a different league to the cut-off route to Taunton which had opened in 1906. While the GWR constantly had supremacy over the London & South Western on the rival routes to Plymouth, the run from London to Birmingham had always been a staunch London & North Western stronghold which even the Midland Railway had failed to penetrate.

In July 1907, No 171 *Albion* was rebuilt to its original form as a 4-6-0 and, during the following two months, twenty new 4-6-0s were constructed and these had long taper boilers with medium smokeboxes. The new engines were numbered 2911–30 and all were named after saints but, although they were far from the first 4-6-0s to be built, they gave their name to what was to become one of the GWR's most highly respected locomotive classes. It mattered not one whit that earlier 4-6-0s had taken names from legendary 'Ladies' and the GWR's directors; the arrival of twenty Saints took precedence and the entire class became known as Saints until extinction in 1953.

The class was boosted by twenty-five more engines between October 1911 and April 1913. These were named after Courts, some of which were the country homes of various GWR directors, but, although the Courts outnumbered the Saints, the adopted generic did not change. The original order was for thirty extra locomotives but Nos 2956–60 were not built and five of the four-cylinder Star class 4-6-0s were constructed instead. The twenty-five new engines had 18½in diameter cylinders and were superheated from new and, before the

TABLE 3.4: THE SAINTS

NO	NAME	BUILT	WDN	FIRST SHED	1922 SHED	LAST SHED
2911	*Saint Agatha*	8/07	3/35	Bristol	Cardiff	Taunton
2912	*Saint Ambrose*	8/07	2/51	Old Oak	Bristol	Weymouth
2913	*Saint Andrew*	8/07	5/48	Old Oak	Cardiff	Swindon
2914	*Saint Augustine*	8/07	1/46	Old Oak	Fishguard	Weymouth
2915	*Saint Bartholomew*	8/07	10/50	Old Oak	Old Oak	Chester
2916	*Saint Benedict*	8/07	7/48	Bristol	Bristol	Tyseley
2917	*Saint Bernard*	8/07	10/34	Old Oak	Ntn. Abbot	Cardiff
2918	*Saint Catherine*	8/07	2/35	Cardiff	Worcester	Leamington
2919	*Saint Cecilia* (a)	9/07	2/32	Cardiff	Old Oak	Taunton
2920	*Saint David*	9/07	10/53	Cardiff	Wolverhampton	Hereford
2921	*Saint Dunstan*	9/07	12/45	Bristol	Bristol	Banbury
2922	*Saint Gabriel*	9/07	12/44	Plymouth	Bristol	Severn Tunnel Jct.
2923	*Saint George*	9/07	10/34	Plymouth	Wolverhampton	Bristol
2924	*Saint Helena*	9/07	3/50	Old Oak	Shrewsbury	Hereford
2925	*Saint Martin*	9/07	(b)	Ntn. Abbot	Worcester	Shrewsbury
2926	*Saint Nicholas*	9/07	9/51	Old Oak	Shrewsbury	Chester
2927	*Saint Patrick*	9/07	12/51	Cardiff	Bristol	Swindon
2928	*Saint Sebastian*	9/07	8/48	Exeter	Old Oak	Westbury
2929	*Saint Stephen*	9/07	12/49	Cardiff	Cardiff	Bristol
2930	*Saint Vincent*	9/07	10/49	Bristol	Bristol	Chester

(a) Renamed *Saint Cuthbert* in October 1907.
(b) Rebuilt as prototype Hall class locomotive December 1924. Finally withdrawn April 1959.

Saint class No 2915 *Saint Bartholomew* is seen receiving a wash and brush up at Swindon shed in 1931.
Photo: Rail Archive Stephenson

TABLE 3.5: THE COURTS

NO	NAME	BUILT	WDN	FIRST SHED	1922 SHED	LAST SHED
2931	*Arlington Court*	10/11	2/51	Exeter	Exeter	Bristol
2932	*Ashton Court*	10/11	6/51	Ntn. Abbot	Bristol	Tyseley
2933	*Bibury Court*	11/11	1/53	Exeter	Wolverhampton	Leamington
2934	*Butleigh Court*	11/11	6/52	Ntn. Abbot	Exeter	Swindon
2935	*Caynham Court*	11/11	12/48	Plymouth	Cardiff	Swindon
2936	*Cefntilla Court*	11/11	4/51	Cardiff	Cardiff	Newport
2937	*Clevedon Court*	12/11	6/53	Fishguard	Exeter	Hereford
2938	*Corsham Court*	12/11	8/52	Fishguard	Bristol	Gloucester
2939	*Croome Court*	12/11	12/50	Exeter	Old Oak	Bristol
2940	*Dorney Court*	12/11	1/52	Fishguard	Cardiff	Cardiff
2941	*Easton Court*	5/12	12/49	Old Oak	Worcester	Westbury
2942	*Fawley Court*	5/12	12/49	Old Oak	Old Oak	Bristol
2943	*Hampton Court*	5/12	1/51	Plymouth	Old Oak	Cardiff
2944	*Highnam Court*	5/12	11/51	Old Oak	Old Oak	Hereford
2945	*Hillingdon Court*	6/12	6/53	Bristol	Cardiff	Cardiff
2946	*Langford Court*	6/12	11/49	Bristol	Cardiff	Westbury
2947	*Madresfield Court*	6/12	4/51	Old Oak	Old Oak	Swindon
2948	*Stackpole Court*	6/12	11/51	Cardiff	Pontypool	Bristol
2949	*Stanford Court*	5/12	1/52	Wolverhampton	Bristol	Swindon
2950	*Taplow Court*	5/12	9/52	Old Oak	Bristol	Bristol
2951	*Tawstock Court*	3/13	6/52	Cardiff	Cardiff	Gloucester
2952	*Twineham Court*	3/13	9/51	Cardiff	Old Oak	Severn Tunnel Jct.
2953	*Titley Court*	3/13	2/52	Gloucester	Pontypool	Chester
2954	*Tockenham Court*	3/13	7/52	Ntn. Abbot	Cardiff	Swindon
2955	*Tortworth Court*	4/13	3/50	Ntn. Abbot	Fishguard	Weymouth

last was delivered, all of the other locomotives which had come under the umbrella of the Saint class had been fitted with Churchward-designed superheaters.

The Schmidt superheater with which No 2901 had been built was found to be most effective but its design seemed hell-bent on prolonging routine maintenance and, furthermore, the royalty payments demanded by Herr Schmidt discouraged extensive use of the devices. Churchward had recognised the advantages of superheating but, as the GWR now had engines which were both modern and of adequate power, there was no immediate necessity for it. This gave Churchward plenty of time to perfect his own design for a superheater which, of course, would provide the added benefit of dispensing with the payment of royalties. In 1908, No 2922 *Saint Gabriel* was fitted with an experimental Churchward superheater, but it was an improved version of this which was subsequently fitted to all of the Saints from 1910.

While the twenty-five new locomotives were under construction between 1911 and 1913, the remaining Swindon-built Atlantics, Nos 172/179–90, were rebuilt as 4-6-0s and, with effect from December 1912, they were renumbered 2972/79–90. To achieve numerical standardisation of a group of engines which had started out as anything other than standard, No 98, by now named *Ernest Cunard*, No 100 *William Dean* and No 171 *Albion* became Nos 2998, 2900 and 2971 respectively under the renumbering scheme of 1912. As a class of seventy-seven, the Saints gained an excellent reputation for strength and speed and were used on heavy express workings all over the GWR system. Their usefulness is reflected in the widespread

TABLE 3.6: ORIGINAL DIMENSIONS OF THE LADIES, THE SAINTS AND THE COURTS

	2901–10	2911–30	2931–55
BUILT:	1906	1907	1911–13
WORKS NOS:	2199–2208	2259–78	2426–35/76–85 2506–10
WEIGHTS FULL (locomotive):	72 tons 0 cwt	72 tons 0 cwt	74 tons 0 cwt
(tender):	40 tons 0 cwt	40 tons 0 cwt	40 tons 0 cwt
TENDER CAPACITY (water):	3500 gallons	3500 gallons	3500 gallons
(coal):	7 tons	7 tons	7 tons
WHEELBASE (locomotive):	27ft 1in	27ft 1in	27ft 1in
WHEEL DIAMETERS (bogie):	3ft 2in	3ft 2in	3ft 2in
(coupled):	6ft 8½in	6ft 8½in	6ft 8½in
CYLINDERS:	(2) 18⅛in × 30in*	(2) 18⅛in × 30in	(2) 18½in × 30in
BOILER PRESSURE:	225 lb/psi*	225 lb/psi	225 lb/psi
HEATING SURFACES (tubes):	1988.7 sq ft*	1988.7 sq ft	1686.6 sq ft
(firebox):	154.3 sq ft*	154.3 sq ft	154.8 sq ft
(s'heater):	*	n/a	286.6 sq ft
SUPERHEATERS FITTED:	1909–11*	1908–12	from new
GRATE AREA:	27.2 sq ft	27.2 sq ft	27.2 sq ft
TRACTIVE EFFORT (at 85% boiler pressure):	23,382 lb*	23,382 lb	24,395 lb
ROUTE AVAILABILITY:	Red	Red	Red
POWER CLASSIFICATION (GWR):	C	C	C
(BR):	4P	4P	4P
SWINDON WORKS DIAGRAMS:	F*	I	R/V

*No 2901 was built with a Schmidt superheater and dimensions were thus: CYS: 18⅜in × 30in ; B/PRESSURE: 200 lb; HEATING SURFACES (sq ft): tubes 1486, firebox 154.9, superheater 307.5; T.E.: 21,457 lb; DIAGRAM: G.

TABLE 3.7: MISCELLANEOUS LOCOMOTIVES OF THE SAINT CLASS

NO	NAME	BUILT	WDN	FIRST SHED	1922 SHED	LAST SHED
2901	*Dean* (a)	2/02	6/32	Bristol	Pontypool	Chester
2998	*Persimmon* (b)	3/03	6/33	Paddington	Exeter	Cardiff

(a) Ex-No 100. Unnamed until June 1902. Renamed *William Dean* in November 1902.
(b) Ex-No 98. Unnamed until 1906. Renamed *Vanguard* in March 1907 and *Ernest Cunard* in December 1907.

allocation of the class at the end of 1913: Bristol had eighteen, Old Oak Common fourteen, Wolverhampton eleven, Cardiff nine and Newton Abbot seven with the rest divided between Exeter, Fishguard, Gloucester and Plymouth.

The Saints were used regularly on the expresses between Paddington and Birmingham and, although two hours was the booked time for the crack trains, the engines were quite adept at turning up at their destinations early. There were several recorded instances of Saints hauling 300 ton trains over the 110½ miles from Birmingham to London in under 115 minutes. Excellent performances by Saints were also recorded regularly between Paddington and Bristol with 360 ton trains completing the 118 mile run ahead of schedule at average speeds of

Main Line.] 13 [Great Western.

For Notes, see page 16; for Continuation of Trains, see pages 14 to 16.

LONDON, READING, OXFORD, DIDCOT, SWINDON, CHIPPENHAM, BATH, BRISTOL, and TAUNTON.—Great Western.

Down. Week Days—*Continued.*

Down.	mrn	mrn	mrn	mrn	mrn	mrn	mrn	mrn
Train		Through Train from Clifton Down (dep. 10 45 mrn.), see page 57.				Minehead, Ilfracombe, and Torquay Express. Luncheon and Tea Car.		Through Train, Birmingham (G. W.) to Torquay and Plymouth. Tea Car, Bristol to Torquay.
PADDINGTON dep.				9 0	9 15			
Ealing (Broadway) "				9 10	9 25			
Reading "			8 42	9 50	10 5			
80 Oxford dep.			8 45	9 35	9F16			
Didcot dep.			9 30	1020	1030			
Steventon			9 38		1038			
Wantage Road ••			9 48		1048			
Challow			10 5		1057			
Uffington 47			1015		11 5			
Shrivenham			1028		1116			
Swindon 59, 60, 70, 122, 123 arr.			1033	1050	1127			
Swindon dep.	9 20		Stop	1057				
Wootton Bassett	9 32							
Dauntsey 41	9 44							
Chippenham 2, 53 arr.	9 54			1117				
Chippenham dep.	10 0			1121				
Corsham	10 10							
Box	10 19							
Bathampton 43	10 27						1145	
Bath • 48, 120, 686 arr.	10 33		mrn	1139			1150	
Bath dep.	10 39		1122	1144			Stop	
Saltford	10 47							
Keynsham	10 53							
St. Anne's Park	11 3							
Stapleton Road 57, 60								
Bristol † 48, 49, 57, 60	11 8		1140	12 2				
450 Liverpool (Ln. St.) dep	Stop							6a45
450 Birkenhead (W.) "								7a0
450 Liverpool (L. St.) "								
450 Manchester (Ln. Rd.) "								
626 " (Central) "								
108 Birmingham (S. H.) "							mrn	1015
626 " (New St.) "	mrn						9 30	
65 Swansea (High St.) "	6 45	6 45					8 55	
65 Cardiff "	9 29	9 2					11 0	
Bristol (Temple Meads) dep.	11 5	1115					1220	1245
Bedminster	11 9	1119					1224	
Flax Bourton		1128					1233	
Nailsea and Backwell	11A20	1135					1239	
Yatton 41	11A27	1145					1250	
Puxton and Worle							1257	
Weston-super-Mare 273 arr.	Runs to Witham, see page 41.	1157					1 5	
Weston-super-Mare dep.		12 5						
Bleadon and Uphill		1212						
Brent Knoll		1222						
Highbridge 122, 123		1233						
Dunball		1241						
Bridgwater 120		1252						
Durston 7		1 5						
Taunton 7, 22, 54 arr.		1 15				1210		1 38
54 Ilfracombe 144 arr.		4p53				3 18		4p53
54 Minehead "						1 55		
22 Exeter (St. David's) "		2 19				1254		2 19
22 Torquay "		3 15				2 7		3 15
22 Paignton "		3 25				2 20		3 25
22 Plymouth (Millbay) "		4 22						4 22
22 Penzance "		7 55						7 55

Down.	aft	aft	mrn	mrn	aft	mrn	mrn
Train		Through Train, Portsmouth to Cardiff, see pages 148, 49, and 61.	Via Badminton, see page 61.		Motor Car, one class only, between Chippenham and Bristol.	Cornish Riviera Limited Express. Via Westbury. Luncheon and Tea Car.	Luncheon Car for Passengers to Bristol or beyond.
PADDINGTON dep.						1030	1045
Ealing (Broadway) "							1055
Reading "							1138
80 Oxford dep.							1120
Didcot dep.							1211
Swindon arr.			III		III		1242
Swindon dep.			11 2	1115	1235		Stop
Wootton Bassett			1113	1126	1246		
Dauntsey 41				1135	1257		
Chippenham arr.				1145	1 10		
Chippenham dep.				1156	Stop		
Corsham				12 6			
Box				1214			
Bathampton 43				1221			
Bath arr.				1227			
Bath dep.		1214		1232			
Saltford				1241			
Keynsham				1247			
St. Anne's Park				1257			
Stapleton Road 57, 60		1234	1249				
Bristol †			1 0	1 2			
626 " (New St.) "					mrn		
65 Swansea (High St.) "					9 40		
65 Cardiff "					1130		
Bristol (Temple Meads) dep.	1252				1 10		
Bedminster					1 14		
Flax Bourton					1 23		
Nailsea and Backwell					1 30		
Yatton 41					1 37		
Puxton and Worle					III		
Weston-super-Mare arr.	1 21						
Weston-super-Mare dep.	1 30						
Highbridge 122, 123	1 48						
Dunball							aft
Bridgwater 120	1 58						2 30
Taunton arr.							2 46
22 Exeter (St. David's) "							4 11
22 Torquay "							5 27
22 Paignton "							5 36
22 Plymouth (Millbay) "						2N37	6N16
22 Penzance "						5 0	1010

Down.	mrn	mrn	noon	mrn	aft	aft	aft
Train	Exeter, Plymouth, Newquay, and Penzance Express. Via Westbury. Luncheon and Tea Car.	Bath, Bristol, and Weston-super-Mare Express.	Torquay and Kingswear Express. Via Westbury. Luncheon and Tea Car.	Thro. Exp., Wolverhampton and Birmingham to Torquay and Penzance, see pages 87, 81, 108, and 24. Tea and Dining Car.	Taunton, Minehead, and Ilfracombe Express. Via Westbury. Luncheon (cold) and Tea Car.		Exeter and Torquay Express.
PADDINGTON dep.	11 0	1115	12 0		12 5		
Reading "					12 50		
80 Oxford dep.					11F20		
Bathampton 43						1 9	
Bath arr.		1k0				1 14	
Bath dep.						1 17	1 38
Saltford						1 26	
Keynsham						1 32	
St. Anne's Park						1 42	
Bristol †		1 15				1 47	1 55
450 Liverpool (Ln. St.) dep				7a40			
450 Birkenhead (W.) "				8a0			
450 Liverpool (L. St.) "				8‖0			
450 Manchester (Ln. Rd.) "				8c10			
626 " (Central) "				[illegible] 20			
108 Birmingham (S. H.) "				1115			
626 " (New St.) "				1120			
65 Swansea (High St.) "		9 40					
65 Cardiff "		1130					
Bristol (Temple Meads) dep.		1 30		1 45			2 5
Weston-super-Mare arr.		1 57					2 32
Weston-super-Mare dep.		2 10					2 39
Bleadon and Uphill		2 16					
Brent Knoll		2 25					
Highbridge 122, 123		2 34					2 58
Dunball		2 41					
Bridgwater 120		2 52					3 12
Durston 7		3 2					
Taunton arr.				2 30	2 55		3 28
54 Ilfracombe 144 arr.	4p53			6 5	6 5		7K5
54 Minehead "				4 5	4 5		5K35
22 Exeter (St. David's) "	2 0			3 19			4 11
22 Torquay "	3 15		3 35	4 25			5 27
22 Paignton "	3 25		3 51	4 36			5 38
22 Plymouth (Millbay) "	3N16			4N45			
22 Penzance "	6 10			7 55			

Down.	mrn	mrn	aft	mrn	aft	aft
Train			Through Train from Sheffield (Victoria) via Great Central Line, see pages 696 and 90. Luncheon and Tea Car.	Through Express, Manchester (London Road) to Torquay; Liverpool (Lime Street) to Newquay; and Birkenhead to Truro, see pages 450 and 24. Tea Car.		
80 Oxford dep.			1212			
Didcot dep.			1238			
Swindon arr.			1 [illegible]			
Swindon dep.			1 20			
Dauntsey 41			1 37			
Chippenham arr.			1 47			III
Chippenham dep.			1 51			1 58
Corsham						2 8
Box						2 16
Bathampton 43						2 23
Bath arr.			2 9			2 29
Bath dep.			2 13		2 21	Stop
Saltford					2 29	
Keynsham					2 35	
St. Anne's Park					2 45	
Bristol †			2 30		2 54	
450 Liverpool (Ln. St.) dep				9 20	Stop	
450 Birkenhead (W.) "				9 35		
450 Liverpool (L. St.) "				9 10		
450 Manchester (Ln. Rd.) "		8‖30		9 25		
626 " (Central) "		8 55		8 55		
626 " (New St.) "		12 2		12 2		
65 Swansea (High St.) "	1045	1045	1045	1045		aft
65 Cardiff "	1250	1250	1250	1250		III
Bristol (Temple Meads) dep.	2 20	2 25	2 38	2 53		2 58
Bedminster						3 2
Flax Bourton		2 37				3 11
Nailsea and Backwell		2 43				3 18
Yatton 41	2 38		2 59			3 25
Weston-super-Mare arr.		3 0	3 10			
Weston-super-Mare dep.					aft 3 25	
Highbridge 122, 123					3 44	
Bridgwater 120					3 57	
Taunton arr.				3 45	4 13	
54 Ilfracombe 144 arr.				7T48	7p48	
54 Minehead "				5K35		
22 Exeter (St. David's) "				4 30	5 23	
22 Torquay "				5 49	6 45	
22 Paignton "				6 0	6 57	
22 Plymouth (Millbay) "				6N16	7N6	
22 Penzance "				1010	1010	

The GWR's Bristol and Taunton lines are shown in this extract from the public timetable for the summer of 1922. The Bristol trains were usually hauled by locomotives of the Saint class while Stars were more common on the through services to the West Country.

over 60 mph. On the West of England route, one legendary adventure involved No 2943 *Hampton Court* which hauled a Summer Saturday train of 535 tons out of Paddington for Plymouth. Congestion on the main line south of Taunton and the need for assistance at Whiteball resulted in the train arriving at its final destination late but, as far as Taunton, the abnormal load had been hauled single-handed and had kept bang on time.

Eventually, however, the increase in the number of four-cylinder Star class 4-6-0s meant that the Saints played less frequent roles on the prestigious main line duties to Birmingham and Plymouth, although the Bristol route was to remain a stronghold of the class until well into the 1920s. Before the First World War, the Saints started to appear in South Wales in increasing numbers. Three of those built in 1911 were allocated from new to Fishguard to help establish fast services to London in anticipation of the port being developed as a transatlantic passenger terminal. The ocean trade failed to materialise but Fishguard still did very nicely from shipping services to and from Ireland and the haulage of the boat trains was regularly entrusted to the Saints.

During the War, displacement of the Saints from some of their traditional haunts enabled their introduction on the non-stop expresses between Paddington and Worcester which were timed at 135 minutes for the 120 mile trip. During the same period, several members of the class were transferred to Shrewsbury shed which serviced routes to Bristol via the Severn Tunnel, to Wolverhampton and also to Chester, and the Saints' enthusiasm for sharply-graded lines made them very popular engines with the local crews. The border route southwards from Shrewsbury had been the run for which the County class 4-4-0s had been originally designed because the line's joint owners, the London & North Western, had initially barred anything larger than the Counties. The border run was a testing duty, not only because of the gradients but also due to the abundance of curves which prevented both the build up of speed on the approach to banks and recovery on the level sections. Loads exceeding 400 tons were commonplace on the route and assistance was rarely available but, nevertheless, the Saints acquitted themselves well.

The grouping of 1923 did not dispense with the competition between railway companies; the rivalry was still there but it was just different names doing battle. One significant target was the mile-a-minute schedule which few companies had achieved consistently, despite the fact that the

Unlike the 'Lady' sequence of Saint class locomotives, the Saints themselves had curved fronts to their running plates. The graceful sweep of the curves is shown by our model, No 2913 *Saint Andrew*, on the catwalk at Old Oak in 1930.
Photo: D. K. Jones Collection

WORCESTER, EVESHAM, CHELTENHAM, KINGHAM, OXFORD, and LONDON.—Great Western.

Up. — Week Days.

Miles from Worcester.	Up.	mrn	mrn	mrn	mrn	mrn (Wolverhampton, Kidderminster, Malvern, and Worcester Express, see pages 98, 102, and 80.)	mrn	mrn	mrn	mrn (Luncheon Car.)	aft	mrn	mrn (Luncheon and Tea Car.) (Hereford, Malvern, Kidderminster, and Worcester Express, see pages 102, 98, and 81.)
	98 Wolverhampton† dep.					7 0	7 0		8 20	8 55			11 20
	98 Kidderminster "					8 11	8 11		9 32	11 12			1 19
	98 Droitwich "					8 28	8 28		9 53	11 35			1 41
	102 Hereford "					7 10	7 10		8 20	10 0		1115	12 50
	102 Malvern (Great) "					8 12	8 12		9 40	11 3		1225	1 34
	Worcester (Shrub Hill) dep.	4 30	6 30		8 10	8 55	9 0		10 20	12 0		1 20	2 0
3¼	Norton Junction								10 26			1 26	
5¼	Stoulton								10 32			1 32	
8	Pershore	h	6 42	7 32	8 23		9 13		10 38	12 14		1 38	
10¾	Fladbury			7 39	8 29			m	10 44		m	1 43	
13¼	Evesham 637	h	6 53	7 48	8 38		9 24	9 15	10 53	12 25	1 5	1 50	
16¾	Littleton and Badsey			7 53	8 43				10 58		1 11	1 55	
28	108 Stratford-on-Avon arr.			8 23	9 14				11 35	1 0		2 21	
	" dep.						8 49		10 35	12 0			
19	Honeybourne 108	h		8 1	8 54		9 34	9 23	11 8	12 36	1 17	2 0	
24¼	Campden	h	7 10	Via Stratford-on-Avon.					11 21			Via Stratford-on-Avon	
26¼	Blockley	h	7 15						11 26				
29¼	Moreton-in-Marsh 109	5 33	7 23				9 54		11 35	12 56			
33¼	Adlestrop		7 32						11 44				
—	104 Cheltenham (St. J.) dep.		6 30				7q25		10 32	12 0			
—	104 Chipping Norton "		7 23			8b19	9 50		11 29	12n50			1s53
36¼	Kingham 104		7 41				10 6		11 54	1 12			
39¼	Shipton ‡		7 52						12 1				
40¾	Ascott-under-Wychwood		7 57						12 5				
44¼	Charlbury		8 5				10 19		12 15				
50¼	Handborough		8 15				10 30		12 27				
54	Yarnton		d				d		12 36				
57¼	Oxford 46, 76, 80 arr.		8 26			10 0	10 40		12 45	1 39			3 4
63	80 Didcot arr.		9 8				11 44		1 32	3 10			
85¼	80 Reading "		9c37				11c23		1c32	2 50			
121¼	80 London (Pad.) 103 "		9 50	11 0		1115	12 5		2 12	2 55		5 0	4 15

Week Days (continued) and Sundays.

Miles from Worcester.	Up.	aft	aft	aft	aft	aft (Dining Car.)	aft	aft (Wednesdays and Saturdays.)	aft	Sundays mrn	Sundays mrn	Sundays aft
	98 Wolverhampton† dep.	12 3	1 15		2 40	4 15	4 20	8 25			8 20	3 58
	98 Kidderminster "	1 19	2 25		3 42	5 17	5 50	9 32			9 40	5 0
	98 Droitwich "	1 41	2 44		4 1	5 37	6 8	9 50			10 0	5 20
	102 Hereford "	1 0	1 0			4 28	4 35	9 22				4 25
	102 Malvern (Great) "	2 3	2 3			5 20	6 5	9 59		m	1050	5 12
	Worcester (Shrub Hill) dep.	2 50	3 10		4 40	6 0	6 40	1050		9 50	1035	5 50
3¼	Norton Junction		3 16		4 46		6 46	c				
5¼	Stoulton		3 22		4 52		6 51					
8	Pershore		3 28		4 58		7 0	11 8		1011	1048	6 3
10¾	Fladbury		3 34		5 4		7 6	b		1017	1054	6 9
13¼	Evesham 637	3 12	3 43	4 36	5 15	6 24	7 15	1123		1028	11 3	6 18
16¾	Littleton and Badsey		3 48	4 41	5 20		7 21					
28	108 Stratford-on-Avon arr.		5 13	5 13	5 55		8v10					
	" dep.	1H35	1 35	5 20	4 57		6 45					
19	Honeybourne 108		3 55	4 55	6A5		7 30			1043	1114	6 32
24¼	Campden		4 8	Via Stratford-on-Avon.	6 18		7 42				1127	6 45
26¼	Blockley		4 13		6 22		7 48				1133	6 51
29¼	Moreton-in-Marsh 109	3 41	4 22		6 30	6 54	7 58				1142	7 7
33¼	Adlestrop		4 31				8 8				1151	7 19
—	104 Cheltenham (St. J.) dep.		3 7		5e10		6 55				7q40	4q53
—	104 Chipping Norton "	3 0	4 15			6 25	7 40		9B55			
36¼	Kingham 104	3 54	4 40			7 6	8 19				1159	7 27
39¼	Shipton ‡		4 46				8 26				12 6	7 35
40¾	Ascott-under-Wychwood		4 50				8 31					
44¼	Charlbury		5 0				8 40				1217	7 45
50¼	Handborough		5 11				8 52				1228	7 58
54	Yarnton	d	5 18									
57¼	Oxford 46, 76, 80 arr.	4 24	5 26			7 35	9 2		1 30		1240	8 10
63	80 Didcot arr.	5 18	6 25			8 44	10 3		2 0		1 17	9 5
85¼	80 Reading "	5 3	6 25			8 25	9 55		2 43		1 47	8 52
121¼	80 London (Pad.) 103 "	5 50	7 17	8 5		9 20	1045		3 30		2 40	9 42

A Arrives Honeybourne at 5 25 aft.
b Motor Car, one class only.
B Via Banbury, one class only.
b Stops on Saturdays to set down.
c By Slip Carriage.
c Stops to set down.
d Passengers for Yarnton and the Witney and Fairford Line travel via Oxford.
H Via Evesham.
h Calls at Pershore, Evesham, Honeybourne, Campden, and Blockley to set down from Worcester and beyond.
m Motor Car, one class only.
n Thursdays only, one class only.
q Via Honeybourne, one class only.
s Saturdays only.
t Change at King's Sutton.
v Via Honeybourne.
† Low Level Station.
‡ Station for Burford (5 miles).

For other Trains BETWEEN Yarnton and Oxford PAGE .....see below

This public timetable was for the summer of 1922 and, a few years earlier, the Saint class 4-6-0s had become established on the express services to Worcester.

No 2917 *Saint Bernard* seems to be missing the barrel of brandy as it sits outside its kennel at Old Oak in the late 1920s.
Photo: Rail Archive Stephenson

Caledonian Railway's Dunalastair 4-4-0s had put the first 60 mph schedule into Bradshaws in the early years of the century. Before 1923, the North Eastern and the Great Central shared the distinction of operating the fastest scheduled trains in the country and these were timed to average 61.5 mph. On 9 July 1923, the GWR introduced a timing of 61.8 mph which, despite being only a fraction faster, was enough to qualify for the number one slot. The new service was the Cheltenham Flyer which, on its inaugural run, consisted of a nine-coach train of 265 tons hauled by No 2915 *Saint Bartholomew*. The train pulled into Paddington three minutes ahead of schedule and the actual average speed on the day was 64.5 mph.

The introduction of the Castle class four-cylinder 4-6-0s in 1923 did not have any immediate effect on the future of the Saints. The Castles were a development of the four-cylinder Star class 4-6-0s and, when compared to the Stars, the Saints had usually proved that they were equal to their bigger brothers and, in certain aspects, superior. The Saints were adequate for most high-speed duties as had been proved with the Cheltenham Flyer but, when prolonged spells of fast running were called for, the Stars were usually preferred as they were acknowledged as having a definite edge in that department. Away from the race track, the Saints proved better than the Stars on both acceleration and uphill haulage and so they were considered to be the more versatile of the two classes. In 1926, a sizeable contingent of Saints was transferred to Swansea's Landore shed and this included the trio from Fishguard as, from that year, Landore took over responsibilities for servicing the Irish boat trains. Fast services on the old Wilts, Somerset & Weymouth line between Westbury and Weymouth were passed to the Saints in 1927 and so the sheds at Westbury and Reading each received a small allocation of the engines.

During the 1920s, several members of the Saint class were treated to modifications of varying degrees. In 1923, No 2933 *Bibury Court* had its blastpipe repositioned and this necessitated moving the chimney forward; it ran in this guise until 1927. From 1925, whistle shields and, from 1927, short safety valve bonnets started to be fitted; one member of the class, No 2930 *Saint Vincent*, was equipped with adjustable horn blocks while another, No 2947 *Madresfield Court*, was fitted with cylinder

Main Line.] 61 [Great Western.

CARMARTHEN, TENBY, NEYLAND, and FISHGUARD HARBOUR. Great Western.

Down. Week Days—Continued.

Down.	mrn	mrn	mrn	mrn	mrn	mrn	mrn	mrn	mrn	mrn	aft	mrn	aft	aft	mrn	aft	mrn	mrn	aft	mrn	aft	aft
		Via Bath, see page 12						To Pontypool Road, see page 102	Via Bath, see page 12	South Wales Express. Breakfast and Luncheon Cars to Landore		To Pontypool Road, see page 102		Saturdays only	Leaves Cheltenham (Malvern Road) at 10 30 mrn, see page 70	Saturdays only	Via Bath, see page 12	Via Bath, see page 12	Through Train Portsmouth to Cardiff, see pages 148, 49, and 13. Except Saturdays			
PADDINGTON ....dep.		5 30	5 30							8 45							7 30	9 0				
Ealing (Broadway) "																	7 43	9 10				
Reading "		6 18	6 18						[illegible]	9 30							8 20	9 50				
12 Oxford ....dep.									7 8								7 8	9 35		m		
Swindon ....dep.		7 22	7 30						8 55								9 13	1057		11 2		
Wootton Bassett			7 42																	1113		
Brinkworth			7 53																	1123		
Little Somerford			8 1																	1131		
Hullavington			8 11																	1141		
Badminton			8 24																	12 8		
Chipping Sodbury	7 50		8 35																	1221		
Coalpit Heath §	7 58		8 43																	1229		
Winterbourne	8 1		8 48																	1233		
Filton Junction 55	8 9		8 56																	1241		
Ashley Hill	8 14		9 1																	1246		
Stapleton Road 57	8 17		9 3																	1249		
Lawrence Hill [49	8 20		9 9																	1253		
Bristol * 12, 43, arr.	8 25	8 27	9 19														1015	12 2		1 0		
Bristol (Tm. Mds.) dep.				9 0			9 12	9 45				11 5					1115	1215			1250	
Lawrence Hill							9 16										1121	1219				
Stapleton Road				9 11			9 20	9 51	10 4			1110 a					1127	1222	1240		1259	
Ashley Hill							9 24										1131	Stop				
Filton Junction							9 32										1140					
Patchway							9 36										1144					
Pilning [71							9 44										1152					
Severn Tunnel Jn. 56 arr.				f			9 57		1030								12 5				1 26	
71 Chepstow 56 ...arr.				1035			1035		1055								1 7					
Severn Tunnel Junc. dep									1035								12 8				1 31	
Magor																	1214					
Llanwern																	1223					
Newport 74, 93, arr				9 55					1049	1117					1142		1233		1 20		1 46	
102, 124, 505 dep				10 0					1053	1123					1147		1239		1 25		1 51	
Marshfield ...[117, 118																					2 0	
Cardiff †111 to 114, arr.				1017					1110	1140					12 4		1256		1 42		2 15	
113 Barry Docks ..arr.									1228	1228		Stop			1 26		1 26		Stop		2 55	
Cardiff (General) ..dep.				1022		1030				1150					1220	1 0	1 8				Stop	2 45
Ely, for Llandaff						1036										1 6	1 15					
St. Fagan's																1 11	1 20					
Peterston						1043										1 17	1 27					
Llantrisant 93, 116						1057									1249	1 24	1 38					
Llanharan						11 4											1 45					
Pencoed						1110											1 51					
Bridgend 72, 73, 112,						1122									1 0	1 41	2 3					
Pyle 75 [119						1135									1 15	1 52	2 18					
Port Talbot & Aberavon						1148								1250	1 28	Stop	2 31					
Briton Ferry 119						1156								1258	1 36		2 39					
Neath 92, 119, 639						12 4								1 7	1 44		2 47					3 40
Skewen														1 14	1 50		2 54					
Llansamlet														1 21	1 56		3 0					
Landore 74 ....arr.						1216				1248				1 26	2 1		3 5					3 55
456 Swansea arr.				1125		1230				1 5				1 35	2 10	aft	3 15					4 5
689 (High Street) dep.					1135	1210				1245			1 15			2 30						3 50
Landore ....dep.						1221				1256												4 0
Cockett					1145	1228							1 25			2 40						
Gowerton 454, 456					1151								1 31			2 46						
Loughor					1156								1 36			2 51			aft			
Llanelly 456 [118					12 5	1247							1 45			3 0			4 0			4 22
Pembrey and Burry Port					1214								1 54			3 9			4 7			
Kidwelly					1224								2 4			3 19						
Ferryside					1232							aft	2 13			3 28						
Carmarthen Junc. ..arr.										1 36		1 50										
90 Carmarthen arr.					1245	1 14				1 53		1 5?	2 25			3 40				aft		
455 dep.											1 45									4 20		
Carmarthen Junc. ..dep.										1 41												
Sarnau											1 57									4 32		
St. Clears											2 6									4 42		5 3
Whitland 56, 59 ...arr.										2 3	2 16									4 52		5 12
59 Tenby ....arr.										3 13	3 1											6 5
Whitland ....dep										2 8	2 27										aft m	
Clynderwen 46											2 39											
Clarbeston Road											2 50										5 10	
Haverfordwest ‡											3 3											
Johnston 58											3 15											
Neyland ....arr.											3 25											
Fishguard & Goodwick										2 45											5 42	
Fishguard Harbour arr.										2 50											5 45	

For Notes, see page 64; for Continuation of Trains, see pages 62 and 64.

The 1922 public timetable for the West Wales line showed that the 8.45am ex-Paddington took under 3 hours to Cardiff, including two stops; the onward leg to Fishguard was, however, somewhat slower. The Saint class locomotives were the usual steeds for these services at the time.

No 2922 *Saint Gabriel* was one of the purpose-built Saints which did not see the birth of British Railways. It was retired in December 1944 still retaining its original inside steam-pipes.

Photo: Rail Archive Stephenson

In May 1931, Saint class No 2935 *Caynham Court* was fitted experimentally with rotary cam poppet valve gear. This was a very rare departure from the norm on the GWR and, perhaps to the relief of the locomotive department, the rotary gear showed no real advantages. The photograph of No 2935 was taken at Swindon in June 1933 and, as can be seen, the non-standard equipment did little for the locomotive's appearance either.

Photo: Rail Archive Stephenson

bypass valves. In 1928, No 2975 *Sir Ernest Palmer* appeared with a pair of cylindrical shields on its front buffer beam and these housed experimental valve spindle guides. Several of the later Saints were paired with the smaller 3,500 gallon tenders which had initially been used only by Nos 2901 – 30 and three of the class, Nos 2912/14/16 each had spells with the giant bogie tender which had been designed for the GWR's only 4-6-2, *The Great Bear*. From 1930, new front ends were fitted to many of the Saints and the most distinctive feature of this modification was the incorporation of outside steam-pipes. A total of forty-one Saints received the new front ends which were intended to have twenty-five year life-spans.

The most significant reconstruction to affect any of the Saints was inflicted on No 2925 *Saint Martin* in December 1924. Charles Collett, Churchward's successor, fitted the engine with driving wheels of a non-standard 6ft 0in and a new style of side-window cab to transform it into what became the prototype for the Hall class; it was eventually renumbered No 4900 as the leader of the numerous and successful class of 4-6-0s. Delivery of the Halls did not commence until four years after the appearance of the prototype and, when they started to displace some of the 4-4-0 classes on passenger duties, it was anticipated that the Saints would also fall victim to the new arrivals. To the consternation of both railwaymen and enthusiasts alike, No 2985 *Peveril of the Peak* was withdrawn in August 1931 and, by the end of the year, No 2910 *Lady of Shalott* and No 2909 *Lady of Provence* had also been retired. To the relief of many, however, this did not signal the wholesale slaughter of the class.

During the 1930s, the Saints were still in regular use on fast passenger trains. They were particularly appreciated on the border route between Newport and Shrewsbury where they earned the nickname of 'Hereford Castles'. Trains of sixteen or seventeen coaches were not unusual on the border route and, apart from banking assistance between Caerleon and Pontypool Road which was usually provided by a 4-4-0, the Saints managed loads of around 450 tons otherwise unaided.

This Saint has a large following. No 2912 *Saint Ambrose* was one of several GWR locomotives to be tried with the giant eight-wheeled tender from the 4-6-2 *Great Bear* and, although this photograph is undated, the evidence of outside steam-pipes places the picture after April 1931. One thing which is a little more certain, however, is that the location is Exeter.

Photo: Rail Archive Stephenson

The 'Court' members of the Saint class were the first of the class to be equipped with superheaters from new. No 2949 *Stanford Court* was built in 1912 and is seen prior to the fitting its outside steam-pipes in 1935.

Photo: Rail Archive Stephenson

A combination of excellent sunlight and a good polish meant that Saint class No 2954 *Tockenham Court* was well prepared for the photographer at Swindon in 1936. No 2954 is seen with the outside steam-pipes which were fitted in 1933 and the engine was to become one of the last survivors of the class.

Photo: Rail Archive Stephenson

The Saints could always be relied on for standby duties at short notice and one member of the class, No 2937 *Clevedon Court*, demonstrated this particularly well. In April 1936, the engine was employed on the sedate task of station pilot at Reading but, on three occasions that month, it had to substitute unexpectedly for failed engines on main line expresses. On the first occasion, No 2937 stood in for a Castle on a non-stop run to Plymouth and, despite the unscheduled engine change at Reading, the train arrived at Plymouth just five minutes outside the booked time. The other two substitutions were both for failed Kings, one on the Cornish Riviera and the other on the Bristolian and, again, the tight schedules were almost maintained even with the locomotive changes. On the Bristolian standby, No 2937 hauled the 225 ton train over the eighty-two miles from Reading to Bristol in seventy-two minutes. Not bad for a twenty-five year old two-cylinder locomotive.

By the time of Nationalisation, thirty of the Saints had reached their sell-by dates and the fitting of the new front ends, which had started in 1930, had done a little to determine the fate of the individual members of the class. The pre-1948 withdrawals included just one recylindered engine while, of the thirty-seven survivors in 1948, only nine had not had the operation. In the best tradition of generalisations, there was one particular exception and this involved the old Reading racer, No 2937 *Clevedon Court*. That locomotive was not fitted with a new front end until June 1948, six months after Nationalisation, but was withdrawn five years later.

The British Railways livery which was selected for the Saints was black with red, cream and grey lining and this categorised them, more or less, as 'any other variety, non-sporting'. Apart from the Kings, which were earmarked for the remarkable ultramarine livery, the only other GWR classes which were scheduled for anything other than black were the Castles and the Stars. The application of the black livery to the Saints might, just conceivably, have been excused by two facts: firstly

Saint class No 2944 *Highnam Court* was photographed at Worcester (Shrub Hill) in February 1931. This locomotive survived until January 1952, thereby becoming one of the last survivors of the class.

Photo: Rail Archive Stephenson

TABLE 3.8: ALLOCATIONS OF SURVIVORS AT MARCH 1950.

NO	SHED	NO	SHED	NO	SHED
2906	Cardiff	2934	Swindon	2948	Bristol
2908	Swindon	2936	Newport	2949	Swindon
2912	Weymouth	2937	Hereford	2950	Bristol
2915	Chester	2938	Gloucester	2951	Gloucester
2920	Hereford	2939	Bristol	2952	Severn Tunnel Jct.
2926	Chester	2940	Cardiff	2953	Chester
2927	Swindon	2943	Cardiff	2954	Swindon
2931	Bristol	2944	Hereford	2979	Newport
2932	Tyseley	2945	Swindon	2981	Banbury
2933	Leamington	2947	Swindon		

TABLE 3.9: YEARLY TOTALS OF SAINT CLASS LOCOMOTIVES

N.B. Totals taken to 31 December of each year.

1906	10	1913	77	1920	77	1927	76	1934	58	1941	53	1948	38
1907	30	1914	77	1921	77	1928	76	1935	54	1942	53	1949	30
1908	30	1915	77	1922	77	1929	76	1936	54	1943	53	1950	25
1909	30	1916	77	1923	77	1930	76	1937	54	1944	51	1951	12
1910	30	1917	77	1924	76	1931	73	1938	54	1945	50	1952	3
1911	40	1918	77	1925	76	1932	69	1939	53	1946	46	1953	0
1912	72*	1919	77	1926	76	1933	62	1940	53	1947	46		

* 1912 total includes Nos 98/100/171–90 which were incorporated in the Saint class at the end of that year.

they were not currently engaged on crack express duties and, secondly, they were not earmarked for lengthy existences. Those possibilities might have held water but for the fact that the Star class engines, which were destined for the dignity of green liveries, were only rarely used for express work by 1948 and, furthermore, the longevity of the Stars was not anticipated to be considerably greater than that of the Saints. The newly-formed Railway Executive worked in mysterious ways but, despite the controversy about the projected livery for the Saints, a number retained their GWR green liveries until withdrawal.

British Railways made short work of the remaining Saints. Apart from No 2925 which had been rebuilt by Collett as the prototype Hall class locomotive, the last Saint to be withdrawn was No 2920 *Saint David* which was retired from Hereford shed in October 1953 with the remarkable mileage of 2,076,297 on the clock. There was, at the time, strong feeling that No 2920 should be preserved as an example of what was considered to be one of the best passenger classes ever designed by the GWR. Considering that nostalgia was not a common trait in those days, it speaks volumes for the high regard in which the Saints were held.

CHAPTER 4

The Stars

George Jackson Churchward enjoyed the contest between the imported French compound locomotives and his own Atlantics. He must have felt a little smug because, although the French machines had attracted the attention of engineers worldwide, extensive comparison tests had shown his own locomotives to be just as useful.

One of the GWR locomotives to be pitted against the compounds in tests was the four-cylinder 4-4-2 No 40 which had been completed at Swindon in April 1906. The idea for using more than two cylinders on non-compound locomotives was not new. As far back as 1862, Haswell's of Vienna had exhibited a conventional four-cylinder locomotive at the London Exhibition and, after a twenty-five year silence, the idea resurfaced in Britain. In 1897, a pair of 4-4-0 engines with four high-pressure cylinders appeared within two months of each other, one on the London & North Western Railway and the other on the Glasgow & South Western. The locomotive superintendent of the L&NWR was Francis Webb, a dynamic young engineer who had long since taken a fancy to compounding, and so a novel cylinder arrangement was no real surprise from him. On the G&SWR, James Manson was, to be realistic, not in the same league as Francis Webb and he was hardly renowned for adventurous engineering. Manson's four-cylinder locomotive took the engineering fraternity aback when it made its debut just before Webb's and, to the surprise of many, the Scottish machine proved to be a very useful creature.

Later in 1897, Dugald Drummond completed a four-cylinder locomotive for the London & South Western Railway but this was a far less conventional contraption than the two earlier ones. On Drummond's locomotive, the driving wheels were uncoupled; the inside cylinders powered the leading axle and the outside cylinders drove the rear axle and so the engine was, technically, a 4-2-2-0. The theoretical advantages of the L&SWR's four-cylinder engine did not materialise in practice and, apart from five similar locomotives which Drummond built in 1901, the experiment was never repeated by either the L&SWR or any other company.

On the GWR, Churchward's four-cylinder 4-4-2 rapidly gained a reputation as one of the very best express passenger designs around and so it came as no surprise when work started to develop the idea in order to produce a four-cylinder 4-6-0. The 4-4-2 was considered an adequate prototype, especially when its performances were analysed in conjunction with those of the two-cylinder 4-6-0s, and so the construction of a formal prototype for a four-cylinder 4-6-0 was considered superfluous. Therefore, a batch of ten 4-6-0s was ordered simultaneously and all were delivered between February and May 1907; the new locomotives were given Nos 4001–10 and all carried names which had originally been borne by the broad gauge 2-2-2s of the Star class over sixty years previously.

Even apart from the wheel arrangements, there were several differences between the 4-6-0s and the 4-4-2 No 40. The most significant internal alteration was the use of Walschaerts valve gear instead of the 'scissors' gear which had been used on No 40 and the change had been prompted by nasty letters from the Midland Railway's head office at Derby. Richard Deeley had designed a type of 'scissors' gear when he was working under the

As would be expected from this official photograph, Star class No 4035 *Queen Charlotte* is in ex-works condition. Although the picture is undated, the tender lettering and the presence of the 'BRD' (Bath Road) shed-code on the frames indicate that it was almost certainly taken in 1946/47. The engine received its 'Castle'-style steam-pipes in 1931.

Star class No 4003 *Lode Star* is now preserved at the National Railway Museum at York. It remained in service until 1951 but this picture, which was taken at Shrewsbury, dates from the mid-1930s.

Photo: Rail Archive Stephenson

leadership of Samuel Johnson at Derby but, with characteristic vanity, Johnson did not want to adopt a device which was not of his own creation. Deeley's invention was left to gather dust but, when he succeeded Johnson in 1904, the idea was resurrected and prepared for use on a new class of 4-4-0s. In 1905, Deeley applied for a patent for his invention and, just before it was granted, 4-4-2 No 40 emerged from Swindon works with an embarrassingly similar type of valve gear.

Although Churchward's scissors gear was of a simpler construction than Deeley's, the similarities were enough for Derby to insist that, should the design dare to show its face at Swindon again, royalties would most definitely be payable. As had been seen with the use of a Schmidt superheater on Saint class No 2901 the previous year, Churchward saw no reason whatsoever why his company should pay royalties for something if he could design something better and, for the Stars, the use of Walschaerts gear was considered not only superior but also somewhat cheaper. The potential problem of the scissors gear was that, as both sides were linked, a breakdown would result in the locomotive being totally incapacitated whereas, with the Walschaerts gear, both sides of the locomotive remained independent and so a dead engine could, at least, be removed from the line rather than cause an obstruction. Every subsequent four-cylinder locomotive to be built for the GWR had Walschaerts gear.

When the new 4-6-0s were delivered, No 4010 *Western Star* was fitted from new with a superheater. Churchward did not repeat the use of the Schmidt device, partly because of fiddly maintenance and partly because of high royalty payments, and the fitment worn by No 4010 was to the Cole design which was of American origin. The Cole superheater was effective but there was no more likelihood of Swindon paying royalties for the repeated use of this than there was with the Schmidt version. Churchward merely wanted to have a close look at the workings of the device and, true to form, he learned enough from it to help with his own superheater design.

Churchward was greatly admired for his ability

to analyse the workings of different engineering designs and to adapt and improve on the originals. Unlike Samuel Johnson and, for that matter, most other contemporaries, Churchward did not possess an ego which denied the existence of competing ideas. This had been seen with his use of Schmidt and Cole superheaters and, previously, with his acquisition of the three French compound locomotives. One of several features of the compounds which appealed to Churchward was the de Glehn design for the front bogie; it used side-control springs and side-bearers instead of the swing-link construction which had been the norm at Swindon. As the swing-link design had been found to cause excessive wear on the pivots and the flanges of the leading coupled wheels, Churchward adopted the French ideas in the design for a new Swindon bogie and, when the next batch of Stars was ordered, the new bogie was incorporated in the plans.

Between March and May 1908, Nos 4011–20 emerged from Swindon complete with the new-style Churchward bogies. The new arrivals were named after knights and the leader of the new batch, No 4011 ***Knight of the Garter***, was the first locomotive to be fitted from new with a standard Swindon superheater which was, again, a product of Churchward's analyses of other designs. Ten more Stars, Nos 4021–30, were built between June and October 1909; these were named after English kings and one of the contingent, No 4021 ***King Edward***, was fitted with an improved version of the earlier superheater. The new superheater was designated Swindon Standard No 3 and not only was it this design which was fitted to all the other Stars between 1909 and 1913 but it also became the standard Swindon design for many years. One of the locomotives which was fitted with a similar superheater in November 1909 was the original four-cylinder engine, No 40, but superheating was far from the most conspicuous change it underwent

A few of the Star class 4-6-0s were retired in the 1930s and these included No 4008 *Royal Star*. This picture was taken at Torquay on 29 May 1932, a little over three years before the engine was put to sleep. Ironically, No 4008 was one of the first of the class to be fitted with elbow steam-pipes but, when this was undertaken in July 1933, withdrawal of the class had already started.

Photo: E. R. Morton

The setting is Shrewsbury Station on a blowy winter day in 1930 and No 4038 *Queen Berengaria* is about to depart with a heavy express train.

Photo: Rail Archive Stephenson

that month. The new boiler, new frames and the conversion of No 40 from 4-4-2 to 4-6-0 placed the locomotive firmly in the Star class. In September 1906, No 40 had been named *North Star* and so its nomenclature fitted in snugly with the other Stars, but it was December 1912 before the engine was renumbered as No 4000.

During the late 1800s and the early 1900s, a large number of locomotive designers seemed to suffer from either jealousy or, in complete contrast, a surfeit of pride and this often manifested itself in the organisation of trials between locomotives of different companies. The obvious purpose of comparison trials was to enable engineers to learn from the work of their contemporaries but, understandably, a lot of individual and corporate pride was at stake and so, for trial purposes, it was normal for participating companies to use the newest possible locomotives. However, when the London & North Western expressed an interest in testing one of the Stars in 1910, the GWR was confident enough of the design that, instead of sending one of the recently-completed locomotives, the engine which was despatched for scrutinisation was three year-old No 4005 *Polar Star*.

During August 1910, No 4005 was pitted against the LNWR's Experiment class 4-6-0 No 1471 *Worcestershire* which had been built at Crewe just seven months previously. The Experiment class had been designed by George Whale in 1905 but No 1471 had been constructed during the incumbency of C.J. Bowen Cooke who had taken over at Crewe after Whale's retirement in 1908. The GWR's engine outclassed the LNWR's in every department and so Bowen Cooke hurried off to create a four-cylinder 4-6-0 for his own company. The outcome of Bowen Cooke's design was the Claughton class which incorporated Churchward's favourite, the Belpaire firebox. The LNWR's No 2222 *Sir Gilbert Claughton* appeared in January 1913 but, although the class went on to become both numerous and well-respected, its long-term fortunes were rather different to those of the GWR's Stars. The Stars were to linger on until 1957 while only four of the Claughtons were to see the 1940s.

The Stars were intended for use on the GWR's high-profile West of England expresses, in particular the non-stop service to Plymouth, but by 1910 the holiday resorts in Devon and Cornwall were becoming very popular and peak-season trains to the West often weighed in at over 500 tons. These loadings were certainly within the capabilities of the two-cylinder Saint class 4-6-0s but, where sustained periods of high-speed running were called for, the four-cylinder Stars had the edge. A further ten Stars, Nos 4031–40, were delivered between October 1910 and March 1911, Nos 4041–45 were added in early summer 1913 and, in the summer of 1914, Nos 4046–60 arrived to bring the class total to sixty. The classification of 'Stars' was continued but the names carried by the new engines were those of English queens, princes and princesses.

All of the new arrivals benefited from the lead of No 4021 and were fitted with Standard No 3 superheaters from new. The first of the 1913 locomotives, No 4041 *Prince of Wales*, was turned out with 15in diameter cylinders instead of the 14¼in which had previously been the norm and, as the larger cylinders proved beneficial, the 15in diameter was gradually adopted as standard for the entire class. Apart from No 4041, the first to carry the larger cylinders from new were the 1914 batch, Nos 4046–60.

On the West of England services, the Stars had little difficulty keeping to a three-hour schedule for the 174 miles from Paddington to Exeter and, even out of the peak holiday season, loadings on that run often exceeded 450 tons. The expresses between Paddington and Bristol tended to be considerably lighter than those to Devon and Cornwall but, nevertheless, the two-hour schedule for the 118 mile trip to Bristol left little chance of regaining time should any be lost. The loadings on the Paddington to Birmingham expresses were, usually, even lighter than those of the Bristol trains. In the years before the First World War, it was uncommon to see a loading in excess of 300 tons on the Birmingham expresses and so the two-hour schedule for the 110 mile run was little more than a casual saunter for the Stars. Although the war effort did not affect the scheduling of passenger trains until 1917, one immediate result of the outbreak of hostilities in 1914 was the renaming of No 4017. Its old name, *Knight of the Black Eagle*, was diplomatically replaced by *Knight of Liege*.

George Churchward retired at the end of 1921. He had been in charge of the locomotive department at Swindon for almost twenty years but his influence had been evident for an even longer period. Churchward had been responsible for the design of some excellent locomotives but his greatest legacy was, arguably, the development of standardisation. Some other railway companies in Britain had managed to achieve a reasonable degree of standardisation but few, if any, had done it in such a stylish manner as the GWR. On 1 January 1922, Charles Collett formally succeeded Churchward as GWR's chief mechanical engineer and he immediately found himself facing a major decision. If Collett wished to make a swift impact upon the engineering world, he would have to break completely with Churchward's principles and stamp his own identity on developments at Swindon. Collett, however, had previously worked as Churchward's deputy and had great respect for his predecessor's work. He therefore viewed a departure from Churchward's tried and tested formulae as trying to mend something which was not broken and, furthermore, superstardom was not for Collett. The outcome was a logical progression of Churchward's ideas which was to last for another twenty-six years.

Before his retirement, Churchward had placed an order for twelve more Star class locomotives but the first did not emerge from Swindon until five months into Collett's reign; the last of the dozen was completed in February 1923. These engines were numbered 4061–72 and were named after abbeys. They were the final Stars to be built and, when they were delivered, the austerity of the war years was still evident in that they wore unlined liveries and their chimneys were cast-iron instead of the traditional Swindon copper-cap design. During the War, the existing Stars had all been reduced to unlined liveries and they had also lost the brass beading from their splashers but, soon after the emergence of the final new Stars in 1923, fully-lined liveries were gradually reintroduced for both the old and the new members of the class. Only the brass beading did not return.

Although Collett had no wish to depart from Churchward's legacy, there was one point about which the two gentlemen had agreed to differ. Churchward had introduced a locomotive braking

Star class 4-6-0 No 4036 *Queen Elizabeth* is seen at its home shed of Old Oak in June 1933 with a high-sided 4,000 gallon tender. It was, however, 1938 before the Stars were regularly paired with such tenders.

Photo: Rail Archive Stephenson

This fine shot of No 4050 *Princess Alice* was taken at Old Oak in 1936 and clearly shows her large tender behind.

Photo: Rail Archive Stephenson

Even the dress of the two spectators does not provide convincing evidence that this is anything other than a pre-Nationalisation picture. However, the style of the coaches which hide underneath the chocolate and cream livery and their complement of SLR-toting passengers give the game away. Castle class No 6080 *Defiant* was, in fact, photographed during the Easter weekend of 1990 at the head of the 'Shakespeare Express'; the picture was taken near Henley-in-Arden on its journey from Stratford to Tyseley.

Photo: Peter Herring

Seven Castle class locomotives are preserved in Britain and one of these is No 5080 which, although having carried the name *Defiant* since January 1941, had started life in May 1939 as *Ogmore Castle*. This picture was taken when the locomotive was on loan to the Gloucester/Warwickshire Railway at Toddington.

Photo: P. Chancellor

The preserved Castle 4-6-0 No 5029 *Nunney Castle* lives at the Didcot Railway Centre. This is fortunate for photographically-minded enthusiasts as the centre is usually at the forefront of special promotions such as night events. In this picture, the locomotive poses on the turntable at Didcot on 26 October 1991.

Photo: P. Chancellor

One of the Castle class 4-6-0s which had an identity crisis was No 5051; born in May 1936, it was christened *Drysllwyn Castle* but, in August 1937, it changed its name by deed poll to *Earl Bathurst*. Its original name was later applied to classmate No 5076 and, later still, to No 7018. In the best tradition of happy endings, the name *Drysllwyn Castle* was eventually given back to the preserved No 5051 and it is in this guise in which it was photographed on Eardington Bank en route to Bridgnorth. With the exception of the third coach, the train provides a wonderful example of the blood and custard colour scheme.

Photo: M. Inger

Preserved Castle class No 5029 *Nunney Castle* is in somewhat better condition than its stone namesake as it performs in the late autumn sunlight at Bearley Junction on 9 November 1991.

Photo: P. Chancellor

This superb double-header was laid on during the GWR's 150th Anniversary celebrations in 1985. The impossibly-named Castle class No 5051 *Drysllwyn Castle* is seen piloting the more-pronounceable Hall class 4-6-0 No 4930 *Hagley Hall* near Dawlish on 4 July of that year.

Photo: Peter Herring

LONDON, BICESTER, OXFORD, BANBURY, LEAMINGTON SPA, WARWICK, and BIRMINGHAM.—Great Western.

Down. — **Week Days—Continued.**

	mrn	mrn	mrn	mrn	mrn	mrn	mrn	mrn	mrn	aft	aft	mrn	mrn	mrn	mrn	mrn	aft	aft	aft	aft	aft	mrn	aft	aft	aft	aft	aft
PADDINGTON ....dep.		9c10	9 45	10 15	10 40									1045		11 20	1250	1210					1218	1 35	2 20		
Ealing (Broadway) "			9 55	10 25										1055				1221					1229				
High Wycombe "		9c42																					1 24				
Princes Risboro' "		10 2																					1 55				
Haddenham "		1012																					2 5				
Brill & Ludgershall A 375 "		1025																					2 18				
Blackthorn "		1031																					2 24				
Bicester §§ 434 arr.		1037					m																2 30				
Bicester dep.		1042					1145																2 36				
Ardley		1050					1155																2 45				
Aynho Park Platform		Stop					12 3																2 53				
130 Bournemouth Cen. dep						7 39									10 0	8 45			9 21					11 21			
143 Portsmouth ¶¶ "		m	6 18			8 22									9 36	9 36								11 20			
130 Southampton Town "	7x35		7 40			8t40									10t54	9 50			10c22					12c22			
47 Basingstoke "			9i35			1080										11B18			12c18					1B30			
32 Reading "			1036			10Z40								1138		12 16		1 24	1 8					2 22			
17 Bristol (T.M.) 108 "								1135					9 35									1125				2 30	
7 Weymouth (T.) "																N55						1030				1030	
17 Swindon "						9 30							1110									1 30					
Didcot dep	1012					11 10			1120					1215		1 7											
Culham	1019								1128					1222		1 14											
Radley 107 [434	1026								1136				12 9	1229		1 22											
Oxford 46, 94, 95, 434 arr.	1035		11 8			11 27			1147				1218	1238	12 50	1 32		1 58	1 42			2 15		2 57			
Oxford dep	1050					11 33			Stop			1152	1228	Stop	12 58	Stop		Stop	1 47	2 10		2 25					
Kidlington 58												12 4								2 24							
Bletchington *												1210								Stop							
Heyford												1218															
Fritwell and Somerton												1225		aft													
Aynho ‡‡												1232		m													
King's Sutton 104							12 9					1239		1 30									2 59				
Banbury ‡104, 434, 590, 680 arr.	1118					12 2	1217					1247	1257	1 37	1 26				2 15			2 53	3 6		3c34		
Banbury dep.						12 7	Stop					1252		Stop	1 29				2 18		2 22	2 58	Stop				
Cropredy												1 2									2 31						
Fenny Compton 590												1 12									2 40						
Southam Road & Harbury												1 21									2 49						
Leamington Spa § 438, 440 arr.					12c14	12 32	aft		aft			1 32		aft	1 53	aft	2 21		2 42		2 58	3 23			3c54		
Leamington Spa dep.						12 36	1245		1255					1 22	1 57	2 35	2 24		2 47		3 3	3 28					4 5
Warwick (Coventry Rd.) ‖						12 41	1250		1 0					1 27		2 40					3 8	3 34					4 10
Hatton 108 arr.							1258		1 9					1 35		2 49					3 15						4 19
108 Stratford-on-Avon arr.							1 20	1 22								3 12										4 9	4 50
Stratford-on-Avon dep.							Stop	1 25	1145									aft								4 13	Stop
Hatton dep.									1 11					1 36				2 8			[illegible]						
Lapworth									1 19					1 45				2 18			3 18						
Knowle and Dorridge									1 26					1 52				2 25			3 26						
Widney Manor														1 57						aft	3 33						aft
Solihull									1 33	1 48	2 0			2 8				2 32		3 10	3 40						4 33
Olton									1 38	1 53	2 5			2 13				2 37		3 15							4 38
Acock's Green and South Yardley		aft					aft		1 42	1 57	2 9			2 21				2 43		3 19			aft				4 42
Tyseley 107		1213					1s7		1 47	2 1				2 25				2 48		3 23			m				4 45
Small Heath & Sparkbrook		1217					1s11		1 52	2 5				2 29				2 52		3 27			3 20				4 48
Bordesley		1220					1s15		1 56	2 9	2 15			2 33				2 56		3 31	3 49		3 23				4 52
Birmngham (Moor St.) ‖‖ arr.											2 18																
" (Sn. Hill) **84 "		1223		12c20	12 40	1 9	1s20	1 56	2 0	2 13				2 37	2 24		2 50	3 0	3 13	3 35	3 53	4 3	3 26		4 20	4 45	4 55
84 Wolverhampton †† arr				12e44	1 9	1 37				3 5					2 47		3 25		3 37						4 45	5 30	5 35
84 Shrewsbury (Gen.) "					1 53	2 33									3 37				4 21						5 33		
84 Chester (General) "					3 10	4 5									4 50				5 40						6 50		
84 Birkenhead (W.) "					3 50	4 50									5 27				6 20						7 30		

Notes printed in the columns of the timetable:

- Restaurant Car from Oxford.
- Through Carriages, Southampton to Scarborough and Glasgow (Queen Street), via G. C. Line, see pages 56, 690, 668, 758, 728, 734, 777, and 790.
- Saturdays only.
- Aberystwyth, Barmouth, and Pwllheli Express, see page 578. Luncheon and Tea Car. Commences on the 14th instant.
- Through Carriages to Aberystwyth, Towyn, and Pwllheli, see pages 84, 461, 578, and 583. Luncheon Car to Shrewsbury. Birmingham and North Exp.
- Through Train, Portsmouth to Birkenhead, see pages 148, 130, 47, 84, and 458.
- Through Train, Taunton to Birmingham, see page 18.
- Except Saturdays.
- Luncheon Car Train. Through Train, Weston-super-Mare to Sheffield, see page 690.
- Bournemouth, Southampton, and Birkenhead and Manchester Express, see pages 137, 131, 47, 85, 458, and 478. Luncheon and Tea Car.
- Leamington Spa and Birmingham Express. Luncheon and Tea Car.
- Through Train from Dover (Marine) (dep. 9 45 mrn.), Folkestone (C.), Ramsgate Town, and Margate Sands to Birkenhead (W.), see pages 227, 229, 246, and 244. Luncheon and Tea Car.
- Arr. Blenheim & Woodstock at 2 35 aft., see page 58.
- Through Train from Weymouth to Birmingham.
- Motor Car, one class only, Princes Risboro' to Banbury.
- Luncheon Car, Paddington to Oxford.
- Tea Car to Wolverhampton. Through Carriages to Aberystwyth and Pwllheli, see pages 85, 579, & 583. Birmingham and North Express.
- Thro' Train, Plymouth to Birmingham and Wolverhampton, see page 18.

For Notes, see page 79; for Continuation of Trains, see pages 78 and 79.

The Star class locomotives were the favoured machines for the London to Birmingham services in the early 1920s. The timetable for the summer of 1922 showed that the fastest trains to Birmingham were the 10.15am, 12.50pm and 2.20pm ex-Paddington.

One of the very last Star class engines in service was No 4061 *Glastonbury Abbey* which survived until March 1957. Here, it is seen being coaled at Oxford on 29 April 1956. It is interesting to note that the pre-Nationalisation feature of the number on the buffer beam is still in place, although the BR shed-code plate has already gone walkabouts.

Photo: E. H. Sawford

TABLE 4.1: ORIGINAL DIMENSIONS OF THE STAR CLASS LOCOMOTIVES

	4001–40 AS BUILT	4041–72 AS BUILT
BUILT:	1907–11	1913–23
WORKS NOS:	2229–38/2300–09/ 2365–74/80–89	2536–40/72–86/ 2915–26
WEIGHTS FULL (locomotive):	75 tons 12 cwt	75 tons 12 cwt
(tender):	40 tons 0 cwt	40 tons 0 cwt
TENDER CAPACITY (water):	3,000 gallons	3,000 gallons
(coal):	7 tons	7 tons
WHEELBASE (locomotive):	27ft 3in	27ft 3in
WHEEL DIAMETERS (bogie):	3ft 2in	3ft 2in
(coupled):	6ft 8½ in	6ft 8½ in
CYLINDERS:	(4) 14¼ in × 26in	(4) 15in × 26in
BOILER PRESSURE:	225 lb/psi	225 lb/psi
HEATING SURFACES (tubes):	1988.7 sq ft*	1686.6 sq ft
(firebox):	154.3 sq ft*	154.8 sq ft
(s'heater):	*	283.4 sq ft
SUPERHEATERS FITTED:	1909–13*	From new
GRATE AREA:	27.1 sq ft	27.1 sq ft
TRACTIVE EFFORT (at 85% boiler pressure):	25,090 lb	27,800 lb
SWINDON WORKS DIAGRAMS:	H/J/K/M/N/Q	S/T/U/A10
ROUTE AVAILABILITY:	Red	Red
POWER CLASSIFICATION (GWR):	D	D
(BR):	5P	5P

*Nos 4010/11/21/31–40 fitted with superheaters from new.

TABLE 4.2: THE STAR CLASS LOCOMOTIVES

NO	NAME	BUILT	WDN	1922 SHED	1948 SHED	LAST SHED
4000	*North Star* (*)	4/06	(a)	Wolverhampton		(a)
4001	*Dog Star*	2/07	1/34	Old Oak Common		Bristol
4002	*Evening Star*	2/07	6/33	Plymouth		Old Oak Common
4003	*Lode Star*	2/07	7/51	Old Oak Common	Swansea	Swansea
4004	*Morning Star*	2/07	4/48	Plymouth	Oxford	Oxford
4005	*Polar Star*	2/07	11/34	Plymouth		Old Oak Common
4006	*Red Star*	4/07	11/32	Old Oak Common		Swansea
4007	*Rising Star* (*)	4/07	9/51	Worcester	Worcester	Worcester
4008	*Royal Star*	5/07	6/35	Old Oak Common		Old Oak Common
4009	*Shooting Star*	5/07	(a)	Newton Abbot		(a)
4010	*Western Star*	5/07	11/34	Old Oak Common		Bristol
4011	*Knight of the Garter*	3/08	11/32	Old Oak Common		Worcester
4012	*Knight of the Thistle*	3/08	10/49	Plymouth	Newton Abbot	Newton Abbot
4013	*Knight of St Patrick*	3/08	5/50	Old Oak Common	Chester	Chester
4014	*Knight of the Bath*	3/08	6/46	Plymouth		Wolverhampton

TABLE 4.2 CONT.

NO	NAME	BUILT	WDN	1922 SHED	1948 SHED	LAST SHED
4015	*Knight of St John*	3/08	2/51	Old Oak Common	Swindon	Swindon
4016	*Knight of the Golden Fleece*	4/08	(a)	Old Oak Common		(a)
4017	*Knight of the Black Eagle* (*)	4/08	11/49	Old Oak Common	Swindon	Swindon
4018	*Knight of the Grand Cross*	4/08	4/51	Plymouth	Wolverhampton	Wolverhampton
4019	*Knight Templar*	5/08	10/49	Wolverhampton	Bristol	Bristol
4020	*Knight Commander*	5/08	3/51	Exeter	Bristol	Bristol
4021	*King Edward* (*)	6/09	10/52	Old Oak Common	Oxford	Oxford
4022	*King William* (*)	6/09	2/52	Plymouth	Swindon	Swindon
4023	*King George* (*)	6/09	7/52	Old Oak Common	Swansea	Swansea
4024	*King James* (*)	6/09	2/35	Old Oak Common		Taunton
4025	*King Charles* (*)	7/09	8/50	Plymouth	Wolverhampton	Wolverhampton
4026	*King Richard* (*)	9/09	2/50	Old Oak Common	Taunton	Taunton
4027	*King Henry* (*)	9/09	10/34	Old Oak Common		Swansea
4028	*King John* (*)	9/09	11/51	Newton Abbot	Westbury	Westbury
4029	*King Stephen* (*)	10/09	11/34	Old Oak Common		Wolverhampton
4030	*King Harold* (*)	10/09	5/50	Old Oak Common	Bristol	Bristol
4031	*Queen Mary*	10/10	6/51	Old Oak Common	Wolverhampton	Wolverhampton
4032	*Queen Alexandra*	10/10	(a)	Old Oak Common		(a)
4033	*Queen Victoria*	11/10	6/51	Old Oak Common	Bristol	Bristol
4034	*Queen Adelaide*	11/10	9/52	Newton Abbot	Bristol	Swindon
4035	*Queen Charlotte*	11/10	10/51	Newton Abbot	Bristol	Bristol
4036	*Queen Elizabeth*	12/10	3/52	Old Oak Common	Swindon	Swindon
4037	*Queen Phillipa*	12/10	(a)	Old Oak Common		(a)
4038	*Queen Berengaria*	1/11	4/52	Newton Abbot	Westbury	Westbury
4039	*Queen Mathilda*	2/11	11/50	Newton Abbot	Swansea	Swansea
4040	*Queen Boadicea*	3/11	6/51	Exeter	Shrewsbury	Shrewsbury
4041	*Prince of Wales*	6/13	4/51	Old Oak Common	Bristol	Bristol
4042	*Prince Albert*	5/13	1/51	Old Oak Common	Bristol	Bristol
4043	*Prince Henry*	5/13	1/52	Wolverhampton	Bristol	Bristol
4044	*Prince George*	5/13	2/53	Plymouth	Shrewsbury	Shrewsbury
4045	*Prince John*	6/13	11/50	Wolverhampton	Westbury	Westbury
4046	*Princess Mary*	5/14	11/51	Newton Abbot	Shrewsbury	Shrewsbury
4047	*Princess Louise*	5/14	7/51	Plymouth	Bristol	Bristol
4048	*Princess Victoria*	5/14	1/53	Wolverhampton	Swansea	Swansea
4049	*Princess Maud*	5/14	7/53	Wolverhampton	Oxford	Wolverhampton
4050	*Princess Alice*	6/14	2/52	Old Oak Common	Swansea	Swansea
4051	*Princess Helena*	6/14	10/50	Old Oak Common	Worcester	Worcester
4052	*Princess Beatrice*	6/14	6/53	Plymouth	Oxford	Shrewsbury
4053	*Princess Alexandra*	6/14	7/54	Plymouth	Wolverhampton	Wolverhampton
4054	*Princess Charlotte*	6/14	2/52	Old Oak Common	Exeter	Plymouth
4055	*Princess Sophia*	7/14	2/51	Old Oak Common	Swindon	Swindon
4056	*Princess Margaret*	7/14	10/57	Old Oak Common	Taunton	Bristol
4057	*Princess Elizabeth*	7/14	2/52	Old Oak Common	Swindon	Swindon

TABLE 4.2 CONT.

NO	NAME	BUILT	WDN	1922 SHED	1948 SHED	LAST SHED
4058	*Princess Augusta*	7/14	4/51	Wolverhampton	Tyseley	Wolverhampton
4059	*Princess Patricia*	7/14	9/52	Plymouth	Gloucester	Gloucester
4060	*Princess Eugenie*	7/14	10/52	Newton Abbot	Wolverhampton	Bristol
4061	*Glastonbury Abbey*	5/22	3/57	Penzance (b)	Shrewsbury	Wolverhampton
4062	*Malmesbury Abbey*	5/22	11/56	Plymouth (b)	Swindon	Swindon
4063	*Bath Abbey*	11/22	(a)	Newton Abbot (b)		(a)
4064	*Reading Abbey*	12/22	(a)	Old Oak Common (b)		(a)
4065	*Evesham Abbey*	12/22	(a)	Exeter (b)		(a)
4066	*Malvern Abbey* (*)	12/22	(a)	Wolverhampton (b)		(a)
4067	*Tintern Abbey*	1/23	(a)	Wolverhampton (b)		(a)
4068	*Llanthony Abbey*	1/23	(a)	Wolverhampton (b)		(a)
4069	*Margam Abbey* (*)	1/23	(a)	Wolverhampton (b)		(a)
4070	*Neath Abbey*	2/23	(a)	Wolverhampton (b)		(a)
4071	*Cleeve Abbey*	2/23	(a)	Old Oak Common (b)		(a)
4072	*Tresco Abbey*	2/23	(a)	Old Oak Common (b)		(a)

NOTES
(a) Locomotive rebuilt as Castle class. Subsequent history is given in Chapter Five.
(b) These allocations are the first ones accredited to the locomotives when they entered service.
(*) Locomotives renamed as follows:
No 4007 renamed *Swallowfield Park* in May 1937.
No 4017 renamed *Knight of Liege* in August 1914.
No 4021 renamed *The British Monarch* in June 1927.
No 4022 renamed *The Belgian Monarch* in June 1927.
No 4023 renamed *The Danish Monarch* in July 1927.
No 4024 renamed *The Dutch Monarch* in September 1927.
No 4025 renamed *Italian Monarch* in October 1927.
No 4026 renamed *The Japanese Monarch* in July 1927.
No 4027 renamed *The Norwegian Monarch* in July 1927.
No 4028 renamed *The Roumanian Monarch* in July 1927.
No 4029 renamed *The Spanish Monarch* in July 1927.
No 4030 renamed *The Swedish Monarch* in July 1927.
No 4066 renamed *Sir Robert Horne* in May 1935 and *Viscount Horne* in August 1937.
No 4069 renamed *Westminster Abbey* in May 1923.

N.B. In October 1927, Nos 4021–24/26–30 had their nameplates changed to omit '*The*'. Nos 4022/23/25/26/28/30 subsequently lost their nameplates in 1940/41.

system which worked not just on the driving wheels but also the carrying wheels of the engine and this had first appeared on the two-cylinder 4-6-0 No 100 in 1902. There was no disputing that Collett was as safety-conscious as Churchward, but the former doubted the advantages of brakes on a bogie while the latter would not hear of their removal. After taking over at the helm, Collett authorised the removal of bogie brakes from all of the GWR's locomotives and the Stars were among the first to be treated.

In August 1923, Collett's four-cylinder Castle class 4-6-0s started to emerge from Swindon. The Castles were more powerful than the Stars and, although there were no regularly-scheduled loadings which were beyond the capabilities of the Stars, the larger boilers of the Castles were worked less hard on the heavier duties. Inevitably, the Castles started to take over on the West of England expresses which were not only the heaviest but also the most widely publicised of the GWR's services. Many of the other express routes from Paddington, however, remained under the highly satisfactory domination of the Stars.

The Castle class became the veritable flavour of the month and, for a time, couldn't be expanded quickly enough. When four members of the Star class, Nos 4009/16/32/37, became due for replacement cylinders in 1925 and 1926, they were not just given new cylinders but were dismantled and subsequently rebuilt to Castle class dimensions. In 1929, No 4000 followed suit to complete its hat-trick of identities: an Atlantic, a Star and a Castle.

The numbers of the Castle class increased steadily and, from 1927, the four-cylinder King class 4-6-0s started to appear. Within a space of four years, the Stars had found themselves overtaken in the pecking order, not once but twice and, during the late 1920s and early 1930s, they became dispersed over most of the GWR system. The knock-on effect was that the poor old two-cylinder Saint class 4-6-0s tended to be the prime candidates for displacement by the Stars. Consequently, the express turns to South Wales, Worcester and Shrewsbury and the faster secondary services from Oxford, Wolverhampton and Weymouth were among the duties which were gradually taken over by the Stars. Despite their relegation from the top-flight workings, the Stars continued to turn in excellent performances on all of the duties to which they were transferred and they were positively welcomed by the crews at their new depots.

During the 1920s, several members of the Star class underwent changes of names. On 28 February 1922, No 4048 *Princess Victoria* borrowed the nameplates of *Princess Mary* from No 4046 just for the day so that it could be used on Royal Wedding duties. In May 1923, No 4069 was renamed *Westminster Abbey* but the most insulting of the renamings involving the Stars were those which were inflicted on Nos 4021–30. All ten had their original names removed in 1927 to avoid confusion with names of new King class locomotives and, instead, the names of various foreign monarchs were applied.

The Stars had impressive haulage capabilities

Star class No 4069 *Westminster Abbey* was built in 1923 and originally carried the name *Margam Abbey*. In 1939, it was rebuilt as a Castle and was consequently renumbered 5089; in that guise it became one of the very last Castles to survive and was not retired until November 1964.

Photo: Rail Archive Stephenson

Main Line.] 23 [Great Western.

LONDON, READING, TAUNTON, EXETER, PLYMOUTH, and PENZANCE.—Great Western.

Down. — Week Days—*continued.*

	mrn	mrn	mrn	mrn	mrn	aft	aft	aft	aft	mrn	mrn	mrn	aft	mrn	aft	mrn	mrn	aft	aft	mrn
12 PADDINGTON ..... dep					5 30								7 30	7 30		9 15	1030			11 0
12 READING ..... "					6 18								8 20	8 20		10 5				
12 OXFORD ..... "													7 8	7 8		9F16				
12 BATH ..... "			6/15		8 10								9 58	10 10						
12 BRISTOL (Temp. Mds.) "			6 50		8 40								1038	10 50						
	mrn	mrn	mrn	mrn	mrn	aft	aft	aft	aft	mrn	mrn	mrn	aft	mrn	aft	aft	aft	aft	aft	aft
Taunton ..... dep			9 0		10 0						1015			11 50		1217				
Norton Fitzwarren			9 6								1027									
Wellington			9 17								1033									
Burlescombe			9 27								1043									
Tiverton Junction 50, 118			9 40								1057									
Cullompton			9 50								11 6									
Hele and Bradninch			10 0								1116									
Silverton			10 7								1122									
Stoke Canon 51											1134									
Exeter (St. David's) * arr.		III	1020		10 37						1142	III	1212	12 27		1254				2 0
40, 51, 141, 142, 144 dep	9 0	10 0			10 45					1110	Stop	1150	1218	12 35		1259		1 40		2 7
Exeter (St. Thomas) 40	9 6	10 6								1116		1155							1 50	
Exminster	9 14	1014								1124		12 3							1 58	
Starcross †	9 22	1022								1134		1211		12s44					2 7	
Dawlish Warren	9 28	1030								1140		1219							2 12	
Dawlish	9 34	1037								1147		1226	1237	12 55		1 19		2 1	Stop	
Teignmouth, for Teignton Bishop's	9 43	1045								1157		1234	1245	1 4		1 28		2 11		
Newton Abbot § 51 ..... arr.	9 52	Stop			11 11					12 6		Stop	1254	1 13		1 37		2 20		
51 MORETONHAMPSTEAD arr.	1053									[illegible]										
51 TORQUAY ..... "	1031				11 52					1256			1 18	2 7		2 7		2 55		
51 PAIGNTON ..... "	1045				12 5					[illegible]			1 25	2 20		2 20		3 3		
51 KINGSWEAR ..... "	11 8				12 35					[illegible]				2 40		2 40		Stop		
Newton Abbot ..... dep	10 6				11 18					1215				1 20						
Totnes 57	1019									[illegible]				1 38						
Brent 54	1042				11 50					1258										
54 KINGSBRIDGE ..... arr.	1120				1 0															
Wrangaton	1048									1 4										
Bittaford Platform	1052									1 8										
Ivybridge	1058									1 14										
Cornwood	11 3									1 19										
Plympton	1113			III						1 29										
Plymouth (Mutley)	1118			1152						1 35										
52, 142 (North Road)	1121			1153	12 16					1 38	aft			2 15			2 37			3 16
(Millbay) ..... arr.	1130					III				1 43	III			2d35	III					
Plymouth (Millbay) ..... dep	Stop				12s10	1 5			1 22		2 10				2 45					
" (North Road)				1154	12 25		1 15										2 44			
Devonport				1158	12 30	1 10	1 21		1 29		2 15				2 50					
Keyham				12 2		1 16			1 33		2 21				2 55					
St. Budeaux Platform				12 5		1 19			1 37		2 24				2 58					
Saltash				12 9	12 39	1 25			1 42		2 27				[illegible]					
Defiance Platform				1212		1 27			1 44											
St. Germans				1220	12 48	Stop			1 53											
Menheniot				1230					2 5											
Liskeard 39					1 7		1 51		2 14											
39 LOOE ..... arr.					2V10		2 25													
Doublebois									2 23											
Bodmin Road 47					1 23		2 8		2 38											
Lostwithiel 50					1 30				2 45											
Par 50					1 42		2 28		2 57											
50 FOWEY ..... arr.									3A5											
50 NEWQUAY					3 28		3 43													5 23
St. Austell					1 55		2 41		3 10											4 36
Burngullow									3 16											
Grampound Road					2 6				3 25											
Probus and Ladock Platform						aft			3 31											
Truro 116 ..... arr.	aft				2 18		3 4		3 40								4 4		aft	4 59
116 FALMOUTH ..... arr.	III	aft			3 6	III	3 57										4 57	aft	III	6 7
Truro ..... dep	1 10	III			2 22	3 25	3 9	3 15									4 9	4 25	4 35	5 5
Chacewater 50	1 24	1 30			2 35	3 38		3 27				aft						4 38	4 48	
Scorrier		1 36			2 41	3 44						III						4 44		
Redruth		1 42			2 48	3 50	3 29					4 0						4 51		5 25
Carn Brea		1 48			2 53	3 55						4 5						4 56		
Camborne		1 54			2 59	4 0	3 39					4 10						5 2		5 35
Gwinear Road 39		2 0			3 6		3 47					4 17					4 36	5 10		5 43
39 HELSTON ..... arr.		3 2					5 20					5 20					5 20			6 30
Hayle		2 8			3 13							4 24						5 18		
St. Erth 39		2 15			3 18		3 56					4 30					4 49	5 23		5 55
39 ST. IVES ..... arr.		2 45			3 45		5 10					5 10					5 10			6 45
Marazion		2 23			3 29		4 5					4 38						5 32		6 4
Penzance ** ..... arr.		2 28			3 35		4 10					4 43					5 0	5 37		6 10

Column notes (printed vertically): To Newquay. — From Newquay, see page 53. — Fridays only. Third Class only. — To Newquay. — Runs on 15th, 22nd, and 29th instant. — Ilfracombe, Minehead, and Torquay Luncheon Car Express. — Cornish Riviera Limited Express. Luncheon and Tea Car. — To Newquay. — Newquay, Falmouth, and Penzance Express. Through Carriage, London to Kingsbridge (arr. 4 40 aft.), see page 24. Luncheon and Tea Car to Truro.

For Notes, see page 26; for Continuation of Trains, see pages 24 to 26.

In this extract from the summer 1922 public timetable, the 10.30am ex-Paddington, the Cornish Riviera Express, is shown. During this period, the fastest and heaviest trains to Devon were most usually hauled by Star class locomotives.

but, on paper, they were subjected to tighter restrictions than the Castles and the Kings. On the routes from Paddington to Bristol, Wolverhampton and Taunton, the Stars were officially permitted 420 tons behind the tender compared to 455 tons for the Castles and 500 tons for the Kings. In South Devon, the Stars had a 288 ton limit on the steepest gradients without assistance while the Castles and Kings were allowed 315 and 360 tons respectively. The loading restrictions were, of course, exceeded regularly by locomotives of all classes, but it was only when a train was over the official weight limit that additional time would be authorised for a journey. Otherwise, the crew had to have a novel excuse for a late arrival.

In practice, the prestige and friendly rivalry among the crews did more for punctuality than any amount of whip-cracking would have done. One well-documented example involved Bristol-based No 4007 *Rising Star* which, in 1935, covered the 118 miles to Paddington with a 280 ton train in less than 109 minutes. The reason for that remarkable run was that the task of hauling the recently-introduced Bristolian had been given to London-based Kings and Castles. The Bristol crews merely wished it to be known that, even with a twenty-eight year-old engine of lower power, they were not incapable of turning on the speed just as impressively as the big boys from Old Oak Common.

Between February 1937 and September 1940, Nos 4063–72 joined the five earlier unfortunates and were rebuilt as members of the Castle class. Unlike the rebuilt locomotives of 1925–29, however, Nos 4063–72 did not retain their original numbers and were, instead, renumbered 5083–92 in the mainstream Castle sequence. The rebuilds kept the same nameplates although, in 1935, No 4066 had been renamed *Sir Robert Horne*. His Lordship's change of title in 1937 required the corresponding renaming of the engine and in August that year, just four months before it was transformed into a Castle, No 4066 became *Viscount Horne*. Another renaming of 1937 involved No 4007 which had its name changed from *Rising Star* to *Swallowfield*

This picture of No 4025 *Italian Monarch* was taken at Reading on 3 April 1937, just over a year before its nameplates were removed as a diplomatic necessity during the War. The engine had originally carried the name *King Charles* but that had been removed in 1927 when the King class engines arrived to hog the limelight.

Photo: D. K. Jones Collection

BRISTOL, BATH, SWINDON, DIDCOT, READING, MAIDENHEAD, SLOUGH, EALING AND LONDON.

Week Days—continued.

THE WHOLE OF THE TRAIN, STEAMER AND ROAD SERVICES ALSO RESTAURANT CARS AND SLEEPING CARS SHEWN IN THIS TIME TABLE ARE SUBJECT TO ALTERATION OR CANCELLATION AT SHORT NOTICE.

Station	p.m.	p.m.	p.m.	p.m.	p.m.	p.m.	a.m.
PENZANCE dep							7 45
Plymouth (North Rd)							10 40
Exeter (St. David's)							12 18
BRISTOL Temple Meads arr							2 10
BRISTOL Temple Meads dep							2 35
Lawrence Hill							
Stapleton Rd.							
St. Anne's Park							
Keynsham & Somerdale							
Saltford							
Oldfield Park							
BATH arr							3 0
BATH dep							3 5
Bathampton							
Bathford Halt							
Box							
Box (Mill Lane)							
Corsham							
Chippenham arr							3 25
Chippenham dep							3 30
Christian Malford Halt							
Dauntsey							
Ashley Hill dep							
Horfield							
Filton Junction							
Winterbourne							
Coalpit Heath							
Chipping Sodbury							
Badminton							
Hullavington							
Little Somerford							
Brinkworth							
Wootton Bassett dep							
SWINDON arr							3 55
SWINDON dep							4 10
Stratton Park Halt							
Shrivenham							
Uffington							
Challow							
Wantage Road				③ Limited accommodation.			
Steventon							
Didcot arr							4 50
Oxford (from Didcot) arr							5 45
Oxford dep		4 30		4 37		③	
Didcot dep						4 38	4 58
Cholsey and Moulsford						4 49	
Goring and Streatley						4 56	
Pangbourne						5 3	
Tilehurst						5 10	
READING arr		5 7	③ Saturdays excepted.	5 18		5 18	5 28
READING dep		5 12					5 32
Twyford							
Maidenhead							
Taplow							
Burnham (Bucks)					③		
Slough					5 20		
Langley (Bucks)					5 26		
Iver	③				5 30		
West Drayton & Yiewsley	5 14		③		5 35		
Hayes and Harlington	5 20		5 30		5 42		
Southall	5 26		5 36		5 48		
Hanwell and Elthorne	5 31		5 41		5 53		
West Ealing	5 34		5 44		5 56		
Ealing (Broadway)	5 37		5 47		6 0		
Acton	5 41		5 51		6 4		
Westbourne Park	5 48		5 58		6 11		
LONDON (Padd'ton) arr	5 52	6 0	6 2		6 15		6 20

Station	p.m.	p.m.	a.m.	p.m.	p.m.	p.m.	p.m.
PENZANCE dep			8 0				
Plymouth (North Rd)			11 15				
Exeter (St. David's)			12 56				
BRISTOL Temple Meads arr			2 55				
BRISTOL Temple Meads dep			3 5			4 0	4 5
Lawrence Hill							
Stapleton Rd.							
St. Anne's Park			3 10				4 10
Keynsham & Somerdale			3 16				4 16
Saltford			3 21				4 21
Oldfield Park			3 27				4 27
BATH arr			3 30			4 15	4 29
BATH dep			3 32	3 40		4 18	4 32
Bathampton			3 37	3 45			4 37
Bathford Halt			STOP	3 47			STOP
Box				3 52			
Box (Mill Lane)				3 54			
Corsham				4 1			
Chippenham arr				4 8			
Chippenham dep				4 40			
Christian Malford Halt				4 48			
Dauntsey				4 53			
Ashley Hill dep							
Horfield							
Filton Junction							
Winterbourne							
Coalpit Heath							
Chipping Sodbury							
Badminton							
Hullavington						Saturdays excepted.	
Little Somerford							
Brinkworth							
Wootton Bassett dep				5 5			
SWINDON arr				5 13			
SWINDON dep		4 30		STOP			
Stratton Park Halt		4 34					
Shrivenham		4 40					
Uffington		4 48					
Challow		STOP					
Wantage Road							
Steventon							
Didcot arr							③
Oxford (from Didcot) arr						7K12	p.m.
Oxford dep							4 55
Didcot dep							5 35
Cholsey and Moulsford							5 45
Goring and Streatley							5 52
Pangbourne							5 59
Tilehurst							6 6
READING arr	③ Saturdays excepted.				③	5 50	6 14
READING dep					5 45	5 52	
Twyford					5 57		
Maidenhead					6 10		
Taplow			③	③	6 15		
Burnham (Bucks)			p.m.	p.m.	6 20		
Slough			5 53	6 0	6 30		
Langley (Bucks)		③		6 5			
Iver		p.m.		6 9			
West Drayton & Yiewsley	③	5 56	6 3	6 15	6 42		
Hayes and Harlington	5 52	6 2		6 22			
Southall	5 58	6 7		6 28			
Hanwell and Elthorne	6 3	6 12		6 33			
West Ealing	6 6	6 16		6 36			
Ealing (Broadway)	6 10	6 19	6 19	6 39	6 56		
Acton	6 15	6 23		6 43			
Westbourne Park	6 22	6 30		6 50			
LONDON (Padd'ton) arr	6 26	6 35	6 30	6 54	7 8	6 40	

Station	p.m.	p.m.	a.m.	a.m.	p.m.	p.m.	p.m.
PENZANCE dep			11 0	9R30			
Plymouth (North Rd)			2 0	1 5			
Exeter (St. David's)		1 5	3 33	2 40			
BRISTOL Temple Meads arr		4 15		4 35			
BRISTOL Temple Meads dep		4 30		STOP	4 40	5 3	
Lawrence Hill							
Stapleton Rd.							
St. Anne's Park		4 36			4 45		
Keynsham & Somerdale		4 43			4 52		
Saltford		4 48			STOP		
Oldfield Park		4 55					
BATH arr		5 0				5 18	
BATH dep	4 45	STOP				5 22	
Bathampton	4 50					5 27	
Bathford Halt	4 52					STOP	
Box	4 57						
Box (Mill Lane)	4 59						
Corsham	5 6						
Chippenham arr	5 13						
Chippenham dep	STOP						
Christian Malford Halt							
Dauntsey							
Ashley Hill dep							
Horfield							
Filton Junction					Saturdays excepted.		
Winterbourne							
Coalpit Heath							
Chipping Sodbury							
Badminton							
Hullavington	For continuation (Mondays to Fridays), see 5.22 p.m. from Chippenham.		Restaurant Car Train. Via Westbury.				
Little Somerford							
Brinkworth							
Wootton Bassett dep							
SWINDON arr							
SWINDON dep							5 45
Stratton Park Halt							5 49
Shrivenham							5 58
Uffington							6 10
Challow							6 15
Wantage Road							6 25
Steventon							6 33
Didcot arr							6 42
Oxford (from Didcot) arr						p.m.	③ 7 12
Oxford dep						5 50	STOP
Didcot dep						6 20	
Cholsey and Moulsford							
Goring and Streatley							
Pangbourne							
Tilehurst	③				③		
READING arr	p.m.		6 32		p.m.	6 48	
READING dep	6 25		6 35		6 45	6 55	
Twyford	6 30				7 2		
Maidenhead	6 48				7 18		
Taplow				③			
Burnham (Bucks)		③ Saturdays excepted.		p.m			
Slough				6 44			
Langley (Bucks)				6 51			
Iver		③		6 55			
West Drayton & Yiewsley		p.m.		7 2			
Hayes and Harlington		6 46		7 12	For continuation see 7.15 p.m. from Maidenhead.		
Southall		6 51		7 18			③
Hanwell and Elthorne		6 55		7 22			p.m.
West Ealing		6 58		7 25			7 34
Ealing (Broadway)		7 1		7 28		7N32	7 38
Acton		7 6		7 34			
Westbourne Park		7 11		7 40			
LONDON (Padd'ton) arr		7 15	7 25	7 44		7 45	7 50

Station	p.m.	p.m.	p.m.	p.m.	p.m.	p.m.	p.m.
PENZANCE dep							
Plymouth (North Rd)							
Exeter (St. David's)							
BRISTOL Temple Meads arr							
BRISTOL Temple Meads dep		5 10			5 30		
Lawrence Hill							
Stapleton Rd.							
St. Anne's Park		5 15					
Keynsham & Somerdale		5 21					
Saltford	③ Saturdays excepted.	5 26					
Oldfield Park		5 32					
BATH arr		5 35			5 45		
BATH dep		5 38			5 48		
Bathampton		5 43					
Bathford Halt		STOP					
Box							
Box (Mill Lane)							
Corsham							
Chippenham arr					6 10		
Chippenham dep	5 22				6 15		
Christian Malford Halt	5 29						
Dauntsey	5 34						
Ashley Hill dep							
Horfield							
Filton Junction							
Winterbourne							
Coalpit Heath							
Chipping Sodbury							
Badminton							
Hullavington				Q. ③ From West Wales.			
Little Somerford							
Brinkworth							
Wootton Bassett dep	5 43						
SWINDON arr	5 55			6 8	6 38		
SWINDON dep	STOP			6 15	6 45		
Stratton Park Halt							
Shrivenham							
Uffington							
Challow							
Wantage Road			③ For continuation, see 7.45 p.m. from Slough.				
Steventon							
Didcot arr							
Oxford (from Didcot) arr						③	
Oxford dep						6 25	
Didcot dep						7 0	
Cholsey and Moulsford						7 10	
Goring and Streatley		③ Saturdays excepted.				7 20	
Pangbourne						7 26	
Tilehurst						7 35	
READING arr				7 15	7 35	7 45	③
READING dep		③		7 20	7 40		7 50
Twyford		p.m.	③				8 5
Maidenhead		7 16	7 16				8 16
Taplow	③	7 20	7 20				
Burnham (Bucks)	p.m.	7 24	7 24				
Slough	7 10	7 34	7 34				
Langley (Bucks)	7 16						
Iver	7 20						
West Drayton & Yiewsley	7 28						
Hayes and Harlington	7 30						
Southall	7 42						
Hanwell and Elthorne	7 46		Saturdays only.				For continuation see 8.20 p.m. from Maidenhead.
West Ealing	7 50						
Ealing (Broadway)	7 53	7 58					
Acton	7 58						
Westbourne Park	8 4						
LONDON (Padd'ton) arr	8 8	8 6		8 10	8 30		

Station	p.m.	p.m.	p.m.	p.m.	p.m.	a.m.	p.m.
PENZANCE dep						11R0	
Plymouth (North Rd)						2R0	
Exeter (St. David's)						3R33	
BRISTOL Temple Meads arr						6 8	
BRISTOL Temple Meads dep		5 32		5 45	5 50	STOP	6 20
Lawrence Hill				5 48			
Stapleton Rd.			5 46	5 50			
St. Anne's Park		5 37			5 56		
Keynsham & Somerdale		5 43			6 3		
Saltford		5 48			6 8		
Oldfield Park		5 54			6 14		
BATH arr		5 57	6 5		6 17		6 36
BATH dep		6 0	STOP		STOP		6 44
Bathampton		6 5					
Bathford Halt		6 7					
Box		6 12					
Box (Mill Lane)		6 14					
Corsham		6 21					
Chippenham arr		6 30					7 5
Chippenham dep		STOP					7 10
Christian Malford Halt							
Dauntsey							
Ashley Hill dep				5 57			
Horfield				6 2			
Filton Junction				6 5			
Winterbourne				6 11			
Coalpit Heath				6 16			
Chipping Sodbury				6 24			
Badminton				6 35			
Hullavington				6 44			
Little Somerford				6 55			
Brinkworth				7 3			
Wootton Bassett dep				7 14			
SWINDON arr				7 25			7 35
SWINDON dep	7 10			STOP			7 44
Stratton Park Halt							
Shrivenham							
Uffington							
Challow							
Wantage Road							
Steventon							
Didcot arr							8 20
Oxford (from Didcot) arr	8 10						9 30
Oxford dep							
Didcot dep							8 25
Cholsey and Moulsford							
Goring and Streatley							
Pangbourne							
Tilehurst							
READING arr			p.m.				8 50
READING dep			7 55		③		8 55
Twyford					p.m.		
Maidenhead					8 20		
Taplow		③			8 25		
Burnham (Bucks)		p.m.			8 29		
Slough		7 45			8 40		
Langley (Bucks)		7 51		③	8 46		
Iver		7 55		p.m.	8 50		
West Drayton & Yiewsley		8 0		8 30	8 56		
Hayes and Harlington		8 7		8 35	9 3		
Southall		8 14		8 40	9 10	③	
Hanwell and Elthorne		8 18		8 44	9 14	p.m.	
West Ealing		8 22		8 47	9 17	9 21	
Ealing (Broadway)		8 25		8 51	9 20	9 26	
Acton		8 30		8 57	9 24	9 32	
Westbourne Park		8 36		9 4	9 30	9 38	
LONDON (Padd'ton) arr		8 40	8 45	9 8	9 34	9 42	9 45

Station	p.m.	p.m.	p.m.	p.m.	p.m.	p.m.	p.m.
PENZANCE dep							
Plymouth (North Rd)							
Exeter (St. David's)					3 55		
BRISTOL Temple Meads arr					7 5		
BRISTOL Temple Meads dep			6 25		STOP	7 10	
Lawrence Hill							
Stapleton Rd.							
St. Anne's Park			6 30			7 16	
Keynsham & Somerdale			6 36			7 23	
Saltford			6 42			7 29	
Oldfield Park			6 49			7 36	
BATH arr			6 55			7 40	
BATH dep	6 53		STOP			7 44	
Bathampton	6 58					7 49	
Bathford Halt	7 0						
Box	7 5						
Box (Mill Lane)	7 7						③
Corsham	7 15						7 53
Chippenham arr	7 22				p.m.		8 0
Chippenham dep	STOP				7 44		
Christian Malford Halt					7 52		
Dauntsey					7 58		
Ashley Hill dep							
Horfield							
Filton Junction				③ Saturdays only.			
Winterbourne							
Coalpit Heath							
Chipping Sodbury							Saturdays only.
Badminton							
Hullavington							
Little Somerford				7 35			
Brinkworth				7 42			
Wootton Bassett dep				7 50	8 9		
SWINDON arr		③			8 20		
SWINDON dep		8 10					
Stratton Park Halt		8 14					
Shrivenham		8 21					
Uffington		8 31					
Challow		8 37					
Wantage Road		8 46					
Steventon		8 53					
Didcot arr		9 0					
Oxford (from Didcot) arr		9 30					
Oxford dep							
Didcot dep							
Cholsey and Moulsford							
Goring and Streatley							
Pangbourne							
Tilehurst			③				
READING arr			p.m.				
READING dep	③		9 50				
Twyford	p.m.		10 4				
Maidenhead	9 10		10 20				
Taplow	9 15		10 26				
Burnham (Bucks)	9 20		10 31				
Slough	9 30		10 38				
Langley (Bucks)	9 37						
Iver	9 42						
West Drayton & Yiewsley	9 50						
Hayes and Harlington	9 55						
Southall	10 0						
Hanwell and Elthorne	10 5						
West Ealing	10 9						
Ealing (Broadway)	10 12						
Acton	10 18						
Westbourne Park	10 24						
LONDON (Padd'ton) arr	10 28						

K—Via Reading. Third class only Didcot to Oxford.
N—Calls to set down passengers only.
R—Restaurant Car for portion of journey.
Q—Calls at Badminton at 5.35 p.m. to pick up passengers for London on notice being given at the station.
③—Third class only.

15

This GWR public timetable was for May 1943 and the 'cancellation' disclaimer of the war years is clearly seen. The fastest scheduled trains from Bristol to Paddington were timed at three hours and the locomotives would have been, most usually, Castles or Stars.

Park but this had nothing to do with any change of status as this locomotive remained a member of the Star class.

During the Second World War, six of the Stars lost their nameplates as a result of wartime diplomacy. In the summer of 1940, Nos 4022 and 4025 had their respective names, *Belgian Monarch* and *Italian Monarch*, removed and, in November that year, Nos 4023, 4028 and 4030 lost their respective names of *Danish Monarch*, *Roumanian Monarch* and *Swedish Monarch*. In January 1941, No 4026 had the name of *Japanese Monarch* removed. These were among the ten locomotives which had lost their original nameplates in 1927 when the King 4-6-0s appeared and, after No 4026 had been rendered anonymous, the only locomotive to retain a similar name theme was No 4021 but, with its name *British Monarch*, there was little likelihood of that one suffering the same fate. The three other Stars which had carried the names of monarchs, Nos 4024/27/29, had saved the authorities the embarrassment of removing nameplates as they had all been scrapped in the 1930s.

At the time of Nationalisation in 1948, forty-seven Stars were still in service and, by then, most of the class had been restored to GWR green liveries after having sported unlined black during the War. The Stars still retained the windowless sides to their cabs and this was a useful feature for identification. Back in 1929, No 4002 *Evening Star* had been fitted with outside steam-pipes of the 'elbow' design which were similar to those of the Castles. Throughout the 1930s and 1940s, the majority of the Stars received the elbow pipes so that, by 1950, the cab sides provided the only swiftly-identifiable differential between the Stars and the Castles.

On 15 November 1950, a royal visit to Swindon was timed to coincide with the borough's Golden Jubilee. The Royal Family's representative on the day was Princess Elizabeth (now Queen Elizabeth II) who, naturally, was treated to a tour of Swindon works although, much to her chagrin, she did not possess the obligatory shed pass for a visit to the locomotive depot. To help offset her disappoint-

By the early 1950s, the remaining Star class engines were usually relegated to secondary duties. In this picture, an unchallenging four-coach load is hauled into Birmingham (Snow Hill) by No 4015 *Knight of St. John* on 25 June 1950.
Photo: D. K. Jones Collection

Star class No 4028 is seen on a down semi-fast, complete with leading clerestory, near Pangbourne in the 1930s. The locomotive had its original name of *King Henry* snaffled in preparation for the arrival of the King class in 1927 and was renamed *Roumanian Monarch*; that name was removed as a diplomatic measure in 1940 and was never replaced. The engine went to its grave anonymously in 1951.

Photo: Rail Archive Stephenson

The awkward-looking elbow steam-pipes were fitted to many of the Star class engines from 1929. The sunlight in this picture of green-liveried No 4034 *Queen Adelaide* at Swindon in 1932 shows the pipes to full disadvantage.

Photo: Rail Archive Stephenson

WOLVERHAMPTON, BIRMINGHAM, OXFORD & LONDON. 81A

Week Days—continued.

Station	a.m.	a.m.	a.m.	a.m.	a.m.	a.m.	a.m.	a.m.	a.m.	a.m.	a.m.	a.m.	a.m.	a.m.	a.m.	a.m.	a.m.	a.m.	p.m.	a.m.	p.m.	noon	a.m.
LIVERPOOL (Land'g Stage) dep												5 30				7 40		8 10					
Birkenhead (Woodside) "												5 50				8 5		8 30					
Chester dep.												7 5				8 55		9 15					
Saltney "												7 10				9 0							
Balderton "												7 15	③										
Rossett "												7 21	8 30			9 10							
Gresford (for Llay) "												7 25	8 34			9 14							
Rhosrobin Halt "													8 39	③									
Wrexham "			7 10									7 40	8 44	9 15		9 25		9 44					
Johnstown and Hafod "			7 16									7 46		9 22									
Wynnville Halt "													STOP	9 25			③						
Ruabon "			7 20									7 55		9 27		9 34	9 38	10 0					
Rhosymedre Halt "																	9 41						
Cefn "			STOP									8 2		STOP		STOP	9 43						
Whitehurst "												8 6					9 46						
Chirk "												8 11					9 49						
Trehowell Halt "			To Barmouth.									8 14				To Barmouth.	9 52						
Weston Rhyn "												8 18					9 55						
Gobowen "												8 28					9 59	10 17					
Whittington (Low Level) "												8 33											
Rednal and West Felton "												8 39					STOP						
Haughton Halt "												8 43											
Stanwardine Halt "												8 49					To Oswestry.						
Baschurch "												8 55											
Oldwoods Halt "												8 59											
Leaton "												9 4											
Shrewsbury arr.												9 12	a.m.					10 39					
Shrewsbury dep.	6 40	7 35		7 55				8 10					9 25					10 47					11 0
Upton Magna "	6 47							8 18															11 8
Walcot "	6 52							8 24															11 13
Admaston "	6 57							8 28															11 18
Wellington "	7‡15	7 53		8 10				8 32	8 55				9 48		10 0			11 5					11 30
New Hadley Halt "	7 20								9 0						10 5								11 35
Oakengates "	7 26			STOP				STOP	9 4						10 9								11 39
Shifnal "	7 36								9 12						10 17					Saturdays excepted.	Saturdays only.	Saturdays only.	11 50
Cosford "	7 45						8 21		9 18						10 23								11 56
Albrighton "	7 49						8 25		9 21						10 27								12 0
Codsall "	7 56	8 12					8 33		9 27						10 34								12 7
Birches and Bilbrook Halt "	7 59						8 36								10 37								12 10
Dunstall Park "	8 5						8 42		9 37						10 43								12 17
WOLVERHAMPTON (Low Level) arr.	8 8	8 23					8 45		9 40				10 14		10 46			11 32					12 20
WOLVERHAMPTON (Low Level) dep.		8 33				8 42				9 55			10 24					11 39		11 45		12 0	
Priestfield "	STOP						STOP		STOP	9 59													STOP
Bilston "						8 48				10 3										11 51		12 6	
Wednesbury "						8 54				10 8										11 56		12 11	
Swan Village "						8 58				10 13										12 0		12 15	
West Bromwich "						9 2				10 18										12 5		12 20	
Handsworth and Smethwick "						9 7				10 24										12 10	12 10	12 25	
Soho and Winson Green "						9 10				10 27										12 13	12 13	12 28	
Hockley "						9 13				10 30										12 16	12 16	12 31	
BIRMINGHAM Snow Hill arr.		8 55				9 16				10 33			10 41	a.m.				11 59		12 20	12 20	12 36	
BIRMINGHAM Snow Hill dep.		9 0			9 6								10 52	11 0				12 5	12 10		12 25		
BIRMINGHAM Moor St. "						STOP				STOP										STOP		STOP	
Bordesley "					9 10									11 3					12 13				
Small Heath and Sparkbrook "					9 14									11 7					12 16				
Tyseley "					9 17									11 10					12 19				
Acock's Green & South Yardley "					9 20									11 13					12 22				
Olton "					9 23									11 16					12 26				
Solihull "					9 28									11 21					12 31		12 36		
Widney Manor "					9 32									11 25							12 40		
Knowle and Dorridge "					9 36									11 29		X			STOP		12 44		
Lapworth "	a.m.				9 42						X			11 34		p.m.					12 49		
Hatton "	9 3				9 49						10 31			11 43		12 4					12 56		
Warwick "	9 10				9 57						10 39			11 51		12 12					1 3		
Leamington Spa arr.	9 15	9 28		a.m.	10 2						10 44		11 22	11 55		12 17		12 31			1 7		
Leamington Spa dep.		9 32		9 45									11 30					12 36					
Southam Road and Harbury "				9 55													Saturdays only.					Saturdays excepted.	
Fenny Compton "				10 5																			
Cropredy "			③	10 15				③															③
Banbury arr.			a.m.	10 23				a.m.					11 56					1 2					p.m.
Banbury dep.			9 0					10 55					12 5					1 6					1 20
King's Sutton "			9 7					11 3															
Aynho (for Deddington) "			9 13				Restaurant Car Train.																
Fritwell and Somerton "		Via Bicester.	9 18																				
Heyford "			9 24															Via Bicester.					
Tackley Halt "			9 30														③					③	
Bletchington "			9 34														p.m.					p.m.	
Kidlington (for Blenheim) "			9 39						③								1 7		③			1 27	
OXFORD arr.			9 48			a.m.			a.m.				12 37				1 16		p.m.			1 36	1 58
OXFORD dep.			10 0			10 20			10 55				12 45						1 22				
Radley "			10 13						11 5										1 35				
Culham "			10 20						11 10										1 40				
Appleford Halt "			10 24						11 14										1 45				
Didcot arr.			10 30				a.m.		11 20	a.m.			1 1						1 52	p.m.			
Didcot dep.							10 50			11 28			1 5							2 0			
Reading arr.						10 58	11 15			11 55			1 30							2 25			
LONDON (Paddington) "		11 30				11 50	12 5			12 45			2 25					2 40		3 15			

X—Third class only (limited accommodation). ③—Third class only. ‡—Arrive 7.2 a.m.

THE WHOLE OF THE TRAIN, STEAMER AND ROAD SERVICES, ALSO RESTAURANT CARS AND SLEEPING CARS SHEWN IN THIS TIME TABLE ARE SUBJECT TO ALTERATION OR CANCELLATION AT SHORT NOTICE.

The GWR public timetable for May 1943 displayed the obligatory disclaimer about cancellations. This extract shows a selection of through workings and the locomotives which were used would have provided a cross-section of the GWR's motive power fleet. Stars, Saints, Castles and Kings were all known to have worked these services.

TABLE 4.3: YEARLY TOTALS OF STAR CLASS LOCOMOTIVES

N.B. Totals taken at 31 December of each year.

1907	10	1915	61	1923	73	1930	68	1937	55	1944	48	1951	20
1908	20	1916	61	1924	73	1931	68	1938	52	1945	48	1952	8
1909	31	1917	61	1925	71	1932	66	1939	49	1946	47	1953	4
1910	38	1918	61	1926	69	1933	65	1940	48	1947	47	1954	3
1911	41	1919	61	1927	69	1934	60	1941	48	1948	46	1955	3
1912	41	1920	61	1928	69	1935	58	1942	48	1949	43	1956	2
1913	46	1921	61	1929	68	1936	58	1943	48	1950	36	1957	0
1914	61	1922	67										

ment, Her Royal Highness was invited to drive a locomotive from the works to the station and the engine which was made available to her was, fittingly, No 4057 *Princess Elizabeth*.

Under the administration of British Railways, the Stars' sphere of operations was considered to be limited. The Kings were continuing to perform superbly on the heaviest and fastest trains while the building of Castles had recommenced. For secondary duties, the Stars were considered overpowered and, furthermore, the introduction of the County class 4-6-0s in 1945 had filled what little gap had been left in the range of motive power. By the early 1950s, the surviving Stars were around forty years-old and withdrawal was creating sizeable gaps in the class, but the need for a major overhaul did not necessarily signal a Star's automatic entry to the cutting yard. Between 1950 and 1952, several members of the class were given the full works treatment, complete with spit and polish, despite the demise of some classmates of similar vintage. In recognition of the Stars being the outstanding locomotives of their day, No 4003 *Lode Star* was set aside after its withdrawal in 1951 and, after restoration, was sent to Swindon Museum as a static exhibit. The three members of the class which were senior to No 4003 had long since been lost; Nos 4001/02 had been retired in the early 1930s while No 4000, which could not lay claim to being a pedigree Star anyway, had by this time been a member of the Castle class for twenty-two years.

After the summer of 1954, however, withdrawals had made such inroads into the class that the only three surviving Stars were Nos 4056/61/62. The trio often appeared on express duties in their final years and they featured in many recorded runs in which 350 ton trains were kept to the schedules which had been set for their younger brethren. No 4062 finally succumbed to retirement in November 1956, No 4061 followed suit in March 1957 but No 4056 *Princess Margaret* survived as a great favourite of Bristol crews until October 1957. The record holder in the mileage stakes was, however, not one of the last three survivors but No 4021, originally *King Edward* but latterly *British Monarch*. When retired at the age of forty-three in 1952, it had covered 2,074,300 miles.

CHAPTER 5

The Castles

Charles Collett succeeded G. J. Churchward at Swindon on 1 January 1922 and the departing chief mechanical engineer's legacy was a stock of locomotives which was the envy of most other British railway companies. As Churchward's chief assistant since 1919, Collett had been closely involved with recent locomotive development on the GWR and, therefore, the new man was more than happy to continue the policies of his tutor.

When Collett took over at the reins, the GWR's crack express passenger services were in the capable hands of Churchward's four-cylinder Star class 4-6-0s and a further dozen Stars had been ordered by Churchward before his retirement. The new batch of Stars was delivered piecemeal during the first fourteen months of Collett's tenure and they brought the total number of locomotives in the much-acclaimed class to seventy-three. It had been anticipated that, for the foreseeable future, the Stars would be more than powerful enough to cope with anything that the traffic department could throw at them but, during the summer of 1922, the loadings of many express trains were so great that even the highly-respected Stars had to be worked to the limit more regularly than the engineering department would have liked. The realisation that there was a genuine requirement for more powerful locomotives than the Stars took some time to sink in at Swindon.

In 1919, Churchward had toyed with the idea of upgrading the Stars by fitting larger boilers but this suggestion had caused severe concern in the GWR's Civil Engineering Department. The boiler favoured by Churchward had been the Standard No 7 which had been fitted to the new 2-8-0 No 4700, but the weight of such a boiler on the frames of a Star class 4-6-0 had been considered unacceptable. The rejection of the idea had not been a major disappointment to Churchward as, at the time, such a locomotive would have been more of an experiment than a necessity.

When Collett was faced with the fact that a more powerful express design was actually required, he returned to Churchward's idea of 1919. After playing with the original calculations, Collett concluded that a boiler which was midway between those of the 2-8-0 and the Stars would provide an adequate increase in power without reaching a prohibitive weight level. It was realised that the proposed boiler could be accommodated on the wheelbase of a Star but, instead of using Churchward's favoured jigsaw technique for the construction of a prototype, Collett chose to adapt the frame design of the Stars to accommodate the new boiler. The restyled frames retained the 27ft 3in wheelbase of the Stars despite being almost one foot longer. The additional length enabled the use of a longer firebox and, much to the eventual delight of crews, a more spacious cab.

Cabs on GWR locomotives were never exactly pie-hot on creature comforts. Back in the days of Joseph and George Armstrong in the 1860s and 1870s, luxuries such as cab sides, let alone roofs, were considered frivolous and were not, therefore, included in their locomotive designs. The brothers Armstrong justified the meagre conditions by citing the dangers from fumes in an enclosed cab but opinion was that, as the brothers had, in their days on the footplate, to endure conditions which were less than five-star, they were not going to let their

No 4096 *Highclere Castle* is seen at Exeter St. Davids on the down relief Cornish Riviera Express (a.k.a. the 10.30 Limited) in September 1931. The locomotive was, at the time, only five years old.

Photo: E. R. Morten

successors have an easier time. Under the administration of William Dean, the general standard of the GWR cabs was improved but the progress did not last as, although Dean's successor, George Churchward, might have made great strides in locomotive development, cabs on Churchward engines were extremely spartan when compared to their counterparts on other railways. The prospect of a larger, more comfortable cab with side windows on the proposed Collett 4-6-0 was welcomed by footplatemen.

Collett's design started to take shape during 1923 and, although the Churchward tradition of utilising standard components was continued to a considerable degree, the new four-cylinder 4-6-0 was to incorporate many features which would readily identify it as a non-Churchward product. Apart from the larger cab, the cylinders were to be 16in in diameter as opposed to the 14½in of the Stars and the steam-pipes to the outside cylinders were to be worn externally. The projected weight of the new locomotive was four and a quarter tons greater than that of the Stars but, as the extra weight was to be evenly distributed, the increase in axle weight would be only a little over one ton. The engineering lads were quick to calculate that the new machine's tractive effort would be 31,625 lb and that figure would regain the title of the country's most powerful passenger locomotive for the GWR.

In the best traditions of propaganda, the GWR itself had pointed to the tractive effort figure of 25,090 lb when, in 1907, it had proclaimed the Stars to be 'the most powerful passenger locomotives in Britain'. The use of the tractive effort figure was highly questionable but the GWR's publicity department felt that it would be unkind to confuse the unqualified general public with such things as drawbar brake horsepower and the like. Having made a rod for its own corporate back, the GWR watched the Lancashire & Yorkshire complete its Hughes-designed 4-6-0s in 1922 and these had a tractive effort of 26,315 lb. Later that same year,

Gresley's first 4-6-2 appeared on the Great Northern and claimed a tractive effort of 29,835 lb while, in December 1922, Raven's Pacifics were completed by the North Eastern Railway to take the title with a tractive effort of 29,918 lb. Much to Swindon's delight, the new 4-6-0 would claim back the blue riband.

It was August 1923 when the machine emerged from Swindon works and, between December that year and April 1924, a further nine were built. The new locomotives were, of course, all superheated and were named after castles but, although being acknowledged as a completely new class, they were designated to continue the numbering sequence of the Stars and, therefore, became Nos 4073–82. The ten members of the Castle class were all allocated to Old Oak Common for duties on the heaviest expresses to Plymouth and, through South Devon, they were allowed loadings of 315 tons unaided as compared to the 288 tons permitted for the Stars. On the more level section eastwards from Taunton, the Castles' loading limit of 455 tons was 35 tons greater than that of the Stars.

In the haulage stakes, the ten Castles did everything that could possibly have been required and, when it came to the public relations department, the GWR milked every last drop of publicity from the locomotives. As if on cue, a royal visit to Swindon works was announced for 28 April 1924 and King George V made no secret of the fact that he fancied himself as an engine driver. No publicist could have staged it better as the last of the ten Castles, No 4082, had been completed just prior to the royal visit and the name attached to the locomotive was none other than *Windsor Castle*. It was that very engine which was used, not only to haul the royal train, but also for the King's footplate debut. Onlookers were heard to remark that His Majesty did a good job of driving No 4082 from the works to the station but it was rumoured that there were the occasional cries from watching railwaymen of 'don't give up your day job'.

TABLE 5.1: ORIGINAL DIMENSIONS OF CASTLE CLASS LOCOMOTIVES

BUILT:	1923–50
WEIGHTS FULL (locomotive):	79 tons 17 cwt
(tender):	40 tons 0 cwt (*)
TENDER CAPACITY (water):	3,500 gallons (*)
(coal):	6 tons (*)
WHEELBASE (locomotive):	27ft 3in
WHEEL DIAMETERS (bogie):	3ft 2in
(coupled):	6ft 8½in (a)
CYLINDERS:	(4) 16in × 26in
BOILER PRESSURE:	225 lb/psi
HEATING SURFACES (tubes):	1885.6 sq ft
(firebox):	163.8 sq ft
(superheater):	262.6 sq ft (b)
GRATE AREA:	30.3 sq ft
TRACTIVE EFFORT (at 85% boiler pressure):	31,625 lb
SWINDON WORKS DIAGRAMS:	W/Y/A5/A7/A18/A19/A20/A22/A23/A26/A30
ROUTE AVAILABILITY:	Red
POWER CLASSIFICATION (GWR):	D
(BR):	7P (c)

NOTES:

(*) Different tenders fitted later. See Table 5.2 for details.

(a) No 5001 ran with 6ft 6in coupled wheels from December 1926 to March 1928 in design trials for the King class locomotives.

(b) Later superheaters varied.

(c) 6P until 31 December 1950.

TABLE 5.2: TENDERS USED BY CASTLE CLASS LOCOMOTIVES

INTRODUCED	WATER	COAL	WEIGHT FULL	NOTES
1923	3,500 galls	6 tons	40 tons 0 cwt	
1926	4,000 galls	6 tons	46 tons 14 cwt	Standard from 1932
1929	3,500 galls	5½ tons	45 tons 3 cwt	Only a few built
1931	4,000 galls	6 tons	49 tons 3 cwt	Only one built
1946	1,950 galls	*	53 tons 3 cwt	* For oil-burning locos
1948	4,000 galls	6 tons	47 tons 6 cwt	Standard from 1948
1949	4,000 galls	6 tons	43 tons 1 cwt	Experimental alloy tank
1952	3,800 galls	6 tons	49 tons 15 cwt	Only two built

The name *Pendennis Castle* originally belonged to a Bulldog class 4-4-0 but was 'requisitioned' for Castle class No 4079. This picture was taken in 1954 and shows the engine taking on water at Shrewsbury before departing with a northbound express. ***Photo: D. K. Jones Collection***

The British Empire Exhibition was a major showcase for the latest technology; the original Castle, No 4073 *Caerphilly Castle*, was exhibited in 1924 and, the following year, No 4079 *Pendennis Castle* did the honours. A neighbour of No 4073 at Wembley in 1924 was LNER 4-6-2 No 4472 *Flying Scotsman* and the vision of the two celebrated locomotives side-by-side prompted arrangements for comparison trials. The period selected for the trials was the last week in April 1925 and, in order to evaluate both types of locomotive fairly, one member of each class was to perform on the GWR and another pair was to be put to the test on the LNER. The away leg was given to GWR No 4079 *Pendennis Castle* and LNER No 4475 *Flying Fox* while the home tie was allocated to GWR No 4074 *Caldicot Castle* and LNER No 4474 *Victor Wild*. Despite the GWR's claim of the Castles being the 'most powerful express locomotives in Britain', the LNER had no doubt that their Pacifics would give the Swindon upstarts a lesson. The result was a severe case of egg on the face at Doncaster.

In every department, the Castles proved superior to the Gresley Pacifics. On home ground, the test track was the Paddington to Plymouth route and, while the LNER locomotive kept perfectly to time, the Castle had the habit of arriving up to fifteen minutes early. The LNER used its main line for its own trials but, whether running to Grantham or through to Doncaster, the Castle had no competition. Admittedly, LNER No 4475 suffered from mechanical problems on its first day but its replacement, No 2545 *Diamond Jubilee*, offered no stiffer challenge and, as well as the timekeeping, the Castles showed a significant superiority in economy. Nigel Gresley, the chief mechanical engineer of the LNER, looked at the average coal consumption figures for the tests on the GWR's lines and, when they showed that his Pacific had used 48 lb of coal per mile as opposed to the 42 lb of the Castle, he was quick to excuse this by citing his locomotive's dislike of the unfamiliar Welsh coal. It was tactfully pointed out to him that the GWR Castles were no more familiar with the Yorkshire coal which had been provided for the tests on the LNER but this had not prevented No 4079 *Pendennis Castle* from using 3.7 lb per mile less than the 57.1 lb of the LNER engine.

Excuses were becoming thin on the ground but the LNER latched on to the fact that the driver of No 4074 *Caldicot Castle* had broken an agreement by exceeding the speed limit on the Plymouth route by over 10 mph on more than one occasion. This grumble was quickly forgotten when the LNER driver in charge of Pacific No 4474 owned up to having exceeded the speed limit by over 10 mph on seventeen occasions. The general humour at Doncaster was not improved when the GWR blatantly contravened an agreement that, whatever the outcome of the tests, no results would be made public without the consent of both railway companies. It was, perhaps, unnecessary for the GWR's directors to capitalise on the results of the trials as the Castles were perfectly adept at performing their own public relations duties. In an attempt to placate the LNER, the GWR supplied Doncaster with details of the Swindon-designed sanding equipment and axle lubrication equipment which had impressed the rivals. The trials were completed just before the opening of the 1925 British Empire Exhibition and, while the LNER decided to exhibit No 4472 *Flying Scotsman* once again, the GWR, rather conspicuously, sent No 4079 *Pendennis Castle* to occupy the adjacent stand.

Prior to the 1925 Empire Exhibition, the Castle class had been boosted by two more locomotives but neither were pedigrees. In April 1925, Star class No 4009 *Shooting Star* had entered Swindon works intent on having simple surgery to replace its cylinders but, when a general anaesthetic had been administered instead of the anticipated local one, it had become obvious that the surgeons had rather more in mind. When No 4009 had regained consciousness, not only did it sport new sixteen-inch diameter cylinders but it also had a larger boiler, extended cab and an extra foot in length. Delighted at being such a big boy, No 4009 had happily accepted its new official classification as a Castle. Identical rebuilding and reclassification was eventually imposed on three other Stars, Nos 4016/32/37, between October 1925 and June 1926 while, in November 1929, No 4000 *North Star* was also similarly treated.

Apart from No 4009, the other locomotive which had been incorporated into the Castle class before the 1925 Empire Exhibition was No 111. This locomotive had started life in February 1908 as the very first 4-6-2 tender locomotive in Britain and had originally been named *The Great Bear*. In view of the highly satisfactory performances of the Star class 4-6-0s prior to 1908, the need for a 4-6-2 had been questioned but the GWR's directors subscribed to the 'big is beautiful' school of thought. Subtlety was not a word they associated with prestige. Despite his detailed knowledge of, and enthusiasm for, large locomotive boilers, Churchward's reaction to the directors' request for a large-boilered 4-6-2 can only be described as underwhelmed.

Nevertheless, the directors had insisted on the construction of the Pacific and, in true Churchward fashion, the jigsaw method of using standard components had been incorporated as much as possible. The cylinders, the superheater, the driving wheels, the bogie and the motion had been taken straight off the shelf and, apart from the massive boiler, the only major new features had been the longer

On an autumn day in 1961, Shrewsbury shed hosted two generations of Castles. Nearest the camera is No 4037 *The South Wales Borderers* which had started life as a member of the Star class in 1910 while, farthest, is No 7015 *Carn Brea Castle* which was not built until after Nationalisation in 1948. The only major difference between the two engines is that the newer one sports a double chimney.

Photo: D. K. Jones Collection

frames, the 3ft 8in diameter trailing wheels and the bogie tender. The GWR's usual practice had been to use its newest and most powerful locomotives on the boat trains to Plymouth as the London & South Western Railway had always been ready to offer competition for those services. With an axle weight of twenty tons, however, No 111 *The Great Bear* had been proclaimed unacceptable on that route even before it had left the works.

The only route which the GWR's civil engineers had passed as suitable for the four-cylinder monster had been the line between Paddington and Bristol but, for the company's directors, this had not been such a bad thing. They may have agreed with Churchward that there had been no real need for the 4-6-2 but the potential propaganda value of having the first Pacific in Britain had been enormous. The Bristol route, although not the most testing of the GWR's services, was the businessman's line and was, therefore, eminently suitable for extracting the maximum publicity from the locomotive. When it entered service, *The Great Bear* had turned out to be a poor steamer and rather underpowered but, in the PR stakes, it became a massive success. Virtually every item of GWR promotional literature carried a picture of the 4-6-2 on its cover and, when a drawing of the locomotive was included in a set of cigarette cards, the nation's smokers took to puffing away like a pack of imprisoned beagles in order to obtain the prized card.

Churchward had remained unimpressed by No 111 despite its prestige value, and he had been heard to remark that the sum of over £5,000 which had been allocated to its construction could have been better spent elsewhere. The locomotive had been constructed in 1908 and the next Pacific did not appear in Britain for another fourteen years. When Britain's second Pacific, Nigel Gresley's 4-6-2 No 1470 *Great Northern*, rolled out of Doncaster works in April 1922, the then-retired George Churchward commented: "There was no need for that young man to build a Pacific; we could have

TABLE 5.3: DIMENSIONS OF 4-6-2 NO 111 AS ORIGINALLY BUILT

BUILT:	1908
WORKS NUMBER:	2279
WEIGHTS FULL (locomotive):	97 tons 0 cwt
(tender):	45 tons 15 cwt
TENDER CAPACITY (water):	3,500 gallons
(coal):	7 tons
WHEELBASE (locomotive):	34ft 6in
WHEEL DIAMETERS (bogie):	3ft 2in
(coupled):	6ft 8½in
(trailing):	3ft 8in
CYLINDERS:	(4) 15in × 26in
BOILER PRESSURE:	225 lb/psi
HEATING SURFACES (tubes):	2673.4 sq ft
(firebox):	158.1 sq ft
(superheater):	545.0 sq ft
GRATE AREA:	41.8 sq ft
TRACTIVE EFFORT (at 85% boiler pressure):	27,800 lb
SWINDON WORKS DIAGRAMS:	A/B/C
ROUTE AVAILABILITY:	Special Red

The GWR's one and only 4-6-2 was No 111 *The Great Bear*. It was constructed in 1908 and rebuilt as a Castle class 4-6-0 in 1924 but, despite such a comparatively long existence as a Pacific, photographs of the machine are relatively rare. Due to its limited sphere of operations, virtually all existing photographs of the 4-6-2 show it either at London or Bristol or en route between those two points and, therefore, I make no excuses for showing it at Paddington station. The picture was taken on 24 August 1910 and shows the locomotive at the head of its regular turn, the 6.30pm to Bristol.

Photo: LCGB/Ken Nunn Collection

sold him ours.''

When the Castles started to appear in 1923, much of the novelty value of the 4-6-2 had disappeared and, in view of its severely-restricted route availability, it was decided that its future would be reviewed when its next major repair or overhaul became due. The last day which No 111 *The Great Bear* spent as a Pacific was 7 January 1924 when, with over half a million miles on the clock, it entered Swindon works for major surgery. It emerged seven months later, still wearing the same number, 111, but as a Castle class 4-6-0 with the new name of *Viscount Churchill.*

Between May and August 1925, ten more Castles were constructed at Swindon. They were given Nos 4083–92 and five of these, Nos 4084–88, were allocated to Laira shed in Plymouth while the others joined their predecessors at Old Oak Common. The next ten were delivered between May and September 1926 and, while the first seven were given Nos 4093–99 to continue the existing sequence, the other three had to start a new sequence by wearing Nos 5000–02. Two of the 1926 batch were dispatched to Laira shed, the others joining their classmates at Old Oak.

In the autumn of 1926, No 5000 *Launceston Castle* was loaned to the LMS but this was not a case of Derby having failed to learn from the embarrassments of Doncaster the previous year. The LMS had reached a crossroads in its locomotive development and it merely wanted to have a close look at the Castle in action on the West Coast main line before deciding which course to pursue. Compound 4-4-0s, the design of which had originated with the Midland Railway, were still in favour with the LMS although 4-6-0s with both London & North Western and Lancashire & Yorkshire pedigrees were found to have specific advantages. Henry Fowler, the chief mechanical engineer of the LMS, had taken the first tentative steps towards designing a compound 4-6-2 but, when the GWR Castle turned in excellent performances northwards from Euston, he readily dropped all plans for his mechanically-complex contraption and, instead, channelled his energies into duplicating the GWR's Castles.

It was not just the performance of the Castle which impressed the LMS hierarchy but, as if to echo events of 1925, the coal consumption of No 5000 was far lower than that of any LMS locomotive. Impatient to see similar performance and economy on his own railway, Fowler asked the GWR if it would construct fifty Castles for the LMS or, failing that, lend the plans to Derby. When the laughter had subsided at Swindon, a polite refusal was dispatched to Derby but, undeterred, Fowler was to pursue the next best option and looked southwards the following year.

At Eastleigh, the main workshop of the Southern Railway, the first of Maunsell's powerful Lord Nelson class 4-6-0s appeared in 1926 and much of the design work had been undertaken by staff who had learned their trade with the GWR at Swindon under the leadership of George Churchward. Naturally, a great deal of Churchward influence had found its way into several Southern designs including the Lord Nelsons and, when Henry Fowler failed to secure the plans of the GWR's Castles, he felt that the next best thing would be a Swindon-influenced Lord Nelson. The Southern was less familiar than the GWR with the old adage linking imitation to flattery and so the plans for the Lord Nelsons were willingly sent to Fowler. The LMS's versions of the Lord Nelsons were to be the famous Royal Scots but, in subtle recognition of the design's origins, the LMS workshop staff initially referred to the Scots as 'Modified Castles'.

Construction of new GWR Castles was resumed between May and July 1927 when Nos 5003–12 emerged. This time, only eight were divided between Old Oak Common and Laira sheds, the other two, Nos 5011/12, being allocated to Newton Abbot. The summer of 1927 saw the appearance of the first six members of Collett's King class 4-6-0s and, within a year, a total of twenty Kings were in action. The Kings were considerably more powerful than the Castles and they were treated to the limelight in the same way as the first Castles had been in 1923 and, previously, the solitary Pacific in 1908. When the Kings became established on the heaviest duties from Paddington to Plymouth, this enabled the Castles to wander from the tightly-knit triangle of Paddington–Bristol–Plymouth. By the end of 1928, Castles started to appear occasionally on workings to South Wales and Wolverhampton and, the following year, they became regulars on the Cheltenham Flyer.

TABLE 5.4: THE CASTLE CLASS LOCOMOTIVES OF THE 1920s

NO	NAME	BUILT	WDN	FIRST SHED	1948 SHED	LAST SHED
111	*Viscount Churchill* (*)	(a)	7/53	Old Oak Common	Old Oak Common	Plymouth
4000	*North Star*	(a)	5/57	Newton Abbot	Wolverhampton	Swansea
4009	*Shooting Star* (*)	(a)	3/50	Plymouth	Old Oak Common	Old Oak Common
4016	*Knight of the Golden Fleece* (*)	(a)	9/51	Wolverhampton	Newton Abbot	Old Oak Common
4032	*Queen Alexandra*	(a)	9/51	Plymouth	Plymouth	Taunton
4037	*Queen Phillipa* (*)	(a)	9/62	Wolverhampton	Old Oak Common	Exeter
4073	*Caerphilly Castle*	8/23	5/60	Old Oak Common	Old Oak Common	Cardiff
4074	*Caldicot Castle*	12/23	5/63	Old Oak Common	Swansea	Old Oak Common
4075	*Cardiff Castle*	1/24	11/61	Old Oak Common	Old Oak Common	Old Oak Common
4076	*Carmarthen Castle*	2/24	2/63	Old Oak Common	Old Oak Common	Llanelli
4077	*Chepstow Castle*	2/24	8/62	Old Oak Common	Newton Abbot	Bristol (SPM)
4078	*Pembroke Castle*	2/24	7/62	Old Oak Common	Swansea	Llanelli
4079	*Pendennis Castle*	2/24	5/64	Old Oak Common	Hereford	Bristol (SPM)
4080	*Powderham Castle*	3/24	8/64	Old Oak Common	Bristol	Southall
4081	*Warwick Castle*	3/24	1/63	Old Oak Common	Swansea	Carmarthen
4082	*Windsor Castle* (*)	4/24	9/64	Old Oak Common	Gloucester	Tyseley
4083	*Abbotsbury Castle*	5/25	12/61	Old Oak Common	Cardiff	Cardiff
4084	*Aberystwyth Castle*	5/25	10/60	Plymouth	Bristol	Cardiff
4085	*Berkeley Castle*	5/25	5/62	Plymouth	Reading	Old Oak Common
4086	*Builth Castle*	6/25	4/62	Plymouth	Worcester	Oxford
4087	*Cardigan Castle*	6/25	10/63	Plymouth	Plymouth	Bristol (SPM)
4088	*Dartmouth Castle*	7/25	5/64	Plymouth	Plymouth	Bristol (SPM)
4089	*Donnington Castle*	7/25	9/64	Old Oak Common	Bristol	Reading
4090	*Dorchester Castle*	7/25	6/63	Old Oak Common	Plymouth	Cardiff East Dock
4091	*Dudley Castle*	7/25	1/59	Old Oak Common	Old Oak Common	Old Oak Common
4092	*Dunraven Castle*	8/25	12/61	Old Oak Common	Worcester	Oxford
4093	*Dunster Castle*	5/26	9/64	Old Oak Common	Bristol	Gloucester
4094	*Dynevor Castle*	5/26	3/62	Old Oak Common	Cardiff	Carmarthen
4095	*Harlech Castle*	6/26	12/62	Plymouth	Swansea	Reading
4096	*Highclere Castle*	6/26	1/63	Plymouth	Bristol	Llanelli
4097	*Kenilworth Castle*	6/26	5/60	Old Oak Common	Penzance	Swansea
4098	*Kidwelly Castle*	7/26	12/63	Old Oak Common	Newton Abbot	Old Oak Common
4099	*Kilgerran Castle*	8/26	9/62	Old Oak Common	Newton Abbot	Llanelli
5000	*Launceston Castle*	9/26	10/64	Old Oak Common	Old Oak Common	Oxley
5001	*Llandovery Castle*	9/26	2/63	Old Oak Common	Cardiff	Old Oak Common
5002	*Ludlow Castle*	9/26	9/64	Old Oak Common	Swansea	Southall
5003	*Lulworth Castle*	5/27	8/62	Old Oak Common	Taunton	Newton Abbot
5004	*Llanstephan Castle*	6/27	4/62	Plymouth	Old Oak Common	Neath
5005	*Manorbier Castle*	6/27	2/60	Old Oak Common	Cardiff	Swindon
5006	*Tregenna Castle*	6/27	4/62	Old Oak Common	Swansea	Carmarthen
5007	*Rougemont Castle*	6/27	9/62	Plymouth	Cardiff	Gloucester
5008	*Raglan Castle*	6/27	9/62	Plymouth	Old Oak Common	Old Oak Common
5009	*Shrewsbury Castle*	6/27	10/60	Plymouth	Plymouth	Swindon

TABLE 5.4 CONT.

NO	NAME	BUILT	WDN	FIRST SHED	1948 SHED	LAST SHED
5010	*Restormel Castle*	7/27	10/59	Plymouth	Cardiff	Reading
5011	*Tintagel Castle*	7/27	9/62	Newton Abbot	Newton Abbot	Old Oak Common
5012	*Berry Pomeroy Castle*	7/27	4/62	Newton Abbot	Exeter	Oxford

NOTES
(*) Locomotives renamed. See Tables 5.7 and 5.8 for details.
(a) Locomotives rebuilt from other classes. See Table 5.6.

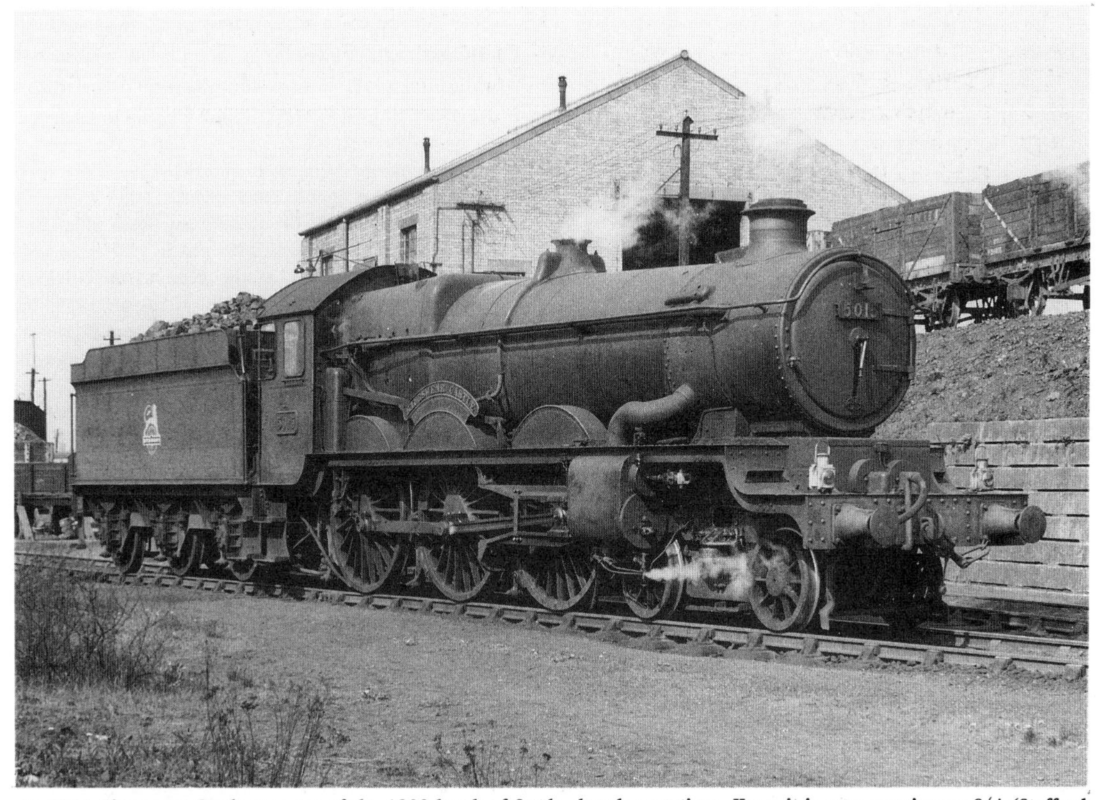

No 5015 *Kingswear Castle* was one of the 1932 batch of Castle class locomotives. Here, it is seen wearing an 84A (Stafford Road) shedplate at Oxford depot on 29 April 1956. Shame about the grime.

Photo: E. H. Sawford

When the GWR required further powerful express locomotives in 1932, it was assumed that the vote would go to another brace of the highly-successful King class 4-6-0s which, by that time, numbered thirty in total. The problem with the Kings, however, was that their axle weights restricted them to the Plymouth, Bristol and Wolverhampton routes only and, therefore, the superior versatility of the Castles swung the vote. Between June 1932 and July 1935, Nos 5013–42 were completed to continue the lineage of the Castles and a handful of the new arrivals were allocated to the previously unheard of outposts of Exeter, Taunton, Cardiff and Shrewsbury sheds.

The new Castles incorporated several minor improvements although not enough to warrant a separate works diagram. One innovation which was introduced on Nos 5033–42 in 1935 was a speedometer and this device became standard on all Castles and Kings from then onwards. Before the use of speedometers, the experience of footplatemen and the observation of mileage posts had sufficed to provide an approximation of a locomotive's speed and it was rare for seasoned crews to be too far adrift in their estimates. In the case of the Castles and the Kings, it was felt that the sheer power of the engines might encourage the boy-racers on the footplates and, in view of the weights of those engines, they were the two classes which could be most dangerous if pushed beyond sensible limits.

In March 1935, No 5005 *Manorbier Castle* joined King class No 6014 *King Henry VII* as an unwilling victim for streamlining, the decision to ruin the stylish lines of the locomotives being solely down to public relations. Both the LMS and the LNER had received much attention because of their well-streamlined engines and, understandably, the GWR's directors did not want their company to be ignored. Charles Collett was most reluctant to alter the cosmetic appearances of the two engines but, mindful of his pension, he carried out his task.

In the name of fashion, No 5005 was fitted with a bulbous cover to its smokebox door, fairings over its outside cylinders and steam-pipes and a wedge front for its cab. Although Collett had proved that he had an eye for external appearances, nobody disputed that he made an absolute pig's ear of streamlining the Castle and the King and it has often been suggested that he deliberately made the work as undignified as possible so that it would not be retained for very long. Whatever the reason for the nightmarish appearances of the two locomotives, the piecemeal removal of the 'customisation' was under way before long. No 5005 started to lose substantial parts of its streamlining in 1937 but it was 1947 before the last trace had disappeared.

Believe it or not, a once-smart Castle class 4-6-0 lurks behind the dustbin lid. In 1935, No 5005 *Manorbier Castle* was subjected to the art deco treatment which was, at that time, all the rage and the picture shows the locomotive passing Dawley at the head of the 10.55am Paddington to Torquay express on 31 August 1935. The 'streamlining' was removed in a piecemeal fashion starting later in 1935 and so this rare shot shows the engine in its complete farcical condition.

Photo: LCGB/Ken Nunn Collection

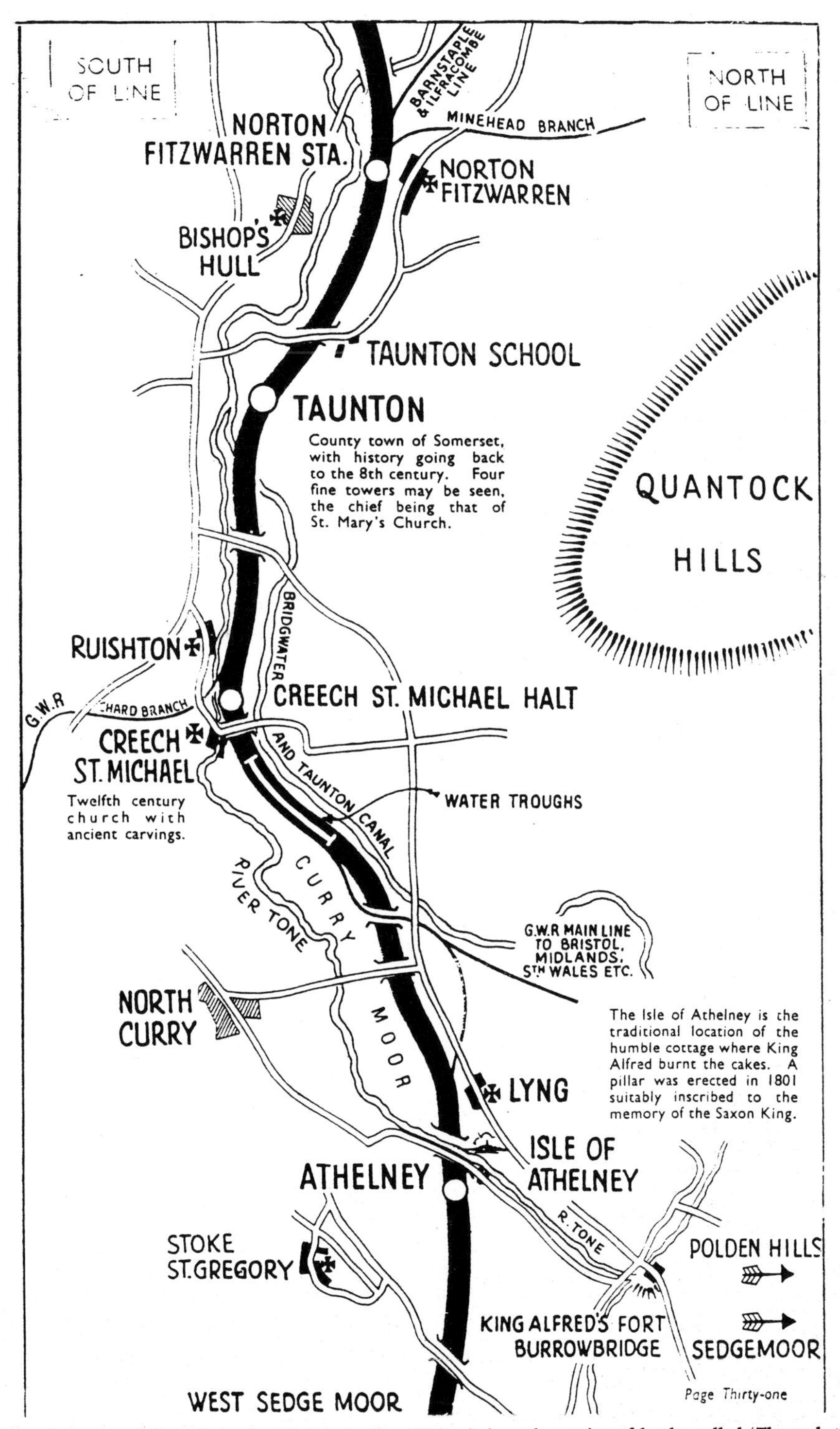

The GWR was well aware of the value of publicity. In the 1930s, it issued a series of books called 'Through the Window' and each one of these provided a commentary on a particular route. This extract is from the Paddington to Penzance book and it explains the delights of southern Somerset to its customers.

TABLE 5.5: THE CASTLE CLASS LOCOMOTIVES OF THE 1930s

NO	NAME	BUILT	WDN	FIRST SHED	1948 SHED	LAST SHED
5013	*Abergavenny Castle*	6/32	7/62	Newton Abbot	Swansea	Neath
5014	*Goodrich Castle*	6/32	2/65	Plymouth	Old Oak Common	Tyseley
5015	*Kingswear Castle*	7/32	4/63	Cardiff	Wolverhampton	Cardiff East Dock
5016	*Montgomery Castle*	7/32	9/62	Old Oak Common	Swansea	Llanelli
5017	*St Donats Castle* (*)	7/32	9/62	Taunton	Worcester	Gloucester
5018	*St Mawes Castle*	7/32	3/64	Old Oak Common	Wolverhampton	Reading
5019	*Treago Castle*	7/32	9/62	Plymouth	Bristol	Wolverhampton
5020	*Trematon Castle*	7/32	11/62	Plymouth	Cardiff	Llanelli
5021	*Whittington Castle*	8/32	9/62	Plymouth	Shrewsbury	Cardiff
5022	*Wigmore Castle*	8/32	6/63	Old Oak Common	Old Oak Common	Wolverhampton
5023	*Brecon Castle*	4/34	2/63	Old Oak Common	Old Oak Common	Swindon
5024	*Carew Castle*	4/34	5/62	Newton Abbot	Bristol	Newton Abbot
5025	*Chirk Castle*	4/34	11/63	Old Oak Common	Bristol	Hereford
5026	*Criccieth Castle*	4/34	11/64	Newton Abbot	Plymouth	Oxley
5027	*Farleigh Castle*	4/34	11/62	Old Oak Common	Old Oak Common	Llanelli
5028	*Llantilo Castle*	5/34	5/60	Plymouth	Plymouth	Plymouth
5029	*Nunney Castle*	5/34	12/63	Old Oak Common	Old Oak Common	Cardiff East Dock
5030	*Shirburn Castle*	5/34	9/62	Exeter	Cardiff	Carmarthen
5031	*Totnes Castle*	5/34	10/63	Wolverhampton	Wolverhampton	Wolverhampton
5032	*Usk Castle*	5/34	9/62	Shrewsbury	Shrewsbury	Old Oak Common
5033	*Broughton Castle*	5/35	9/62	Wolverhampton	Chester	Oxford
5034	*Corfe Castle*	5/35	9/62	Newton Abbot	Newton Abbot	Old Oak Common
5035	*Coity Castle*	5/35	5/62	Cardiff	Old Oak Common	Swindon
5036	*Lyonshall Castle*	5/35	9/62	Cardiff	Old Oak Common	Old Oak Common
5037	*Monmouth Castle*	5/35	3/64	Old Oak Common	Old Oak Common	Bristol (SPM)
5038	*Morlais Castle*	6/35	9/63	Old Oak Common	Old Oak Common	Reading
5039	*Rhuddlan Castle*	6/35	6/64	Old Oak Common	Old Oak Common	Reading
5040	*Stokesay Castle*	6/35	10/63	Old Oak Common	Old Oak Common	Bristol (SPM)
5041	*Tiverton Castle*	7/35	12/63	Plymouth	Plymouth	Old Oak Common
5042	*Winchester Castle*	7/35	6/65	Old Oak Common	Old Oak Common	Gloucester
5043	*Barbury Castle* (*)	3/36	12/63	Old Oak Common	Old Oak Common	Cardiff East Dock
5044	*Beverston Castle* (*)	3/36	4/62	Old Oak Common	Old Oak Common	Cardiff
5045	*Bridgwater Castle* (*)	3/36	9/62	Old Oak Common	Old Oak Common	Wolverhampton
5046	*Clifford Castle* (*)	4/36	9/62	Cardiff	Cardiff	Wolverhampton
5047	*Compton Castle* (*)	4/36	9/62	Swansea	Newton Abbot	Wolverhampton
5048	*Cranbrook Castle* (*)	4/36	8/62	Bristol	Bristol	Llanelli
5049	*Denbigh Castle* (*)	4/36	3/63	Worcester	Cardiff	Bristol (SPM)
5050	*Devizes Castle* (*)	5/36	8/63	Worcester	Plymouth	Bristol (SPM)
5051	*Drysllwyn Castle* (*)	5/36	5/63	Swansea	Swansea	Llanelli
5052	*Eastnor Castle* (*)	5/36	9/62	Cardiff	Cardiff	Bristol (SPM)
5053	*Bishop's Castle* (*)	5/36	7/62	Shrewsbury	Wolverhampton	Cardiff
5054	*Lamphey Castle* (*)	6/36	10/64	Old Oak Common	Cardiff	Gloucester
5055	*Lydford Castle* (*)	6/36	9/64	Old Oak Common	Old Oak Common	Gloucester
5056	*Ogmore Castle* (*)	6/36	11/64	Old Oak Common	Old Oak Common	Oxley
5057	*Penrice Castle* (*)	6/36	3/64	Newton Abbot	Plymouth	Old Oak Common

TABLE 5.5 CONT.

NO	NAME	BUILT	WDN	FIRST SHED	1948 SHED	LAST SHED
5058	*Newport Castle* (*)	5/37	3/63	Newton Abbot	Newton Abbot	Gloucester
5059	*Powis Castle* (*)	5/37	6/62	Exeter	Exeter	Shrewsbury
5060	*Sarum Castle* (*)	6/37	4/63	Wolverhampton	Plymouth	Old Oak Common
5061	*Sudeley Castle* (*)	6/37	9/62	Shrewsbury	Shrewsbury	Cardiff
5062	*Tenby Castle* (*)	6/37	8/62	Wolverhampton	Newton Abbot	Llanelli
5063	*Thornbury Castle* (*)	6/37	2/65	Worcester	Worcester	Oxley
5064	*Tretower Castle* (*)	6/37	9/62	Newton Abbot	Shrewsbury	Gloucester
5065	*Upton Castle* (*)	7/37	1/63	Exeter	Old Oak Common	Old Oak Common
5066	*Wardour Castle* (*)	7/37	9/62	Old Oak Common	Old Oak Common	Old Oak Common
5067	*St Fagans Castle*	7/37	7/62	Old Oak Common	Swindon	Reading
5068	*Beverston Castle*	6/38	9/62	Bristol	Swindon	Oxford
5069	*Isambard Kingdom Brunel*	6/38	2/62	Old Oak Common	Old Oak Common	Plymouth
5070	*Sir Daniel Gooch*	6/38	3/64	Old Oak Common	Wolverhampton	Old Oak Common
5071	*Clifford Castle* (*)	6/38	10/63	Newton Abbot	Newton Abbot	Bristol (SPM)
5072	*Compton Castle* (*)	6/38	10/62	Newton Abbot	Swansea	Wolverhampton
5073	*Cranbrook Castle* (*)	7/38	2/64	Plymouth	Shrewsbury	Cardiff East Dock
5074	*Denbigh Castle* (*)	7/38	5/64	Old Oak Common	Bristol	Bristol (SPM)
5075	*Devizes Castle* (*)	8/38	9/62	Wolverhampton	Wolverhampton	Bristol (SPM)
5076	*Drysllwyn Castle* (*)	8/38	9/64	Exeter	Bristol	Southall
5077	*Eastnor Castle* (*)	8/38	7/62	Old Oak Common	Taunton	Llanelli
5078	*Lamphey Castle* (*)	5/39	11/62	Plymouth	Newton Abbot	Neath
5079	*Lydford Castle* (*)	5/39	5/60	Old Oak Common	Newton Abbot	Old Oak Common
5080	*Ogmore Castle* (*)	5/39	4/63	Old Oak Common	Cardiff	Llanelli
5081	*Penrice Castle* (*)	5/39	10/63	Wolverhampton	Old Oak Common	Cardiff East Dock
5082	*Powis Castle* (*)	6/39	7/62	Bristol	Bristol	Old Oak Common
5083	*Bath Abbey*	(a)	1/59	Swansea	Bristol	Worcester
5084	*Reading Abbey*	(a)	7/62	Weymouth	Bristol	Old Oak Common
5085	*Evesham Abbey*	(a)	2/64	Old Oak Common	Old Oak Common	Bristol (SPM)
5086	*Viscount Horne*	(a)	11/58	Wolverhampton	Shrewsbury	Worcester
5087	*Tintern Abbey*	(a)	8/63	Old Oak Common	Old Oak Common	Llanelli
5088	*Llanthony Abbey*	(a)	9/62	Shrewsbury	Wolverhampton	Wolverhampton
5089	*Westminster Abbey*	(a)	11/64	Swansea	Swansea	Oxley
5090	*Neath Abbey*	(a)	5/62	Plymouth	Plymouth	Old Oak Common
5091	*Cleeve Abbey*	(a)	10/64	Bristol	Bristol	Tyseley
5092	*Tresco Abbey*	(a)	7/63	Gloucester	Worcester	Cardiff East Dock
5093	*Upton Castle*	6/39	9/63	Old Oak Common	Swansea	Old Oak Common
5094	*Tretower Castle*	6/39	9/62	Newton Abbot	Newton Abbot	Bristol (SPM)
5095	*Barbury Castle*	6/39	8/62	Plymouth	Plymouth	Shrewsbury
5096	*Bridgwater Castle*	6/39	6/64	Bristol	Weston	Worcester
5097	*Sarum Castle*	7/39	3/63	Shrewsbury	Shrewsbury	Cardiff East Dock

NOTES:
(*) Locomotives renamed. See Tables 5.7 and 5.8 for details.
(a) Locomotives rebuilt from other classes. See Table 5.6.

Between March 1936 and July 1939, forty-five new Castles were constructed. A large proportion of these followed the trend and were allocated to Old Oak Common, Laira and Newton Abbot sheds but the others were divided between several of the GWR's other main depots. The new locomotives took Nos 5043–82 and 5093–97, the gap from Nos 5083–92 being filled by the rebuilding of ten Star class 4-6-0s. The Stars that had been selected for surgery were the last ten to have been built, Nos 4063–72, which had been delivered between November 1922 and February 1923. Unlike the five other Stars which had been rebuilt as Castles between 1925 and 1929, Nos 4063–72 were renumbered in the conventional Castle sequence. They did, however, retain their original names and in order to differentiate between these ten and the two unrebuilt 'Abbeys' which remained members of the Star class, the conversions bore the legend 'Castle Class' in small letters underneath their nameplates.

By the late 1930s, the Castles had started to spread their wings a little. Apart from regular turns on the Cheltenham Flyer, the Castles had gained a strong foothold on the Bristolian despite the use of Kings in the early days of the service. The Bristolian was a fast train but it was seldom heavily loaded and so the muscle power of the Kings was considered rather superfluous. Although the Cornish Riviera Express remained a preserve of the Kings

Castle class No 5057 *St. Fagans Castle* stands at Bristol Temple Meads. The date is June 1949 and the changes of the Nationalisation era are already evident in the tender lettering and the smokebox numberplate.
Photo: Rail Archive Stephenson

TABLE 5.6: LOCOMOTIVES REBUILT FROM 4-6-2(*) OR STAR CLASS

NO	DATE	NO	DATE	NO	DATE	NO	DATE
111(*)	9/24	4032	4/26	5085	7/39	5089	10/39
4000	11/29	4037	6/26	5086	12/37	5090	4/39
4009	4/25	5083	6/37	5087	11/40	5091	12/38
4016	10/25	5084	4/37	5088	2/39	5092	4/38

Even allowing for the perspective of the photograph, No 5088 *Llanthony Abbey* looks positively majestic when compared to the functional-looking ex-LMS Jubilee class 4-6-0. The picture was taken at Shrewsbury on 3 August 1953 and the clearly-superior Castle is on a Birkenhead-bound express. Never let it be said I am at all biased.

Photo: E. R. Morten

For much of its life, No 5058 *Earl of Clancarty* was based at Newton Abbot or Plymouth. This picture was taken in July 1937 when the locomotive was only a couple of months old and shows it hauling a named train southwards from Bristol Temple Meads towards its home territory. One interesting item in the picture is the top of the old central tower of the entrance concourse at Temple Meads; it is glimpsed behind the locomotive's tender. Sadly, the tower was destroyed by fire during a wartime air-raid.

Photo: Rail Archive Stephenson

for many years, the Castles remained popular for many other expresses to Devon and Cornwall and were, later, to take command of the Torbay Express.

The latter half of the 1930s and the early 1940s saw a number of the Castle class locomotives renamed and three of these were the original Star class rebuilds, Nos 4009, 4016 and 4037, which were renamed in 1936, 1938 and 1937 respectively. No 4009 did not only receive a new name, *A1 Lloyds*, but was also renumbered as No 100; No 4016 was renamed *The Somerset Light Infantry (Prince Albert's)* and No 4037 received the name *The South Wales Borderers*.

Twenty-one members of the class were renamed between July and November 1937 although six of them were only a matter of months old. The reason for this mass renaming was vanity. The locomotives concerned were Nos 5043–63 and it was the last of these, No 5063 *Thornbury Castle* which, inadvertently, sparked the unrest. When Stanley Baldwin retired as Prime Minister in 1937 he was given a peerage and, as he and his father had both served on the board of the GWR, it was decided to rename No 5063 *Earl Baldwin*. Quite innocuous, or so it would seem, but the renaming seemed to spread an air of insecurity in other titled circles. When construction of the 3200 class 4-4-0s from cannibalised Duke and Bulldog 4-4-0s commenced in 1936, a total of twenty earls of the realm had proudly consented to have their names carried on the 'new' locomotives. Although most of the titled gentlemen couldn't tell a saddle tank from a lavatory brush, some well-meaning individual pointed out to them that the Castle class engine which carried the name *Earl Baldwin* was an infinitely grander machine than the mongrel contraptions which bore their names. Mayhem ensued and, as a sop to the offended nobles, the names of the earls were transferred to Castles Nos 5043–62.

The poor old Duke class 4-4-0s had become victims of the Castles once again. Back in 1923, Nos 3282, 3300 and 3301 had had their respective

It's a pity that the local Hell's Angels abandoned their bikes near the railings at Dawlish as they must have missed the vision of No 5059 *Earl of St. Aldwyn* at the head of a southbound express. The picture was taken on 3 August 1957.
Photo: E. R. Morton

nameplates of *Chepstow Castle, Pendennis Castle* and *Powderham* removed in deference to the newly-arrived 4-6-0s. In 1930, Nos 3280 *Tregenna* and 3305 *Tintagel* were also rendered anonymous despite the fact that, like No 3301 *Powderham*, it was not overly difficult to see that the word 'Castle' was missing from the name.

Two of the Castle names which were displaced by the vanity of the earls were reused on Nos 5064/65 later in 1937 while the rest were to reappear in future years. Between October 1940 and January 1941, twelve further Castles, Nos 5071–82, were involved in a renaming scheme which replaced the names of Castles by those of aircraft which had become famous in the Battle of Britain. During the War years, the Castles and the Kings were the only GWR classes to avoid being relegated to a black livery although one compromise was the loss of the lining-out.

Charles Collett retired early in 1941, by which time he had been eligible for a bus pass for five years. The GWR tradition of continuity meant that

TABLE 5.7: RENAMING OF CASTLE CLASS LOCOMOTIVES

NO	NEW NAME	NO	NEW NAME
5043	*Earl of Mount Edgcumbe*	5061	*Earl of Birkenhead*
5044	*Earl of Dunraven*	5062	*Earl of Shaftesbury*
5045	*Earl of Dudley*	5063	*Earl Baldwin*
5046	*Earl Cawdor*	5064	*Bishop's Castle*
5047	*Earl of Dartmouth*	5065	*Newport Castle*
5048	*Earl of Devon*	5071	*Spitfire*
5049	*Earl of Plymouth*	5072	*Hurricane*
5050	*Earl of St Germans*	5073	*Blenheim*
5051	*Earl Bathurst*	5074	*Hampden*
5052	*Earl of Radnor*	5075	*Wellington*
5053	*Earl Cairns*	5076	*Gladiator*
5054	*Earl of Ducie*	5077	*Fairey Battle*
5055	*Earl of Eldon*	5078	*Beaufort*
5056	*Earl of Powis*	5079	*Lysander*
5057	*Earl Waldegrave*	5080	*Defiant*
5058	*Earl of Clancarty*	5081	*Lockheed Hudson*
5059	*Earl of St Aldwyn*	5082	*Swordfish*
5060	*Earl of Berkeley*		

N.B. Some of the names removed from Nos 5043–63 were later used on Nos 5071–82. When subsequently removed from Nos 5071–82, they appeared for a third time on post-War Castles. Full details are given in Table 5.8.

TABLE 5.8: LATER USES OF DISPLACED NAMES OF CASTLE CLASS LOCOMOTIVES

NAME	ORIGINALLY CARRIED BY	REMOVED ON	LATER CARRIED BY	REMOVED ON	LATER CARRIED BY
Barbury Castle	5043	9/37	5095		
Beverston Castle	5044	9/37	5068		
Bridgwater Castle	5045	9/37	5096		
Clifford Castle	5046	8/37	5071	9/40	5098
Compton Castle	5047	8/37	5072	11/40	5099

TABLE 5.8 CONT.

NAME	ORIGINALLY CARRIED BY	REMOVED ON	LATER CARRIED BY	REMOVED ON	LATER CARRIED BY
Cranbrook Castle	5048	8/37	5073	1/41	7030
Denbigh Castle	5049	8/37	5074	1/41	7032
Devizes Castle	5050	8/37	5075	10/40	7002
Drysllwyn Castle	5051	8/37	5076	1/41	7018
Eastnor Castle	5052	7/37	5077	10/40	7004
Bishop's Castle	5053	8/37	5064		
Lamphey Castle	5054	9/37	5078	1/41	7005
Lydford Castle	5055	8/37	5079	11/40	7006
Ogmore Castle	5056	9/37	5080	1/41	7035
Penrice Castle	5057	10/37	5081	1/41	7023
Newport Castle	5058	9/37	5065		
Powis Castle	5059	10/37	5082	1/41	7024
Sarum Castle	5060	10/37	5097		
Sudeley Castle	5061	10/37	7025		
Tenby Castle	5062	11/37	7026		
Thornbury Castle	5063	7/37	7027		
Tretower Castle	5064	9/37	5094		
Upton Castle	5065	9/37	5093		

the automatic replacement was Collett's chief assistant, Frederick W. Hawksworth, who had been born in Swindon and had spent his entire career on the GWR. The War years were not a good time for a new chief mechanical engineer to make his mark but this was not of tremendous concern to Hawksworth as, like Collett, he did not yearn for stardom. Under George Churchward, solid foundations had been laid for a long-term policy of standardisation and Collett had provided superb continuity of Churchward's ideas. In common with his predecessor, Hawksworth saw no reason whatsoever to implement major changes just for their own sakes.

After the War, Hawksworth ordered that construction of the Castles should recommence and Nos 5098/99 finished off the old numbering sequence when they appeared in May 1946. Thirty-eight more Castles were added and these started with No 7000 although, by the time of Nationalisation, only No 7007 had been reached. No 7008 was delivered five months after the GWR had been gobbled up by British Railways and, when the very last Castle, No 7037, left Swindon works, the GWR had been nominally extinct for two years and seven months. During 1946/47, five of the class had been converted to oil-burners in preparation for the predicted coal shortage but all had been restored to a traditional diet by November 1948.

The post-War Castles incorporated several detail

TABLE 5.9: THE CASTLE CLASS LOCOMOTIVES OF THE POST-WAR YEARS

NO	NAME	BUILT	WDN	FIRST SHED	1948 SHED	LAST SHED
5089	*Clifford Castle*	5/46	6/64	Swansea	Swansea	Oxley
5099	*Compton Castle*	5/46	2/63	Old Oak Common	Old Oak Common	Gloucester
7000	*Viscount Portal*	5/46	12/63	Newton Abbot	Newton Abbot	Worcester
7001	*Denbigh Castle* (*)	5/46	9/63	Cardiff	Cardiff	Oxley
7002	*Devizes Castle*	6/46	3/64	Swansea	Swansea	Worcester
7003	*Elmley Castle*	6/46	8/64	Swansea	Swansea	Gloucester

Charles Collett would have loved to have seen this picture. From left to right are No 6024 *King Edward I*, No 5029 *Nunney Castle* and mixed traffic Hall class 4-6-0 No 6998 *Burton Agnes Hall* and all three were photographed together at Didcot while being prepared on 15 August 1991 in readiness for an open day at Old Oak Common shed in London.

Photo: Robert Falconer

The first and last of the classic Great Western express passenger designs were photographed together at Old Oak Common in September 1985. No 6000 ***King George V*** displays the famous bell with which it was presented during its trip to America in 1927 but its shedplate for Gloucester (Barnwood) is somewhat less of a genuine piece of heritage as it owes more to the engine's ownership by Messrs. Bulmers of Hereford than to its working history. When this picture was taken, even the renewal of the original broad gauge 4-2-2 ***Iron Duke*** had vanished over ninety years earlier and so the one which is seen here is, of course, the National Railway Museum's working replica.

Photo: Peter Herring

Three of Charles Collett's 'Kings' are in preservation and one of these is No 6024 ***King Edward I***. This picture shows the locomotive at the head of the Stratford-bound 'Shakespeare Express' at Wilmcote on 16 April 1990.

Photo: Robert Falconer

TABLE 5.9 CONT.

NO	NAME	BUILT	WDN	FIRST SHED	1948 SHED	LAST SHED
7004	*Eastnor Castle*	6/46	1/64	Gloucester	Gloucester	Reading
7005	*Lamphey Castle*	6/46	9/64	Worcester	Worcester	Worcester
7006	*Lydford Castle*	6/46	12/63	Shrewsbury	Shrewsbury	Old Oak Common
7007	*Ogmore Castle* (*)	7/46	2/63	Wolverhampton	Wolverhampton	Worcester
7008	*Swansea Castle*	5/48	9/64	Oxford		Old Oak Common
7009	*Athelney Castle*	5/48	3/63	Swansea		Gloucester
7010	*Avondale Castle*	6/48	3/64	Oxford		Reading
7011	*Banbury Castle*	6/48	2/65	Bristol		Oxley
7012	*Barry Castle*	6/48	11/64	Swansea		Oxley
7013	*Bristol Castle* (*)	7/48	2/65	Old Oak Common		Gloucester
7014	*Caerhays Castle*	7/48	2/65	Bristol		Tyseley
7015	*Carn Brea Castle*	7/48	4/63	Swindon		Old Oak Common
7016	*Chester Castle*	8/48	11/62	Cardiff		Cardiff East Dock
7017	*G.J. Churchward*	8/48	2/63	Old Oak Common		Old Oak Common
7018	*Drysllwyn Castle*	5/49	9/63	Swansea		Old Oak Common
7019	*Fowey Castle*	5/49	2/65	Bristol		Oxley
7020	*Gloucester Castle*	5/49	9/64	Cardiff		Southall
7021	*Haverfordwest Castle*	6/49	9/63	Swansea		Old Oak Common
7022	*Hereford Castle*	6/49	6/65	Cardiff		Gloucester
7023	*Penrice Castle*	6/49	2/65	Cardiff		Oxley
7024	*Powis Castle*	6/49	2/65	Old Oak Common		Oxley
7025	*Sudeley Castle*	8/49	9/64	Old Oak Common		Worcester
7026	*Tenby Castle*	8/49	10/64	Wolverhampton		Tyseley
7027	*Thornbury Castle*	8/49	12/63	Plymouth		Reading
7028	*Cadbury Castle*	5/50	12/63	Swansea		Llanelli
7029	*Clun Castle*	5/50	12/65	Newton Abbot		Gloucester
7030	*Cranbrook Castle*	6/50	2/63	Old Oak Common		Old Oak Common
7031	*Cromwell's Castle*	6/50	7/63	Plymouth		Worcester
7032	*Denbigh Castle*	6/50	9/64	Old Oak Common		Old Oak Common
7033	*Hartlebury Castle*	7/50	1/63	Old Oak Common		Old Oak Common
7034	*Ince Castle*	8/50	6/65	Bristol		Gloucester
7035	*Ogmore Castle*	8/50	6/64	Shrewsbury		Old Oak Common
7036	*Taunton Castle*	8/50	9/63	Old Oak Common		Old Oak Common
7037	*Swindon*	8/50	3/63	Swindon		Swindon

NOTES:

(*) Locomotives renamed. See Tables 5.7 and 5.8 for details.

N.B. The final shed allocation of several Castles of all periods shows them to be resident at depots which were not usually associated with express passenger locomotives. For example:

1) Bristol SPM: (St Philip's Marsh) took the allocation of Bath Road when that shed closed to steam in September 1960.
2) Cardiff East Dock shed took the allocation of Canton when that shed closed to steam in September 1962.
3) Oxley, Wolverhampton: took the allocation of Stafford Rd. when that shed closed to steam in September 1963.

Despite being only three years old, Oxford-based No 7010 *Avondale Castle* looks like a neglected veteran as it enters Wellington with a Bournemouth to Birkenhead express on 14 May 1951.

Photo: E. R. Morten

TABLE 5.10: CASTLE CLASS LOCOMOTIVES CONVERTED TO OIL-BURNING

100A1	1/47 to 9/48	5079	1/47 to 10/48	5091	10/46 to 11/48
5039	12/46 to 9/48	5083	12/46 to 11/48		

differences to their predecessors and these included new designs of superheaters and mechanical lubricators. The early years of British Railways saw a minor flurry of renaming among the Castles but this time, there were more sensible reasons for the changes. In the first two months following Nationalisation, No 7001 and No 7007 were renamed *Sir James Milne* and *Great Western* to commemorate the now-extinct railway company — the choice of No 7007 was rather appropriate as it had been the very last passenger locomotive to have been built at Swindon under the régime of the GWR.

On 13 February, 1952, the name of *Windsor Castle* was transferred from No 4082 to No 7013 as it was considered a more suitable handle for the locomotive which had been earmarked for hauling the funeral train of the late King George VI. The nameplates of No 4082 and No 7013 were never restored to the 'correct' engines. Fifteen months prior to the funeral, the King's daughter, H.R.H. Princess Elizabeth, had officiated at the Golden Jubilee of the borough of Swindon and part of the celebrations had involved her naming No 7037, the last Castle class locomotive ever to be built. Most appropriately, the name chosen had been *Swindon*. The royal connection with the Castle class, which had started with King George V driving No 4082 *Windsor Castle* in 1924, had involved three generations of the same family.

Three other Castles had their names changed in the 1950s. No 5017, No 5066 and No 7005 were the locomotives involved and their respective new names and the dates of the changes were: *The Gloucestershire Regiment 28th/61st* in April 1954, *Sir Felix Pole* in April 1956 and *Sir Edward Elgar* in August 1957.

108 LONDON, OXFORD, BIRMINGHAM, WOLVERHAMPTON,

Week Days—continued.

		a.m.	a.m.	p.m.	a.m.	a.m.	a.m.	a.m.	p.m.	a.m.	p.m.	p.m.	p.m.	p.m.	a.m.	p.m.	a.m.	p.m.	p.m.	p.m.	p.m.	p.m.	p.m.	p.m.	p.m.
		Via Bicester. Calls at High Wycombe at 9.49 a.m. Restaurant Car to Shrewsbury.				Via Bicester.		(3)	Saturdays only.		Saturdays excepted.		Saturdays only.		Restaurant Car London to Oxford.		Via Bicester. Restaurant Car Train.		(3)		(3)		X Saturdays excepted.		
LONDON (Paddington)	dep.	9 10				9K10	9 15								9 45		11 10								
Reading	"						10 5								10 38										
Didcot	arr.						10 28								11 3										
	dep							10 38							11 6										
Appleford Halt	"						STOP	10 45																	
Culham	"							10 50																	
Radley	"							10 58																	
OXFORD	arr.							11 7							11 25										
	dep.														11 35				12 25						
Kidlington (for Blenheim)	"																		12 35						
Bletchington	"																		12 39						
Tackley Halt	"																		12 43						
Heyford	"																		12 49						
Fritwell and Somerton	"																		12 55						
Aynho (for Deddington)	"					(3) 11¶20													1 0						
King's Sutton	"					11 25													1 6		(3) 1 24				
Banbury	arr.	10 49				11 32									12 13		12 34		1 12		1 30				
	dep.	10 53													12 18		12 39								
Cropredy	"																								
Fenny Compton	"																								
Southam Road and Harbury	"																								
Leamington Spa	arr.	11 17													12 42		1 3								
	dep.	11 21	11 32							11 47				12 30	12 47		1 8						1 20	1 30	
Warwick	"		11 36							11 52				12 34									1 24	1 34	
Hatton	"		11 47							12 2				12 43									1 34	1 48	
Lapworth	"									12 10				12 51								1 36		1 51	
Knowle and Dorridge	"		STOP							12 16				12 57								1 42	STOP	1 57	
Widney Manor	"									12 20				1 1								1 46		2 1	
Solihull	"									12 25		12 50		1 5						1 35		1 50		2 5	
Olton	"									12 29		12 54		1 9						1 39		1 54		2 9	
Acock's Green & South Yardley	"									12 32		12 57		1 12						1 42		1 57		2 12	
Tyseley	"								12 19	12 35		1 0		1 15						1 45		2 0		2 15	
Small Heath & Sparkbrook	"								12 22	12 38		1 3		1 18						1 48		2 3		2 18	
Bordesley	"								12 26	12 42		1 6		1 21						1 51		2 6		2 21	
BIRMINGHAM Moor Street	arr.																								
BIRMINGHAM Snow Hill	arr.	11 50							12 30	12 46		1 10		1 26	1 16		1 37			1 55		2 10		2 25	
	dep.	11 56			11 58				12 37		12 55		1 15				1 43	1 50							
Hockley	"				12 1													1 53						STOP	
Soho and Winson Green	"				12 4						1 0							1 56							
Handsworth and Smethwick	"				12 8				12 43		1 4		1 21					2 0							
West Bromwich	"				12 13				12 48		1 9		1 26					2 5							
Swan Village	"				12 16				12 52		1 12		1 30					2 9							
Wednesbury	"				12 21				12 57		1 16		1 34					2 14							
Bilston	"				12 26				1 2		1 21		1 39					2 20							
Priestfield	"				12 30				1 5		1 24							2 24							
WOLVERHAMPTON (Low Level)	arr.	12 15	p.m.		12 34				1 9		1 29		1 45				2 2	2 28					p.m.		
	dep.	12 22	12 30						1 18								2 9						2 35		
Dunstall Park	"		12 33						1 21														2 38		
Birches and Bilbrook Halt	"		12 39						1 27														2 44		
Codsall	"		12 42						1 30														2 47		
Albrighton	"		12 48						1 36														2 53		
Cosford	"		12 52						1 40														2 57		
Shifnal	"		12 58						1 46														3 3		
Oakengates	"		1 8						1 55														3 12		
New Hadley Halt	"		1 11				p.m.		1 58														3 16		
Wellington	"	12 47	1 15				1 41		2 2								2 36						3 20		
Admaston	"						1 45																		
Walcot	"						1 51																		
Upton Magna	"						1 57																		
Shrewsbury	arr.	1 4					2 5										2 52								
	dep.	1 10		1 40													2 58								4 15
Leaton	"			1 48																					
Oldwoods Halt	"			1 51																					
Baschurch	"			1 58																					
Stanwardine Halt	"			2 1																					
Haughton Halt	"			2 7																					
Rednal and West Felton	"			2 13																					
Whittington (Low Level)	"			2 19																					
Gobowen	"	1 37		2 26													3 28								4 39
Weston Rhyn	"			2 30																					
Trehowell Halt	"																								
Chirk	"			2 34																					
Whitehurst	"			2 37																					
Cefn	"			2 40																				(3)	
Rhosymedre Halt	"																							p.m.	
Ruabon	"	1 52		2 47												3 25	3 36							4 44	4 51
Wynnville Halt	"			2 49																				4 46	
Johnstown and Hafod	"			2 52																				4 49	
Wrexham	"	2 3		3 0												3 35	3 48							4 55	5 2
Rhosrobin Halt	"																								
Gresford (for Llay)	"			3 8																					
Rossett	"			3 12																					
Balderton	"			3 18																					
Saltney	"			3 25																					
Chester	arr.	2 24		3 31													4 11								5 22
Birkenhead (Woodside)	arr.	3 5		4 50													4 50								6 11
LIVERPOOL (Landing Stg.)	"	3 23		5 8													5 8								6 38

K—Change at High Wycombe.
X—Third class only (limited accommodation).
(3)—Third class only.
¶—Aynho Park.
§—Arrive 8.51 a.m.

Although this extract from the autumn 1947 GWR timetable does not show the two-hour Birmingham expresses, the faster services would have still been hauled by Kings or Castles as far as Wolverhampton and, from there, Stars or Saints would have taken over.

For mere Englishmen who like to see vowels in their reading matter, *Dryslwyn Castle* was inevitably referred to as No 7018. This picture shows the engine, complete with straight-sided tender, alongside County class 4-6-0 No 1000 *County of Middlesex* at Landore shed in Swansea in July 1950. When the picture was taken, No 7018 was only just over a year old. Despite being taken in the summer, it seems that a stiff breeze is presenting problems for the engine cleaner's workout with his hula-hoop.
Photo: Rail Archive Stephenson

By the mid-1950s, the Castles were on express duties over most of the GWR system although, on the Welsh Border route, they performed less impressively than the Stars and even the two-cylinder Saints. The introduction of diesel-hydraulic traction in 1958 did more to displace the Kings than the Castles as it was the former which were subjected to the more severe route restrictions. By 1958, the Saints and the Stars had all disappeared and, apart from the two-cylinder Hall class 4-6-0s, the Castles were the only express locomotives available for widespread use. One notable duty performed by a Castle in the late 1950s was at the head of the last steam-hauled Bristolian which ran on 12 June 1959. The locomotive was No 5085 *Evesham Abbey*.

In September 1955, one of the King class locomotives had been fitted with an experimental double chimney which had been intended to work in conjunction with a redesigned blastpipe. The experiment was a success but it was not just the Kings which benefited as, between 1956 and 1960, sixty-six members of the Castle class also received double chimneys. Yet, while some Castles were being fitted with double chimneys others were being withdrawn. The first member of the class to have been retired was No 100 *A1 Lloyds*, formerly No 4009 *Shooting Star*, which was scrapped in March 1950, five months before the last Castle was built. Two other Star rebuilds were retired in 1951 and the rebuilt Pacific No 111, went in 1953 leaving No 4037 and Nos 5083–92 as the surviving non-pedigree Castles. Of the thoroughbred Castles, Nos 4073/74 were scheduled to be put to the torch in 1955 but a second opinion revealed that both were positively in the pink and they went on to see, respectively, another five and eight year's service. The first purpose-built Castle to succumb was No 4091 *Dudley Castle* which went in January 1959.

The reprieve of No 4073 *Caerphilly Castle* was fortuitous as it gave the authorities the opportunity

BATH AND BRISTOL. 27

Week Days—continued.

	a.m.	p.m.	a.m.	a.m.	a.m. X	a.m.	a.m.	a.m.	p.m.	p.m.	a.m.	a.m.	a.m.	a.m.	p.m.
Notes						Restaurant Car Train.				Saturdays only.	"CORNISH RIVIERA EXPRESS." Restaurant Car Train. (Via Castle Cary.)		Restaurant Car Train.	"TORBAY EXPRESS" Restaurant Car Train. (Via Castle Cary.)	Restaurant Car Train.
LONDON (Paddington) dep.						9 45					10 30		10 45	11 0	
Slough ,,							9a57					10 40			
Maidenhead ,,					9 52		10 24					11 0			
Reading arr.					10 9	10 34	10 44					11 24	11 28		
READING dep.						10 38		10 50					11 30		
Tilehurst ,,								10 56							
Pangbourne ,,								11 2							
Goring and Streatley ,,								11 8							
Cholsey and Moulsford ,,								11 16							
Didcot arr.						11 3		11 25							
Oxford arr.						11 25									
Oxford (for Didcot) dep.				10 40											
Didcot dep.				10 46											
Steventon ,,				10 54											
Wantage Road ,,				11 0											
Challow ,,				11 9											
Uffington ,,				11 15											
Shrivenham ,,				11 24											
Stratton Park Halt ,,				11 31											
SWINDON arr.				11 35									12 21		
SWINDON dep.			11 25							12 20			12 25		
Wootton Bassett ,,			11 35							12 30					
Brinkworth dep.			11 43												
Little Somerford ,,			11 48												
Hullavington ,,			11 58												
Badminton ,,			12 10												
Chipping Sodbury ,,			12 20												
Coalpit Heath ,,			12 29												
Winterbourne ,,			12 33												
Filton Junction arr.			12 40												
Horfield ,,			12 44												
Ashley Hill ,,			12 47												
Dauntsey dep.															
Christian Malford Halt ,,															
Chippenham arr.															
Chippenham dep.	11 55														
Corsham ,,	12 3														
Box (Mill Lane) ,,	12 9														
Box ,,	12 11														
Bathford Halt ,,	12 16														
Bathampton ,,	12 18														
BATH arr.	12 23												1 5		
BATH dep.	12 24								12 45				1 8		
Oldfield Park ,,	12 27														
Saltford ,,	12 33														
Keynsham and Somerdale ,,	12 38														
St. Anne's Park ,,	12 44														
BRISTOL Stapleton Road arr.			12 49						1 5						
BRISTOL Lawrence Hill ,,			12 53												
BRISTOL Temple Meads arr.	12 48		12 58										1 30		
BRISTOL Temple Meads dep.		12 55												p.m.	1 45
Exeter (St. David's) arr.		2 40									p.m.			2 20	3 24
Plymouth (North Road) ,,		4 35									3 10			4F35	5 0
PENZANCE ,,											5 35			7F40	7 40

This is an extract from the GWR public timetable for the autumn of 1947 and, by then, the Castles predominated on services between London and Bristol. Although this page shows that two trains to Devon and Cornwall were named, the Bristolian is conspicuous by its absence.

This fine view of beautiful Birmingham shows No 7036 ***Taunton Castle*** entering Snow Hill station on an unidentified working on 28 September 1961. Despite being only eleven years old when the picture was taken, the locomotive had only two years left to live.

Photo: M. John Stretton

72 · LONDON, GLOUCESTER, NEWPORT, CARDIFF,

Week Days—continued.

Station	a.m.	a.m.	a.m.	p.m.	a.m.	a.m.	p.m.	a.m.	a.m.	p.m.	p.m.	a.m.	a.m.	a.m.	a.m.	p.m.	a.m.		p.m.	a.m.	p.m.	p.m.	p.m.
Notes	Saturdays only.		Through Train from Kingswear (depart 7.0 a.m.—see pages 56 and 66).			Saturdays only.		Saturdays only.		Saturdays excepted. Buffet Rail Car (Third class only—limited accommodation).		Through Train Portsmouth and Southsea to Cardiff.	(Via Salisbury)—See page 40.				Restaurant Car London to Fishguard Harbour. Via Badminton.	Tuesdays, Thursdays and Saturdays only.		Restaurant Car Train.			Saturdays excepted.
LONDON (Paddington) dep.								9 15				9P15					1135			10 45			
Reading „	③ 6 40							10 5				10P 5								11 30			
Didcot „	7 45							10 32				10P32			10 45								
Swindon arr.	8 48							11 5				11P 5			11 35					12 21			
SWINDON dep.	STOP	9 25						11 20				11P10	11E25	11E25		12 5					12 30		
Purton „																12 14							
Minety and Ashton Keynes „																12 22							
Oaksey Halt „																12 28							
Kemble „						③		11 40								12 32					12 50		
Chalford „						11 0		11 53													1 4		
St. Mary's Crossing Halt „						11 2																	
Brimscombe „						11 4		11 57															
Brimscombe Bridge Halt „						11 6																	
Ham Mill Crossing Halt „						11 9																	
Bowbridge Crossing Halt „						11 11																	
Stroud „						11 15		12 5													1 12		
Downfield Crossing Halt „						11 17																	
Cashes Green Halt „						11 19																	
Ebley Crossing Halt „						11 21																	
Stonehouse „						11 25		12 10															
GLOUCESTER arr.						11 40		12 26													1 30		
CHELTENHAM SPA (St. James') arr.						12 3		12 50													1 55		
CHELTENHAM SPA (St. James') dep.					10 40				11 30										12 30				
GLOUCESTER dep.					11 18	STOP		STOP	12 45										1 0		STOP		
Oakle Street „					11 19				12 54														
Grange Court „				③	11 24				12 58														
Westbury-on-Severn Halt „					11 27																		
Newnham „					11 30				STOP										1 15				
Awre (for Blakeney) „					STOP																		
Lydney ¶ „																			1 30				
Woolaston „							X																
Tutshill Halt (for Beachley) „							12 31																
Chepstow „							12 35												1 43				
Portskewett „							12 42																
Caldicot Halt „							12 46							X									
Severn Tunnel Junction arr.							12 48					p.m.		p.m.					1 56				
BRISTOL Temple Meads dep.		11†2	11 15									12L33		1 7									
BRISTOL Lawrence H. „			11 20									12L38		1 13									
BRISTOL Stapleton Rd. „			11 24									1 18		1 17									
Ashley Hill „														1 20									
Horfield „														1 24									
Filton Junction „												1W18		1 28									
Patchway „			11 36											1 32									
Pilning (High Level) „														1Q40									
Severn Tunnel Junc. arr.			11 53									1 40											
Severn Tunnel Junction dep.			11 57				12 50					1 42		STOP					1 57				
Undy Halt „							12 53																
Magor „							12 56																
Llanwern „							1 3																
NEWPORT arr.			12 16			p.m.	1 10	p.m.	p.m.			2 0					2 10		2 13				
NEWPORT dep.			12 20			1 0		1 12	1 30		1 55	2 2					2 12		2 17				
Marshfield „			12 29						1 39			2 12											
CARDIFF (General) arr.			12 39		p.m.	1 20		1 30	1 49		2 14	2 23					2 30		2 36		p.m.		
CARDIFF (General) dep.				12 50	1 5					2 5							2 35				2 54		
Ely (Main Line) „				12 55	1 10						STOP	STOP									2 59		
St. Fagans „				1 0	1 15																3 4		
Péterston „					1 20																		
Llantrisant „					1 30																		
Llanharan „					1 36																		
Pencoed „					1 45																		
Bridgend arr.					1 52																		
Bridgend dep.					1 55					2J35													
Pyle „	p.m.				2 6																		
Port Talbot (General) „	1 35				2 19												3 24						
Briton Ferry „	1 43				2 26																	3 35	
Neath (General) „	1 51				2 33					3K0							3 34					3 41	
Skewen „	1 57				2 39																	3 47	
Llansamlet „	2 3				2 45																	3 53	
Landore „	2 9				2 51									③								3 59	
SWANSEA (High St.) arr.	2 14				2 56					3 14				p.m.			3 55					4 4	
SWANSEA (High St.) dep.														3 35			4 2						4 10
Cockett „														3 44									
Gowerton „														3 48									4 24
Loughor „														3 53									
Llanelly „														4 3			4 24						4 34
Pembrey and Burry Port „														4 10									4 42
Kidwelly „														4 21									4 54
Ferryside „														4S30									5 2
CARMARTHEN arr.														4S40			4 50						5 14
CARMARTHEN dep.																	4 54						
Sarnau „																							
St. Clears „																							
Whitland arr.																							
Pembroke Dock arr.																							
Whitland dep.													③										
Clynderwen „											③		p.m.										
Clarbeston Road „											p.m.		5 5										
Haverfordwest (B) dep.											4 40												
Johnston (Pem.) „											5 1												
Milford Haven arr.																							
Neyland arr.											5 10												
Wolf's Castle Halt dep.													5 17										
Welsh Hook Halt „													5 21										
Mathry Road „													5 26										
Jordanston Halt „													5 31										
Fishguard and Goodwick arr.													5 38										
FISHGUARD HARB. „													5 41				6 0						

B—For St. David's.
E—Via Badminton (change at Filton Junction).
J—Calls at Bridgend to pick up passengers for Swansea (High Street) and beyond.
K—Calls at Neath (General) to set down passengers from Cardiff (General).
L—Change at Stapleton Road.
P—Change at Bath.
Q—Pilning (Low Level).
S—Saturdays only.
W—Calls to pick up passengers only.
X—Third class only (limited accommodation).
③—Third class only.
†—Arrival time.
¶—About 300 yards to Lydney Junction Station (S. & W. Line).

This GWR public timetable was for autumn 1947, just months before Nationalisation came into effect. In the late 1940s, Castles predominated on the fastest services to South Wales. This extract shows that the solitary through train to Fishguard ran only on three days of the week.

to appreciate what a remarkable engine it had been. When the locomotive was finally withdrawn from Cardiff shed in May 1960, the way had been prepared for it to become an exhibit at the Science Museum in South Kensington. A contemporary of No 4073 was No 4079 *Pendennis Castle* which also escaped the torch. It was purchased privately after withdrawal from Bristol in May 1964 and maintained in running order but, sadly for British enthusiasts, it now lives in Australia. No 5029 *Nunney Castle* and No 5051 *Earl Bathurst* were both rescued from Dai Woodham's yard in Barry by the Great Western Society and have been restored to running order at the Didcot Railway Centre. The Barry mortuary also provided No 7027 *Thornbury Castle*, No 5043 *Earl of Mount Edgcumbe* and No 5080 *Defiant*, the last two of which were acquired by the Birmingham Railway Museum.

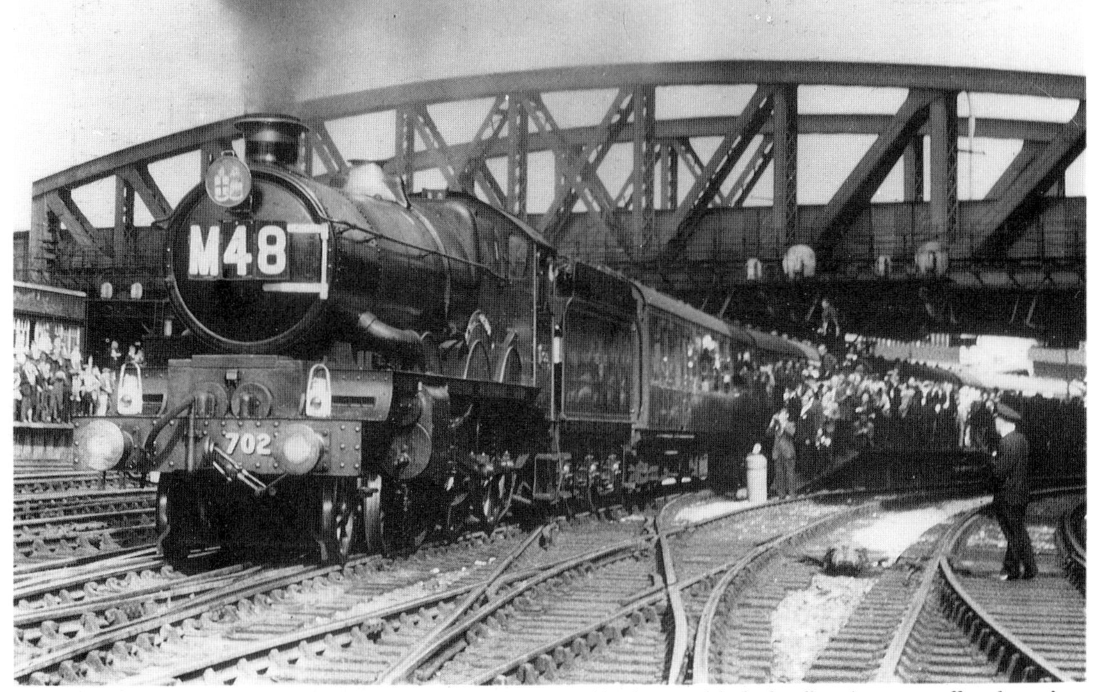

There is no truth in the rumour that British Railways tried to use this picture with the heading: 'even our off-peak services are in demand'. The reason for the lemming-covered platform is that No 7029 *Clun Castle* is leaving Paddington on the last scheduled steam working from the station. The date was 11 June 1965 and the train was the 4.15pm to Banbury. The locomotive was, of course, suitably polished and it wore the GWR's coat of arms on its smokebox.

Photo: Rail Archive Stephenson

TABLE 5.11: YEARLY TOTALS OF CASTLE CLASS LOCOMOTIVES

N.B. Totals taken at 31 December of each year.

Year	Total	Year	Total	Year	Total	Year	Total	Year	Total	Year	Total	Year	Total
1923	2	1930	46	1936	91	1942	131	1948	151	1954	167	1960	155
1924	11	1931	46	1937	104	1943	131	1949	161	1955	167	1961	152
1925	23	1932	56	1938	116	1944	131	1950	170	1956	167	1962	97
1926	35	1933	56	1939	130	1945	131	1951	168	1957	166	1963	49
1927	45	1934	66	1940	131	1946	141	1952	168	1958	165	1964	12
1928	45	1935	76	1941	131	1947	141	1953	167	1959	162	1965	0
1929	46												

MONDAYS TO FRIDAYS—continued

Table 61

Table 61—*continued* LONDON, READING, DIDCOT, OXFORD, SWINDON, CHIPPENHAM, BATH SPA, BRISTOL and TAUNTON

	am	am	am	am	am	am	am	am	am	am	am	am	am	am	am	am	am		am	am	am	am
Notes		TC Paddington to Penzance				Via Melksham and Bradford-on-Avon (Tables 62 and 72); Runs 25th July to 26th August inclusive	Runs 4th July to 2nd September inclusive; TC Swindon to Weston-super-Mare				TC Swansea to Weston-super-Mare	RC Paddington to Bristol; RC Paddington to Torquay and Paignton. TC Paddington to Torquay and Paignton	THE BRISTOLIAN. Limited accommodation. RC and TC Paddington to Bristol						RC and TC Paddington to Bristol	TC Portsmouth to Bristol (Table 72)	TC Paddington to Taunton. For continuation, see 12 40 pm from Bristol (T.M.); TC Paddington to Weston-super-Mare; RC Paddington to Weston-super-Mare	TC Paddington to Newquay and Falmouth (Tables 81, 99 and 101); Via Castle Cary (Table 62); RC Paddington to Plymouth (to Newquay on Fridays)
PADDINGTON .. dep		5 30	5 30						6 25	7 10		7 30	8 45		8 0	8 0			9 5		9 15	9 30
Reading General ... dep		6 18	6 38						7 40	8 5		8 12			9 0	9 10			9 43		10 0	10 7
Tilehurst			6 45						7 47							9 16						
Pangbourne			6 51						7 53							9 22						
Goring and Streatley			6 57						7 59							9 29						
Cholsey and Moulsford			7 4						8 7							9 37						
Didcot .. arr		6 42	7 15						8 16	8 28		8 35			9 24	9 47					1023	
152 Oxford .. arr		7 27	7 50						8 48	8 48		9 11			9 43	1011					1045	
152 Oxford .. dep			Stop					7 10				8 5			Stop	Stop					9 55	8X50
Didcot .. dep		6 45						7 45				8 37									1025	
Steventon								7 54														
Wantage Road								8 5														
Challow								8 17														
Uffington								8 23														
Shrivenham	7 0							8 35														
Stratton Park Halt	7 7							8 42														
Swindon .. arr	7 17	7 20						8 48				9 6							1035		1050	
Swindon .. dep	Stop	7 25		7 35			8 45					9 10					9 57		1038		11 3	
Wootton Bassett				7 44			8 57										10 7					
Dauntsey				7 52													1015					
Christian Malford Halt				7 57													1019					
Chippenham .. arr		7 50		8 6			9 13					9 30				am	1025				1126	
Chippenham .. dep		7 53		8 8		8 40	9 14					9 32				10 8	Stop				1131	
Corsham				8 18								9 40				1015						
Box (Mill Lane)				8 24												1022						
Box				8 27												1025						
Bathford Halt			am	8 32																		
Bathampton			8 17	8 35		9 20										1031				1134		
Bath Spa .. arr	am	8 12	8 22	8 41		9 25	9 32					9 52			am	1036	am		1110	1140	1150	
Bath Spa .. dep	8 0	8 16	8 25	8 43	9 10	9 26	9 35					9 55			1027	1037	1050		1112	1143	1152	
Oldfield Park	8 3		8 28	8 46		9 29	9 40									1040				1146		
Saltford	8 9		8 34	8 52		9 35										1046						
Keynsham and Somerdale	8 14		8 39	8 57		9 40										1051						
St. Anne's Park	8 20		8 45	9 3		9 45										1056				1156		
Stapleton Road																						
Lawrence Hill																						
Bristol (Temple Meads) arr	8 26	8 34	8 51	9 11	9 26	9 51						1013	1030		1045	11 2	1110		1130	12 5	1211	
164 Liverpool (L.St.)B . dep					Stop	Stop													Stop			
164 Manchester (L.Rd.)B „																						
„ (Cen.). „																						
164 Birkenhead (W.) .. „																						
164 Chester (General). „																			am			
164 Shrewsbury .. „																			6X25			
152 Birmingh'm (S.H.) 169 „																						
„ (New St.) „					am						7 48											
104 Swansea (High St.). „					6 30						6 45								8 45			
104 Cardiff (General).. „					8 5	am					8 43								10 8			
Bristol (Temple Meads) dep		8 50	9 0		9 45	9 55					10 12	1020		1040					1135			
Bedminster			9 5		9 49									1045					1140			
Parson Street			9 8		9 52									1049					1143			
Flax Bourton			9 17																1152			
Nailsea and Backwell			9 23											11 0					1157			
Yatton			9 31		10 6									1110					12 5			
Puxton and Worle			9 37																1211			
Weston Milton Halt			9 42																1216			
Weston-super-Mare General arr			9 46		1018	10L26	10L34				10L42			1122					1220			
Weston-super-Mare General dep			9 51									cc										
Bleadon and Uphill			9 56																			
Brent Knoll			10 3																			
Highbridge and Burnham-on-Sea			1010																			
Dunball			1016																			
Bridgwater		9 32	1025									1114										
Durston		9 42	1034																			
Creech St. Michael Halt																						
Taunton .. arr		9 55	1046									1132										1152
84 Ilfracombe .. arr		1 48										3 40										3 40
82 Minehead „		1132	1240									1240										1 16
81 Exeter (St. David's) „		1048										1215										1233
81 Torquay „		1210										1 20										1 47
81 Paignton „		1218										1 30										1 55
81 Plymouth (N'thRd) „		1245										2R 0										2 0
81 Penzance „		4 25										4R55										4 55

For SATURDAY TRAINS, pages 159 to 169

For SUNDAY TRAINS, pages 170 to 172 **For Notes, page 173**

The Western Region public timetable for summer 1955 showed the Bristolian, the 8.45am ex-Paddington. Castles were the usual locomotives on Bristolian duties.

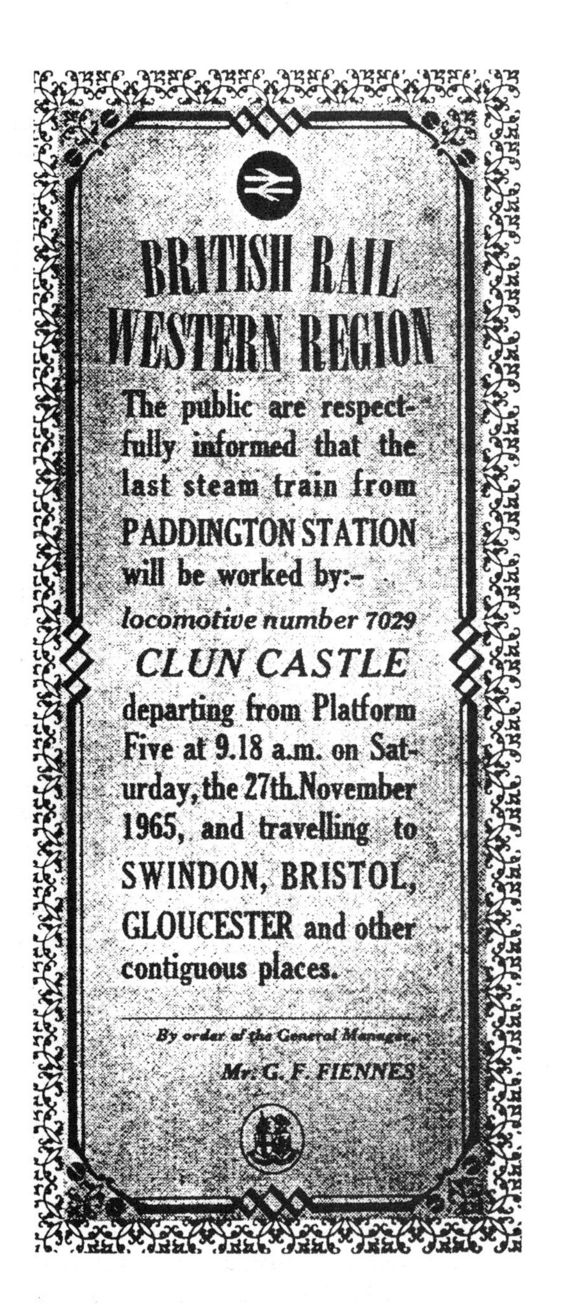

BRITISH RAIL
WESTERN REGION
The public are respectfully informed that the last steam train from
PADDINGTON STATION
will be worked by:-
locomotive number 7029
CLUN CASTLE
departing from Platform Five at 9.18 a.m. on Saturday, the 27th. November 1965, and travelling to
SWINDON, BRISTOL, GLOUCESTER and other contiguous places.

By order of the General Manager,
Mr. G. F. FIENNES

A recent transfer from Birmingham to the Great Central Railway has been No 7029 *Clun Castle* which was bought privately in January 1966 and kept in working order. This locomotive was, arguably, one of the most suitable candidates for preservation although four others had genuine claims. The very first Castle, No 4073, had quite rightly been preserved while Nos 7007 and 7037 were, respectively, the last passenger locomotives to be built by the GWR and the very last Castle. No 4037 also had a claim despite its non-pedigree background; with a mileage of 2,429,722, it held the distance record for any ex-GWR locomotive. The claim held by No 7029 was that it had outlived all the other Castles by six months and, although it was officially withdrawn in December 1965, it performed its last British Railways duty on 1 January 1966 when it took charge of the 5pm train from Gloucester to Cheltenham.

Gloucester shed had become a popular allocation for several Castles in their last months, but one 'final' duty performed by No 7029 was bathed in a little more limelight. On 11 June 1965, it was decked out with GWR's coat of arms for the privilege of hauling the 4.15pm train from Paddington to Banbury. This was the very last scheduled steam working at Paddington.

A commemorative brochure was issued by the Western Region to mark the end of steam at Paddington and, these days, copies have the status of collectors' items. However, I would emphasise that my copy is only available for a fee which would guarantee a retirement income! The cover of the brochure stated that the only surviving Castle, No 7029 *Clun Castle*, was to officiate on the special working and it did not go unnoticed that the last scheduled steam-hauled service into Paddington, which had taken place on 11 June 1965, had been hauled by the same locomotive.

CHAPTER 6

The Kings

By the mid 1920s, the railway companies of Britain had made considerable progress with designs for express passenger locomotives. The more questionable acquisitions from the grouping had, in the main, been weeded out and the drawing offices at Swindon, Derby, Doncaster and Eastleigh were all concentrating on bigger and more powerful engines for prestigious passenger duties. The 1920s might have been the decade when the motor car and the charabanc had started to challenge the railways on rural routes but, when it came to long-distance travel, the railways had no serious competition.

On the LMS, Henry Fowler resumed occupancy of the chair at Derby in 1925 with the realisation that he had to escape from the old Midland policy of smaller engines. At Doncaster, Nigel Gresley was turning out excellent Pacifics for the LNER while down on the Southern Railway, the first of Maunsell's Lord Nelson 4-6-0s emerged from Eastleigh in 1926. Maunsell's four-cylinder locomotive had a nominal tractive effort of 33,500 lb which was, at the time, greater than any other British passenger locomotive, but the rare occurrence of the Southern being top of the form was, predictably, short-lived. In June 1927, Charles Collett's four-cylinder 4-6-0 No 6000 *King George V* rolled gracefully out of Swindon works and the GWR's publicity machine was not slow to announce that the locomotive had a record-breaking tractive effort of 40,300 lb.

When the first of the Castle class locomotives had appeared less than four years earlier, it had been anticipated that they would be capable of hauling the heaviest trains on the fastest schedules. Despite the Castles being the most powerful express engines of their day, the traffic department at Swindon had its sights set on train loadings which were looked on elsewhere as rather adventurous. The optimism with which the traffic officers were endowed was, occasionally, a little over the top. It was explained to them that, although it might just be possible to design a locomotive which could haul thirty-coach trains, the expense of reconstructing all the main-line stations to accommodate such trains would be rather high. Nevertheless, a degree of increase in the weights of the trains was on the cards and locomotives even more powerful than the Castles were needed.

The three routes which were earmarked for heavier trains were Paddington to Wolverhampton via Bicester, Paddington to Plymouth via Bristol and the alternative route to Plymouth via Westbury. The prospect of heavier trains and larger locomotives meant increased axle weights but, although those routes could accept the axle weight of the Castles without grumbling, they would require strengthening if they were to be used by anything heavier. While many other railway companies saw frequent verbal fisticuffs between locomotive and civil engineering departments, things were somewhat more civilised at Swindon. After consultations between Collett and J.C.Lloyd, the chief civil engineer, it was confirmed that, despite the safety limit on axle loadings of twenty tons, all main-line overbridges which the GWR had constructed since 1904 were, in fact, designed to accept up to twenty-two tons. Lloyd was asked to check whether these limits could safely be increased by half a ton and he calculated that, with the exception of just four bridges in mid-Somerset, a twenty-two and a half

Brand new King class No 6000 *King George V* basks outside Swindon works in July 1927 before its celebrated trip to America. The ex-works condition is clearly evident and even dear old *North Star* looks uncharacteristically neglected by comparison.
Photo: Rail Archive Stephenson

ton axle weight was permissible. Lloyd was given the task of upgrading those four bridges and Charles Collett was sent away to design a locomotive to the limit of the newly-agreed axle loading.

The locomotive which was the subject of Collett's new design became known as the 'Supercastle'. It was calculated that, if the boiler pressure were 250 lb as opposed to the 225 lb of the Castles and if the cylinders were 16¼in × 28in as opposed to 16in × 26in, the nominal tractive effort would be a stupendous 39,100 lb. But the chairman of the GWR, Sir Felix Pole, was not satisfied. The GWR's publicity machine used tractive effort figures when making claims about the power of locomotives and, although the projected 39,100 lb of the Supercastle would beat Maunsell's Lord Nelsons hands-down, it was known that Fowler had a mighty steed in the advance-planning stage for the LMS. To be absolutely sure of the GWR regaining its crown, Sir Felix Pole insisted on a tractive effort of no less than 40,000 lb. Collett returned to the drawing board and swiftly calculated that, with 6ft 6in coupled wheels instead of the Castle's standard 6ft 8½in, the new locomotive's tractive effort would be to 40,300 lb. The expense of retooling at Swindon to enable the manufacture of non-standard components was considered well worth it as the prestige and publicity value of the Supercastle would be substantial. When the wraps later came off Fowler's competing product at Derby, a very handsome Royal Scot was revealed but its tractive effort was 33,150 lb, less than even Maunsell's 4-6-0s let alone Collett's project.

In all the fields of engineering, the stretching of existing limits presents unforeseen problems and, in its day, the case of the Supercastle was no exception. It had been anticipated that a new design of bogie would be required as the standard Churchward-style bar-frame bogies had developed a tendency to break rivets and, when thoughts turned to a new design, the popular choice for strength was a plate-frame bogie. The snag was that the inside plate-frames would not squeeze under the pair of inside cylinders but it was realised, however, that there was nothing in the rule book to say that a frame couldn't go partly inside and partly outside. The product of this piece of lateral thinking was the highly-distinctive bogie which had outside bearings to the leading axle and inside bearings to the trailing one. This feature became a boon to myopic schoolboy enthusiasts who, having suffered the taunts of so-called 'chums' after failing to differentiate between a Hall and a Grange at a distance, could readily distinguish a Castle from a King at one thousand paces.

As completion of the first of the new engines drew nearer, it was realised that a proper class designation would be required and, for a brief period, the class became referred to as 'Cathedrals' in anticipation of a name theme. The popular vote for cathedrals was seriously considered but, when arrangements were being made for the first of the class to be exhibited in the United States, it was felt that nothing could be more patriotic than the names of English kings. Appropriately, the first to be completed, No 6000, was named after the reigning monarch, *King George V*, and the plan was that each of the other locomotives would carry the names of kings in reverse chronological order.

The naming of the Kings was taken very seriously. Ten of the Star class 4-6-0s, Nos 4021-30, carried the names of English kings and these were promptly changed to 'monarchs' in order to avoid confusion; Duke class 4-4-0 No 3257 *King Arthur* also lost its name in deference to the newcomers.

The class leader, No 6000, emerged from Swindon works in June 1927 and, the following month, Nos 6001 – 05 were completed. All six locomotives were given the obligatory running-in turns before being let loose on the watching public and it was 20 July when No 6000 was first given charge of the Cornish Riviera Express. The crew was Driver Young and Fireman Pearce of Old Oak Common and, in view of the impending trip to America, No 6000 was designated a one-crew locomotive so that the foot-platemen could have every chance to familiarise themselves with the engine. Messrs. Young and Pearce had already had their passages to America

The class leader, No 6000 *King George V*, is shown in action at an unidentified location in September 1931.
Photo: E. R. Morten

booked and so they were as keen as the team at Swindon to take every opportunity for familiarisation.

On the Plymouth route, the Kings were allowed 500 tons behind the tender as far as Taunton and this compared with the 455 tons and 420 tons which had been set for the Castles and Stars respectively. On the section between Taunton and Plymouth, the going got considerably tougher and, although the loading of the Kings was reduced to 360 tons unaided, this was still 45 tons better than the Castles and 70 tons up on the Stars. The Kings were the first locomotives to haul ten-coach trains up the Devon banks without assistance and, as a bit of exhibitionism, No 6001 *King Edward VII* took 400 tons up Rattery, Hemerdon and Dainton unaided on 22 July 1927. At long last, the schedule for the Cornish Riviera Express could be safely reduced to exactly four hours for the 225½ miles from Paddington to Plymouth. Apart from the main line to Plymouth, the Kings had another duty in Devon and this was on the section between Newton Abbot and Kingswear; although unquestionably a main line, the final run-in to Kingswear was only single track.

However, not everything was hunkydory with the Kings. Crews came up with stories of rough rides and excessive rolling and, at first, this baffled the locomotive department. When the bogie of No 6003 *King George IV* left the track between Reading and Newbury on 10 August 1927, it was looked on as a blessing in disguise as the train itself remained on the track and there were no casualties. The section of track was known to be in good condition and so the cause of the Kings' erratic behaviour could be narrowed down to the bogie. A thorough investigation revealed that, although the theory of the bogie was sound, in practice there was minimal leeway for either wear in the axleboxes or anything less than perfect track. The addition of coil springs to the bogies did the trick.

After its initial trials and the respringing of its bogie, No 6000 was fitted with Westinghouse brake apparatus so that it would be able to work main-line trains during its visit to America. In order to get to America, the locomotive's boiler and chassis

No 6016 *King Edward V* shows little intention of stopping at Exeter St. Davids. The train is the down Cornish Riviera Express and the date is September 1931.

Photo: E. R. Morten

had to be separated as there was not one single crane at Cardiff Docks which was able to lift the complete engine on board its ship. The transatlantic trip was to commemorate the centenary of the Baltimore & Ohio Railroad Company and the honour of leading the procession was given to No 6000 as it was representing the country in which the steam engine had originated. A second Swindon product which also appeared at the exhibition was a replica of *North Star*. This replica was of neither the 4-4-2 of 1906 nor the 4-6-0 rebuild of 1909 but of Daniel Gooch's 2-2-2 of 1837. The Centenary Exhibition lasted from 24 September to 15 October 1927 and was a great success, but it was only afterwards that the real work started. No 6000 had left an excellent impression on all who had seen it on the circular exhibition track but the curiosity was about how it would perform on the main line.

The Baltimore & Ohio did not show No 6000 any favours. For its first test run after the end of the Centenary Exhibition, the locomotive was given a 272-mile triangular trip from Baltimore to Washington, on to Philadelphia and then back to Baltimore. The load may have been only seven coaches including the dynamometer car but, because of the American penchant for sturdy construction, that train weighed in at very nearly 550 tons. Needless to say, the Old Oak Common crew of Messrs. Young and Pearce were not exactly familiar with the route or its idiosyncrasies and the locomotive was equally unfamiliar with a diet of poor-quality coal but, despite the obstacles, *King George V* performed magnificently.

An indication of the impression which the locomotive left behind in America was that, shortly after its departure, a number of the Baltimore & Ohio's locomotives appeared with copper-capped chimneys. How very Swindon! In order to commemorate its visit, No 6000 was presented with an inscribed brass bell for its buffer beam and two medals for its cab sides. The bell and the medals have remained a distinctive feature of the locomotive, apart from a few brief periods when the bell was stolen, usually as a prank.

It was February 1928 before any more Kings were built but, within less than five months, the class totalled twenty locomotives. Although the Wolverhampton run had been one of the three intended routes for the Kings, they did not appear on that line until June 1928. As soon as it was delivered from Swindon works, No 6019 *King Henry V* was allocated to Wolverhampton to become the first member of the class which saw regular rostering on Birmingham expresses. From Paddington, the loading was usually close to 500 tons but coaches were detached at both Banbury and Leamington so that the final twenty-three miles into Birmingham were often completed with less than 400 tons behind the tender. The schedule for the 110½ miles between Paddington and Birmingham was just under two hours but, although the Kings rarely had any difficulty with this timing, the lower-powered Castle class locomotives also managed it regularly.

Between May and August 1930 ten additional Kings, Nos 6020–29, were constructed at Swindon to complete the class. The celebrity status of the class was still dominated by No 6000 *King George V* and this resulted in its appearance at a variety of special events over the years. For example, in 1931, the locomotive was used to help promote the Empire Marketing Board's 'Buy British Week'.

On 9 September 1935, No 6000 was the locomotive in charge of the inaugural Bristolian which left Paddington at 10am for a two-hour run to Bristol. The train consisted of six ocean liner coaches and its introduction was timed to coincide with the GWR's centenary celebrations. There was, however, one event which had eluded the social diary of No 6000 and this was the centenary of the Lancashire & Yorkshire Railway which had been celebrated in September 1930. The GWR's representative at the L&Y's shindig had been No 6029 *King Stephen* which, at the time, was only a few weeks old. The locomotive had been stabled and serviced at Agecroft shed and this became the most northerly point to be seen by a King until 1948.

For several years, the Kings were left to perform impressive main-line work in peace but, in March 1935, No 6014 *King Henry VII* was selected as one of two subjects for the indignity of the current trend for Art Deco treatment. Similarly to No 5005 *Manorbier Castle*, the graceful lines of No 6014 were hidden underneath a bulbous smokebox cover and fairings over the cylinders, buffer beams, steam-pipes and the top of the firebox. Even the

TABLE 6.1: ORIGINAL DIMENSIONS OF THE KING CLASS LOCOMOTIVES

BUILT:	1927–1930
WEIGHTS FULL (locomotive):	89 tons 0 cwt
(tender):	46 tons 14 cwt
TENDER CAPACITY (water):	4,000 gallons
(coal):	6 tons
WHEELBASE (locomotive):	29ft 5in
WHEEL DIAMETERS (bogie):	3ft 0in
(coupled):	6ft 6in
CYLINDERS:	(4) 16¼in × 28in
BOILER PRESSURE:	250 lb/psi
HEATING SURFACES (tubes):	2007.5 sq ft
(firebox):	193.5 sq ft
(superheater):	313 sq ft
GRATE AREA:	34.3 sq ft
TRACTIVE EFFORT (at 85% boiler pressure):	40,300 lb
ROUTE AVAILABILITY:	Double Red
POWER CLASSIFICATION (GWR):	Special
(BR):	7P (8P after 31.12.1950)
SWINDON WORKS DIAGRAMS:	Z: As built
	A6: Streamlined
	A24: Four-row superheaters
	A29: ditto plus double chimneys

TABLE 6.2: KING CLASS LOCOMOTIVES

NO	NAME	BUILT	WDN	NO	NAME	BUILT	WDN
6000	*King George V*	6/27	12/62	6015	*King Richard III*	6/28	9/62
6001	*King Edward VII*	7/27	9/62	6016	*King Edward V*	6/28	9/62
6002	*King William IV*	7/27	9/62	6017	*King Edward IV*	6/28	7/62
6003	*King George IV*	7/27	6/62	6018	*King Henry VI*	6/28	12/62
6004	*King George III*	7/27	6/62	6019	*King Henry V*	7/28	9/62
6005	*King George II*	7/27	11/62	6020	*King Henry IV*	5/30	7/62
6006	*King George I*	2/28	2/62	6021	*King Richard II*	6/30	9/62
6007	*King William III*	3/28*	9/62	6022	*King Edward III*	6/30	9/62
6008	*King James II*	3/28	6/62	6023	*King Edward II*	6/30	6/62
6009	*King Charles II*	3/28	9/62	6024	*King Edward I*	6/30	6/62
6010	*King Charles I*	4/28	6/62	6025	*King Henry III*	7/30	12/62
6011	*King James I*	4/28	12/62	6026	*King John*	7/30	9/62
6012	*King Edward VI*	4/28	9/62	6027	*King Richard I*	7/30	9/62
6013	*King Henry VIII*	5/28	6/62	6028	*King Henry II***	7/30	11/62
6014	*King Henry VII*	5/28	9/62	6029	*King Stephen***	8/30	7/62

*Locomotive renewed 1936.

**Locomotives renamed:

No 6028 became *King George VI* in January 1937

No 6029 became *King Edward VIII* in May 1936

One of the GWR's few failures was in the field of streamlining. The cosmetic carbuncles were applied to No 6014 *King Henry VII* in 1935 but, thankfully, they started to be removed bit by bit after only a few months. This picture was taken at Torquay on 24 July 1936 and it shows that the cylinder and steam-pipe skirting had already been dispensed with, as had the tender cowlings. The last of the 'optional extras' such as the wedge-front cab remained until 1953. Despite the embarrassing subject matter, the picture is an excellent one of a rarely-photographed machine.

Photo: E. R. Morten

original nameplate was replaced by a straight one in the name of 'modernisation'. Mercifully, however, the removal of the tacky additions started just five months later and continued in a piecemeal fashion so that, apart from the wedge-fronted cab, the locomotive was returned to normality by 1943.

The total number of Kings in service did not exceed thirty but a thirty-first was constructed in 1936. The reason was that, on 15 January that year, No 6007 *King William III* was badly damaged in an accident at Shrivenham and the cost of repair was considered to be uneconomical. The locomotive was nominally written off but the replacement No 6007, which was added to stock on 24 March at a cost of £5,362, incorporated the boiler, frame and tender of the original. The Shrivenham accident had happened when No 6007 was at the head of the 8.40pm Penzance to Paddington sleeper. A few minutes before the train passed Shrivenham box, the signalman had accepted a coal train but, in the darkness and the mist, the poor fellow had misread the tail lamp of the coal train. Unknown to both the signalman and the crew of the King, the coal train divided and the tail section was stationary on the line when No 6007 approached at 60mph. The inevitable collision ensued and the engine driver and a passenger were killed and several other passengers and the fireman seriously injured.

In May 1936, No 6029 *King Stephen* was renamed *King Edward VIII* but, by the time the new nameplates had been cast and fitted to the locomotive, the gentleman after whom the engine was renamed had decided that monarchy wasn't really his cup of tea. Undeterred by having named a locomotive after an uncrowned monarch, the GWR did not hesitate to rename No 6028 *King Henry II* as *King George VI* when the Duke of York succeeded to the throne. The renaming took place in January 1937.

Apart from the unfortunate accident involving No 6007 in 1936, the only other major accident involving a member of the class happened at Norton Fitzwarren near Taunton on the night of 3/4 November 1940 and, tragically, it resulted in considerable loss of life. The thirteen-coach 9.50pm express from Paddington to Plymouth was being hauled by No 6028 *King George VI* and was put on the relief line at Taunton so that an overdue newspaper train could overtake. The use of the relief line by expresses was accepted practice but, on the fateful night, the driver of the express misinterpreted the audible warnings from the automatic train control apparatus in his cab and made the assumption that his train had been reinstated on the official main line when, in fact, it was still on the relief line. It was only when the newspaper train overtook that the driver of the express realised his mistake. At that moment, his train was travelling at 45mph and was almost at the point where the relief and main lines merged and, as the last van of the newspaper train passed, the express hit the trap points which protected the main line. The train was derailed and coaches were overturned across all four tracks; twenty-seven people including the fireman were killed and many others were seriously injured. It was a tragic case of human error and, when it was later revealed that the driver's house had been destroyed in an air raid the previous night, there was much public sympathy for the man who had reported for work despite being under such stress.

After the grouping of 1923, interchange trials had become all the rage and, not altogether surprisingly, these had a new lease of popularity after Nationalisation. No 6018 *King Henry VI* was one of the GWR locomotives which went walkabout and, in May 1948, it was in action on the ex-LNER line between Kings Cross and Leeds. The performance of No 6018 was satisfactory but not spectacular and, as something rather special had been anticipated from the machine but had not been delivered, the Swindon hierarchy chose to blame the untypical diet of Yorkshire coal for the lack of fireworks. The Western Region's bluff was called later the same year when the North Eastern Region insisted that another King should perform trials but with the benefit of Welsh coal. This time, the locomotive was No 6001 *King Edward VII* but the improvements in performance and economy were, embarrassingly, minimal.

The second triallist, No 6001, was one of four Kings to be painted in the experimental post-Nationalisation express livery of ultramarine with black and white lining. By the end of 1948, almost the entire class was sporting the new livery and, while blue might have been perfectly acceptable to East Anglia or mid-Scotland in pre-grouping days, the reaction in the West of England was highly disapproving. Thankfully, the alternative livery of Brunswick green soon started to be reapplied to the Kings and, by 1954, all of the class were more presentable. Of the eleven locomotive classes which were earmarked for the controversial livery, the Kings were the only GWR representatives on the list. Seven of the classes were of LNER origin, two of LMS origin and the other was the Southern's Merchant Navy 4-6-2s.

One other decree which overruled Swindon was that the practice of painting locomotive numbers on buffer beams should cease and, instead, front numberplates should be carried on smokebox doors in LMS style. The Kings were the first complete class of former- GWR locomotives to be fitted with smokebox numberplates but it made very little difference when the engines were on duty; the traditional train reporting numbers, which were carried in metal frames on the smokebox doors, totally obscured the locomotives' numbers.

All members of the class had, of course, been superheated from new but, in 1948, No 6022 *King Edward III* was fitted with a rebuilt boiler which had a high-degree superheater with a heating surface half as great again as the original superheater. The locomotive used the Somerset cut-off route for most of its trials later that year but the results were inconclusive. Although the performance showed an improvement, the difference was not significantly greater than would have been expected from a recently reboilered engine. Nevertheless, when the other members of the class became due for reboilering, they received the high-degree superheaters.

[A List of Passenger Fares is exhibited at each Station.]

105

ORDINARY AND MONTHLY TICKET FARES.

From and to LONDON (Paddington).

Ordinary Return Tickets available for 3 months are also issued.

NOTE.—The fares shewn below are liable to alteration. In cases where there is more than one route the fares given are generally by the shortest route.]

Station	Ordinary Single 1st.	Ordinary Single 3rd.	Monthly Return 1st.	Monthly Return 3rd.
Aberdare	43/3	26/1	52/5	34/11
Aberdovey	57/2	34/4	69/-	46/-
Abergavenny	40/8	24/5	49/2	32/9
Aberystwyth	59/11	36/-	72/3	48/2
Abingdon	15/7	9/5	18/11	12/7
Acton	—	0/7½	—	0/9½
Aldermaston	11/7	6/11	14/3	9/6
Ashburton	53/7	32/2	64/5	42/11
Avonmouth Dock	32/1	19/3	37/8	25/1
Aylesbury	—	5/10	—	8/-
Bala	52/7	31/6	63/6	42/4
Banbury	17/5	10/5	21/2	14/1
Bangor	61/1	36/8	73/6	49/-
Barmouth	59/5	35/7	71/8	47/9
Barnstaple	48/-	28/9	57/11	38/7
Barry	41/3	24/10	49/8	33/1
Basingstoke	12/3	7/5	14/9	9/10
Bath	27/4	16/5	33/2	22/1
Beaconsfield	—	3/5	—	4/7
Bedwyn	17/-	10/3	20/9	13/10
Bicester	13/9	8/3	16/6	11/-
Birkenhead (Woodside)	49/8	29/10	59/9	39/10
Birmingham (Snow Hill)	28/5	17/-	34/5	22/11
Bodmin	65/1	39/-	78/2	52/1
Bourne End	—	4/1	—	5/7
Bourton-on-Water	23/4	14/1	28/6	19/-
Bradford-on-Avon	24/11	15/-	30/5	20/3
Brecon	46/9	28/1	56/6	37/8
Bridgend	44/4	26/8	53/3	35/6
Bridgnorth	35/2	21/1	42/3	28/2
Bridgwater	37/10	22/8	45/6	30/4
Bridport	36/11	22/2	44/8	29/9
Bristol (Temple Meads)	30/2	18/1	36/9	24/6
Bromyard	33/-	19/10	40/-	26/8
Burnham (Bucks)	—	3/4	—	4/7
Caernarvon	63/2	38/-	76/3	50/10
Cahirciveen	—	—	—	—
Calne	24/11	15/4	30/9	20/6
Campden	24/10	14/11	29/11	19/11
Cardiff (General)	39/1	23/6	47/3	31/6
Cardigan	68/3	41/-	82/3	54/10
Carmarthen	58/5	35/-	70/3	46/10
Chard	36/8	22/1	44/-	29/4
Cheddar	32/10	19/9	43/2	28/9
Cheltenham Spa	29/3	17/7	35/6	23/8
Chepstow	35/6	21/4	42/9	28/6
Chester (General)	45/10	27/7	55/2	36/9
Chippenham	24/-	14/5	28/11	19/3
Chipping Norton	18/10	12/3	27/8	18/5
Cholsey & Moulsford	12/5	7/6	15/2	10/1
Cirencester	23/9	14/2	28/6	19/-
Clevedon	34/2	20/6	41/5	27/7
Clifton Down	31/-	18/8	36/9	24/6
Colnbrook	—	2/2	—	3/1
Compton	15/9	9/6	19/3	12/10
Cookham	—	4/1	—	5/7
Cork	—	—	—	—
Corwen	49/8	29/10	59/9	39/10
Craven Arms	39/1	23/6	47/3	31/6
Criccieth	65/6	39/3	79/-	52/8
Dartmouth	53/3	32/-	64/5	42/11
Dawlish	47/-	28/2	56/6	37/8
Denham	—	2/1	—	2/9
Devizes	22/-	13/2	26/9	17/10
Devonport	57/6	34/6	69/5	46/3
Didcot	13/9	8/3	16/6	11/-
Dolgelley	57/-	34/3	68/5	45/7
Dorchester	34/7	20/1	41/11	27/11
Droitwich Spa	29/3	17/7	35/6	23/8
Dudley	30/8	18/5	36/9	24/6
Dulverton	41/11	25/1	50/3	33/9
Ealing Broadway	—	0/8½	—	1/1
Evesham	27/4	16/5	33/2	22/1
Exeter (St. David's)	43/11	26/4	52/9	35/2
Exmouth (via Starcross)	46/8	28/-	56/-	37/4
Falmouth	73/11	44/5	89/2	59/5
Faringdon	18/1	10/10	22/-	14/8
Fenny Compton	19/8	11/9	23/11	15/11
Festiniog	57/11	34/10	69/11	46/7
Fishguard Harbour	61/3	36/9	73/6	49/-
Fowey	66/3	39/10	79/11	53/3
Frome	26/-	15/8	31/3	20/10
Gerrards Cross	—	2/8	—	3/8
Gloucester	29/3	17/7	35/6	23/8
Gobowen	43/8	26/3	52/9	35/2
Goring & Streatley	11/7	6/11	14/3	9/6
Greenford	—	0/11½	—	1/3
Hagley	31/-	18/8	37/8	25/1
Hanwell & Elthorne	—	0/11½	—	1/3
Harlech	62/-	37/3	74/11	49/11
Hartlebury	31/-	18/8	37/8	25/1
Hatton	23/11	14/5	28/11	19/3
Haverfordwest	64/4	38/7	77/2	51/5
Hayes & Harlington	—	1/4½	—	1/10
Helston	77/-	46/3	92/9	61/10
Henley-on-Thames	—	5/7	—	7/5
Hereford	36/11	22/2	44/8	29/9
Highbridge	37/1	22/3	44/8	29/9
High Wycombe	6/11	4/2	8/9	5/10
Holyhead	67/5	40/5	80/9	53/10
Hungerford	15/10	9/6	19/3	12/10
Ilfracombe	51/6	30/11	62/-	41/4
Iver	—	1/11	—	2/8
Ivybridge	54/5	32/8	65/8	43/9
Kidderminster	31/-	18/8	37/8	25/1
Kilkenny	—	—	—	—
Killarney	—	—	—	—
Kingsbridge	56/2	33/9	67/6	45/-
Kingswear	52/11	31/10	63/11	42/7
Kington	39/8	23/11	47/11	31/11
Lampeter	59/11	36/-	72/3	48/2
Langley (Bucks)	—	2/6	—	3/8
Leamington Spa	22/4	13/6	27/2	18/1
Ledbury	33/2	19/11	40/-	26/8
Leominster	36/2	21/9	43/8	29/1
Limerick	—	—	—	—
Liskeard	61/9	37/1	74/5	49/7
Lismore	—	—	—	—
Liverpool (Land'g St'ge)	50/7	30/4	60/8	40/5
Llandilo	53/1	31/11	63/11	42/7
Llandudno	57/11	34/10	69/11	46/7
Llanelly	53/1	31/11	63/11	42/7
Llangollen	47/-	28/2	56/6	37/8
Llanidloes	50/9	30/5	61/2	40/9
Looe	64/-	38/5	77/2	51/5
Loudwater	—	4/1	—	5/7
Ludlow	38/1	22/10	46/-	30/8
Lydney	34/2	20/6	41/5	27/7
Maidenhead	6/4	3/10	7/11	5/3
Maiden Newton	34/7	20/10	41/11	27/11
Malvern (Great)	31/5	18/10	38/2	25/5
Manchester	46/10	28/2	56/6	37/8
Market Drayton	40/7	24/4	48/9	32/6
Marlborough	19/5	11/8	23/6	15/8
Marlow	—	4/6	—	6/2
Marshfield	37/5	22/6	45/2	30/1
Maryborough	—	—	—	—
Melksham	24/6	14/8	29/6	19/8
Merthyr	43/3	26/1	52/5	34/11
Milford Haven	66/7	40/-	79/11	53/3
Minehead	42/11	25/9	51/6	34/4
Monmouth (Troy)	37/2	22/4	45/2	30/1
Moretonhampstead	50/6	30/4	60/8	40/5
Moreton-in-Marsh	23/6	14/1	28/6	19/-
Much Wenlock	38/6	23/1	46/5	30/11
Neath (General)	48/10	29/3	58/9	39/2
Newbury	13/9	8/3	16/6	11/-
Newent	31/11	19/1	38/8	25/9
Newport (Mon.)	36/2	21/9	43/8	29/1
Newquay	71/4	42/11	85/11	57/3
Newton Abbot	49/-	29/4	58/9	39/2
Newtown	47/8	28/7	57/6	38/4
Neyland	66/7	40/-	79/11	53/3
Oakengates	35/9	21/6	43/2	28/9
Oswestry	44/4	26/8	53/3	35/6
Oxford	16/3	9/10	19/9	13/2
Paignton	51/1	30/8	61/6	41/-
Pangbourne	10/8	6/5	12/11	8/7
Pembroke Dock	66/7	40/-	79/11	53/3
Penarth	39/10	23/11	47/11	31/11
Penmaenmawr	58/6	35/1	70/3	46/10
Penzance	77/6	46/7	93/3	62/2
Plymouth	57/6	34/6	69/5	46/3
Pontypool Road	38/4	22/11	46/5	30/11
Pontypridd	40/9	24/6	49/2	32/9
Portishead	33/1	19/11	40/-	26/8
Port Talbot (General)	47/4	28/6	57/-	38/-
Pwllheli	67/7	40/7	81/5	54/3
Radstock	28/1	16/10	34/-	22/8
Reading	9/3	5/7	11/2	7/5
Rhyl	53/6	32/2	64/5	42/11
Ross-on-Wye	33/11	20/4	40/11	27/3
Rosslare Harbour	—	—	—	—
Ruabon	45/7	27/4	55/2	36/9
Ruislip & Ickenham	—	1/10	—	2/5
St. Austell	67/2	40/4	80/9	53/10
St. Germans	59/7	35/11	71/8	47/9
St. Ives	77/1	46/3	92/9	61/10
Shepton Mallet	29/8	17/10	35/11	23/11
Shrewsbury	39/1	23/6	47/3	31/6
Slough	4/9	2/10	6/-	4/-
Soho & Winson Green	28/9	17/3	34/11	23/3
Southall	—	1/0½	—	1/6
Southampton	20/2	12/1	24/5	16/3
Southam Road	20/10	12/7	25/3	16/10
Staines	—	2/8	—	3/8
Stourbridge Town	31/1	18/8	37/8	25/1
Stourport-on-Severn	31/8	19/-	38/2	25/5
Stratford-on-Avon	23/11	14/5	28/11	19/3
Stroud	26/3	15/9	31/8	21/1
Swansea (High Street)	50/10	30/6	61/2	40/9
Swindon Junction	19/10	12/-	23/11	15/11
Taplow	—	3/6	—	4/10
Taunton	36/7	22/-	44/-	29/4
Tavistock	57/8	34/7	69/5	46/3
Teignmouth	47/9	28/8	57/6	38/4
Tenby	65/4	39/2	78/8	52/5
Tidworth	19/9	11/10	23/11	15/11
Torquay	50/7	30/4	60/8	40/5
Totnes	51/4	30/10	62/-	41/4
Trowbridge	24/6	14/8	29/6	19/8
Truro	70/11	42/7	85/6	57/-
Twyford	—	4/9	—	6/5
Uxbridge (Vine Street)	—	2/1	—	2/9
Valencia Harbour	—	—	—	—
Wadebridge	65/1	39/-	78/2	52/1
Wallingford	12/11	8/-	16/-	10/8
Warrington	46/8	28/-	56/-	37/4
Warwick	22/10	13/10	27/8	18/5
Waterford	—	—	—	—
„ (by Direct Boat	—	—	—	—
Wellington (Salop)	36/7	22/-	44/-	29/4
Wellington (Som.)	38/4	22/11	46/-	30/8
Wells	30/11	18/7	37/3	24/10
Welshpool	44/3	26/7	53/3	35/6
West Drayton	—	1/8½	—	2/3
West Ealing	—	0/9½	—	1/2
Weston-super-Mare	35/-	21/-	42/3	28/2
Weymouth	36/6	21/11	44/-	29/4
Whitchurch (Hants)	15/2	9/3	18/5	12/3
Whitland	61/3	36/9	73/6	49/-
Winchester	16/10	10/1	20/3	13/6
Windsor & Eton	—	3/5	—	4/7
Witham	27/4	16/5	33/2	22/1
Wolverhampton (L.L.)	31/6	19/-	38/2	25/5
Worcester	29/3	17/7	35/6	23/8
Wrexham	45/10	27/7	55/2	36/9
Yeovil (Pen Mill)	32/-	19/2	38/8	25/9

The cost of travel on the GWR was spelt out in the timetables and this page is taken from the summer 1943 edition. For those of you who are fortunate to be much younger than me, it should be explained that 20 shillings made one pound and 12 pence made one shilling; a shilling was equal to 5p. Thus, 43/3 (43 shillings and 3 pence) was the equivalent of £2.16p while 15/7 (15 shillings and 7 pence) was the equivalent of 78p. In those days, the word 'inflation' was something one associated only with balloons.

Immediately after Nationalisation, the Kings were selected for British Railways's experimental livery of ultramarine. Despite being a mono picture, the blatantly different tone can be seen in this shot of No 6015 *King Richard III* at Swindon shed in 1950. I make no apology for the lack of sharpness in this photograph as pictures of ultramarine Kings are rare.

Photo: D. K. Jones Collection

King class No 6022 *King Edward III* was photographed at Old Oak in August 1956, just three months after being fitted with its double chimney. The 'lion and wheel' emblem of the period is clearly defined.

Photo: Rail Archive Stephenson

EXETER, PLYMOUTH, TRURO AND PENZANCE. 35

Week Days—continued.

Station	a.m.	a.m.	a.m.	a.m.	a.m.	p.m.	p.m.	a.m.	a.m.	a.m.	a.m.	p.m.	a.m.	a.m.	a.m.	a.m.	p.m.	a.m.	p.m.	a.m.	p.m.	p.m.	p.m.
LONDON (Paddington) dep.	5 30									9 5			9 15	9 35	10 30	10 40		11 0		11 10			
Reading „	6 20								8§15	9 55			10 12	10 22									
Swindon „	7 25		7V40		7V40				9 20	10 53			11 20										
Bath „	8 19	8 27	9 27		10 5				11 0	11 34	11 43		12 10				12 24						
Bristol (Temple Meads) arr.	8 35	8 51	9 50		10 20				11 20	11 50	12 5		12 27				12 48						
BRISTOL (Temple Meads) dep.	8 50	9 0	10 15		10 35				11 25		12 15	12 22	12 45				STOP		1 5			1 22	1 25
Bedminster „		9 5	10 19						11 31		12 19	12 25	12 49										1 2[illegible]
Parson Street „		9 10	10 21						11 33			12 27	12 51										1 31
Long Ashton „																							
Flax Bourton „		9 19	10 28						11 42			12 36	1 2										1 40
Nailsea and Backwell „		9 24	10 35						11 47			12 41	1 7										1 45
Yatton „		9 30	10 41						11 55		12 36	12 48	1 22										1 51
Puxton and Worle „		9 39	10 50						12 1		12 43	12 58	1 32										STOP
Weston Milton Halt „		9 43	10 54						12 5		12 47	1 2	1 37										
Weston-super-Mare arr.		9 46	11 0						12 8		12 50	1 5	1 40									1 5[illegible]	
Weston-super-Mare dep.		9 50						11 15			12 53										1 50		
Bleadon and Uphill „		9 55						11 20													1 55		
Brean Road Halt (F) „								11 25			B										H		
Brent Knoll „		10 3						11 30			1 4										2 4		
Highbridge „		10 10						11 40			1 10										2 12		
Dunball „		10 16						11 49			1 16										2 17		
Bridgwater „	9 37	10 22			11 20			11 57			1 22								1 50		2 26		
Durston „	9 47	10 35						12 8			1 32										2 36		
Creech St. Michael Halt „								12 15													2 42		
TAUNTON arr.	10 0	10 45			11 40			12 25			1 44			12 42		1W30			2 10	2 20	2 50		
TAUNTON dep.	10 8				11 45		12 15	STOP								1W33			2 15				
Norton Fitzwarren „																							
Wellington „	10 20						12 29																
Burlescombe „							12 38																
Sampford Peverell „							12 47																
Tiverton Junction „	E						12 53																
Cullompton „							1 0																
Hele and Bradninch „							1 9																
Silverton „							1 13																
Stoke Canon „																							
EXETER St. David's arr.	10 54				12 27		1 25									2 12		2 35	2 55				
EXETER St. David's dep.	11 0			11 25	12 34	1 20									P	2 18		2 42	3 2				
EXETER St. Thomas „				11 29	12 38	1 24																	
Exminster „				11 37	12 45	1 31																	
Starcross (for Exmouth) „				11 45	12 52	1 38																	
Dawlish Warren „				11 50	12 57	1 43																	
Dawlish „				11 54	1 2	1 47										2 37							
Teignmouth „	11 25			12 2	1 10	1 55										2 45							
Newton Abbot arr.	11 36			12 12	1 20	2 5										2 55			3 30				
Torquay arr.	12 44			12 44	1 52	2 31										3 18			4 1				
Newton Abbot dep.	11 44			12 20	1 28														3 35				
Totnes „	12 4			12 37	1 48																		
Brent „	12 22			12 52														3 45	4 10				
Wrangaton „				12 57																			
Bittaford Platform „				1 1																			
Ivybridge „				1 6																			
Cornwood „				1 11																			
Plympton „				1 19																			
PLYMOUTH (North Road) arr.	12 45			1 26	2 26										3 25		p.m.	4 10	4 35				p.m.
PLYMOUTH (North Road) dep.	12 55														3 30		3 40	4 20	4 45				5 20
Devonport „	1 0																3 44		4 49				5 24
Dockyard Halt „																							
Ford Halt „																							
Keyham „																	3 48						5 27
St. Budeaux Platform „																	3 52						5 30
Saltash „	1 7																3 57						5 35
St. Germans „	1 19																4 6						5 44
Menheniot „	1 31																4 17						5 55
Liskeard „	1 40														4 1		4 25	4 50	5 19				6 3
Doublebois „	1 48																4 33						6 11
Bodmin Road „	1 59																4 43	5 8	5 36				6 21
Lostwithiel „	2 6																4 50	5 15	5 43				6 30
Par „	2 17														4Y30		5 0	5 25	5 55				6 40
Newquay arr.	3 21														5L37		6Q40	6 40	7 12				
St. Austell dep.	2 28														4 40		5 11		6 6				6 53
Grampound Road „	2 40																5 24		6 20				7 5
Probus & Ladock Platform „	2 45																5 30						
Truro arr.	2 53														5 5		5 40		6 32				7 17
Falmouth arr.	3 49							p.m.							5 50				7 14				8 10
Truro dep.	3 0							4 25							5 8		5 45		6 40				
Chacewater „	3 12							4 36									5 56		6 50				
Scorrier „	3 17							4 41									6 1		6 55				
Redruth „	3 23							4 46							5 26		6 6		7 1				
Carn Brea „	3 27							4 50									6 10						
Camborne „	3 33							4 54									6 14		7 10				
Gwinear Road „	3 39							4 59							5 38		6 19		7 16				
Hayle „	3 47							5 6									6 26		7 24				
St. Erth „	3 52							5 10							5 50		6 31		7 29				
St. Ives arr.	4 15							5 30							6 25		6 50		7 55				
Marazion dep.	4 1							5 20									6 39		7 38				
PENZANCE arr.	4 5							5 25							6 0		6 44		7 45				
Notes			For continuation see Weston-super Mare dep. 11.15 a.m.			Saturdays only.					Saturdays only.	Saturdays only.		Via Westbury. Saturdays only, and runs June 26th to September 4th (inclusive) only. Through Carriages London to Minehead.	Via Castle Cary. Restaurant Car to Penzance.	Via Castle Cary. Restaurant Car to Kingswear.		Via Castle Cary. Saturdays only, and runs June 26th to September 4th (inclusive) only. Through Train to Newquay.		Via Castle Cary. Saturdays only, and runs June 28th to October 2nd (inclusive) only. Through Carriages London to Minehead.		Saturdays only.	

For complete service between Plympton, Plymouth and Saltash, see page 49.

In this extract from the GWR public timetable for May 1943, the 10.30am Paddington to Penzance is conspicuous by having lost its title of the Cornish Riviera Express. During the 1940s, the Kings predominated on the fastest and heaviest trains to the South-West.

On 15 July 1950, two members of the class were in the news. For an awayday to Exeter, the King and Queen travelled in the royal train which, due to the unavailability of No 6028 was hauled by No 6021 *King Richard II*. Also in the West Country, No 6027 *King Richard I* was involved in a minor accident that day when, at the head of the second portion of the Cornish Riviera Express, it struck a farm tractor which had broken down on a level crossing near Westbury, Wiltshire. No real damage resulted and there was no likelihood of injuries whatsoever, but the incident received considerable media coverage because one of the train's passengers was Winston Churchill who was en route to Plymouth to chair a conference on safety.

On 1 January 1951, the Kings received the British Railways power classification 8P. Because of their 'Double Red' restriction, they had never strayed from the trunk routes for which they had originally been built. However, piecemeal upgrading of the Welsh Border route had been undertaken over the years and, by 1951, that route was pronounced capable of accepting the Kings. The first of the class to work through the Severn Tunnel was the celebrity No 6000.

In an attempt to improve the draughting of the Kings, No 6001 *King Edward VII* was fitted with a smaller diameter blastpipe and, correspondingly, its original chimney liner was replaced by a longer, narrower one. Tests were undertaken both at work and on the rolling road test rig at Swindon and, on showing a marked improvement in steaming, almost all of the class was similarly treated. The new draughting system had been fitted to No 6001 in October 1952 and, in July the following year, the locomotive performed a remarkable feat under test conditions when it hauled a twenty-five coach train between Stoke Gifford and Reading at an average speed of 60mph. Not bad for an 800 ton loading!

In 1954, the Bristolian was reintroduced and, naturally, the locomotives which were earmarked for the train were the Kings. In preparation for the reappearance of the named train, No 6003 *King George IV* was tested on dynamometer runs and the engine confirmed that the proposed 105-minute schedule could be handled comfortably. The relative ease of hauling the Bristolian was reflected in 1955 when No 6018 *King Henry VI* was in charge of the train and became the first of the class to top the 100 mph mark. Despite their fine work, the Kings were soon ousted from Bristolian duties by the Castles but this was simply because the train's loadings were rarely in excess of nine coaches and it was felt that the Kings were being wasted on the duty. The Cornish Riviera Express was one of the heavier turns which needed the Kings more than the Bristolian and when No 6015 *King Richard III* was in charge of a Riviera early in 1956, it notched up 109mph on Lavington Bank, east of Westbury.

After the wear and tear of a few years' service had taken its toll on the draughting arrangements, it was discovered that the increased exhaust pressures were resulting in a loss of power. In order to overcome this, the idea of a double chimney was mooted and, in September 1955, No 6015 *King Richard III* was fitted with the experimental device. This solved the problem and all of the Kings received double chimneys by early 1958. However, the exhaust was not the only problem to be encountered by the Kings in the mid-1950s. Early in 1956, several members of the class suffered bogie failures and this set the alarm bells ringing at Swindon to such an extent that all but three of the class were abruptly taken out of service. It was discovered that many of the bogies were suffering from weld failures and, after more extensive inspections, several main axles were found to be showing signs of imminent fractures. The offending bogies and axles were all repaired and the locomotives were returned to service.

Although sets of Timken roller bearings had been ordered with the intention of modifying the axles and bogies of the Kings, they were not fitted. The last modification to be carried out to the class remained the fitting of the double chimneys. By 1958, the construction of diesel-hydraulic locomotives was underway and the decree from Swindon was that any significant modifications to main-line steam locomotives should be suspended. Swindon made no secret of the fact that the new diesels were intended for the fastest services on the high-profile routes which had previously been the preserve of the Kings. As the Kings were too heavy to be transferred to secondary routes, even the most hardened optimist must have been aware that the days of these great locomotives were numbered.

58 PENZANCE, TRURO, PLYMOUTH, EXETER, TAUNTON,

Week Days—continued.

For Through Train Service from Penzance, Plymouth, and Torquay to Birmingham (G.W.) and Wolverhampton, via Stratford-on-Avon, see page 132.

Station	p.m.	p.m.		p.m.	p.m.	noon	a.m.		p.m.	p.m.	p.m.	p.m.	p.m.	p.m.	p.m.	a.m.		p.m.	p.m.	a.m.	p.m.	p.m.	p.m.
				Saturdays only.			Restaurant Car Train. "CORNISH RIVIERA EXPRESS." Via Castle Cary.					Through Train Plymouth to Liverpool (Lime Street). (See page 131.)			Through Carriages Paignton and Torquay to Birmingham (G.W.) and Wolverhampton. (a) (Forward from Exeter at 2.57 p.m.)	Restaurant Car Train.	Through Train Penzance and Plymouth to Birmingham (G.W.) and Wolverhampton. (See page 132).		Through Carriages Kingswear and Torquay to London. (Forward from Exeter at 3.30 p.m.)	Restaurant Car Train. Via Westbury.	Restaurant Car Train.		
PENZANCE dep.							9 45									10 40				11 5			
Marazion "																				11 9			
St. Ives dep.							9 20									10 25				10 25			
St. Erth dep.							9 55									10 50				11 18			
Hayle "																10 54							
Gwinear Road "							10 8									11 3							
Camborne "																11 9				11 35			
Carn Brea "																							
Redruth "																11 18				11 44			
Scorrier "																							
Chacewater "																11 27							
Truro arr.							10 33									11 37				12 1			
Falmouth dep.							9 55									11 0				11 0			
Truro dep.							10 38									11 42				12 5			
Probus & Ladock P'form "																							
Grampound Road "																							
St. Austell "																12 8				12 31			
Newquay dep.							10 10									11 15				11 15			
Par dep.							11 10									12 17				12 40			
Lostwithiel "																12 27				12 52			
Bodmin Road "																12 37							
Doublebois "														S 12 30									
Liskeard "																12 58				1 17			
Menheniot "														12 45									
St. Germans "														12 55									
Saltash "														1 8									
St. Budeaux Platform "														1 12									
Keyham "														1 15									
Ford Halt "																							
Dockyard Halt "														1 18									
Devonport "														1 20									
PLYMOUTH (North Road) arr.							12 7							1 24		1 30				1 48			
PLYMOUTH (North Road) dep.							12 15				12 25	1 0				1 35				1 55			
Plympton "											12 35												
Cornwood "											12 47												
Ivybridge "											12 52												
Bittaford Platform "											12 57												
Wrangaton "											1 1												
Brent "											1 6												
Totnes "											1 20												
Newton Abbot arr.											1 38	1 50								2 50			
Torquay dep.						12 0				12 51		12 51			1 44				2 17				
Newton Abbot dep.						12 35				1 20		1 55			2 4				2 35	2 55			
Teignmouth "						12 45				1 30					2 14				2 48				
Dawlish "						12 52				1 38					2 22				2 56				
Dawlish Warren "						12 56				1 44													
Starcross (for Exmouth) "						1 2				1 48													
Exminster "						1 8				1 55													
EXETER St. Thomas "						1 15				2 2													
EXETER St. David's arr.						1 20	1 35			2 8		2 25			2 40	2 50			3 15	3 25			
EXETER St. David's dep.	1 0						1 38					2 30				2 57		S 3 5		3 30			
Stoke Canon "	1 6																	3 11					
Silverton "	1 13																	3 18					
Hele and Bradninch "	1 17																	3 23					
Cullompton "	1 25																	3 31					
Tiverton Junction "	1 31																	3 38					
Sampford Peverell "	1 36																	STOP					
Burlescombe "	1 42																						
Wellington "	1 52																						
Norton Fitzwarren "	2 1																						
TAUNTON arr.	2 8											3 10				3 37				4 10			
TAUNTON dep.									2 25			3 15				3 40				4 15			
Creech St. Michael Halt "									2 30														
Durston "									2 35														
Bridgwater "									2 46			3 33											
Dunball "									2 52														
Highbridge "									3 0														
Brent Knoll "									3 10														
Brean Road Halt (F) "									3 20														
Bleadon and Uphill "									3 24														
Weston-super-Mare arr.									3 28														
Weston-super-Mare dep.				2 35					3 33												4 35		
Weston Milton Halt "				2 39					3 36														
Puxton and Worle "				2 44																			
Yatton "		2 40		2 52					3 48												4 47	5 10	
Nailsea and Backwell "		2 47		3 0					3 55													5 17	
Flax Bourton "		2 51		3 5																		5 21	
Long Ashton "																							
Parson Street "		2 58		3 12																		5 29	
Bedminster "		3 1		3 16																		5 32	
BRISTOL (T. Meads) arr.		3 5		3 20					4 16			4 18				4 35					5 12	5 36	
Bristol (Temple Meads) dep					3 55								4 32					p.m. 5 3			5 25		5 50
Bath arr					4 20								4 57					5 18			5 43		6 17
Swindon "					5D55																6 33		7L21
Reading "																				6 30	7 28		
LONDON (Padd.) "							5 0													7 20	8 15		

After the War, the naming of trains was reintroduced. This page from the GWR's public timetable for autumn 1947 shows that the Cornish Riviera Express now stops at Exeter.

Despite the official withdrawal of all of the King class locomotives in 1962, No 6018 *King Henry VI* was removed from storage and was steamed again on 28 April 1963 in order to haul an SLS special. This picture was taken at Swindon shed while the locomotive was taking refreshment in preparation for the final leg of the journey back to Birmingham.

Photo: P. Chancellor

Table 152— *continued*

LONDON, OXFORD, BANBURY, LEAMINGTON SPA, STRATFORD-UPON-AVON, BIRMINGHAM, WOLVERHAMPTON, SHREWSBURY and CHESTER

Week Days—*continued*

Station		1	2	3	4	5	6	7	8	9
		am	am	pm	am	am	am	am	am	pm
PADDINGTON	dep	9 10			8z 0		9d15		10 10	
High Wycombe		9 46				9 23				
Princes Risborough						9 45				
Ilmer Halt										
Haddenham (Bucks)										
Dorton Halt										
Brill and Ludgershall										
Bicester North AA	arr	10 20								
	dep	10 21								
Ardley										
Aynho Park Platform										
63 Bournemouth Central	dep						6 32	8 5		
63 Portsmouth and Southsea								7 29		
63 Southampton Central							7 47	8 56		
63 Basingstoke							9N 2	9 48		
61 Reading General					9 10		10d 0			
61 Bristol (Temple Meads) 169										
62 Weymouth Town										
61 Swindon					8 50					
Didcot	dep				9 50		10 30			
Appleford Halt										
Culham										
Radley					10 2					
Oxford	arr				1011	1037	10 45	1054		
	dep				1014			1056		
Kidlington, for Blenheim					1023					
Bletchington					1029					
Tackley Halt					1033					
Heyford					1039					
Fritwell and Somerton					1045					
Aynho, for Deddington					1050					
King's Sutton					1056					
Banbury General	arr	10 40			11 2				11 22	
	dep	10 42							11 23	
Cropredy										
Fenny Compton										
Southam Road and Harbury										
Leamington Spa General	arr	11 7								
	dep	11 10	1120							
179 Stratford-upon-Avon	arr		1153							
	dep	10N52								
Birmingham (Snow Hill)	arr	11 40							12 10	
	dep	11 45							12 14	
Wolverhampton (Low Level)	arr	12 4							12 33	
	dep	12 1[illegible]		1230					12 40	1250
Dunstall Park				1233						1253
Birches and Bilbrook Halt				1238						1258
Codsall				1241						1 1
Albrighton				1247						1 7
Cosford				1251						1 11
Shifnal				1257						1 17
Oakengates West				1 7						1 27
New Hadley Halt				1 10						1 30
Wellington		12 37		1 15						1 35
159 Crewe	arr									
159 Manchester (London Rd.)										Stop
Notes		RC Paddington to Shrewsbury. TC Paddington to Stratford-upon-Avon, arr 11 53 am. TC Paddington to Birkenhead	TC Paddington (dep 9 10 am) to Stratford-upon-Avon	Saturdays only	Except Saturdays	Via Thame (Table 60)	Except Saturdays. RC Paddington to Didcot	Runs 16th July to 27th August inclusive. Saturdays only. RC and TC Bournemouth (Cen.) to Newcastle (Table 39)	Except Saturdays Via Bicester North. CAMBRIAN COAST EXPRESS. RC and TC Paddington to Aberystwyth	Except Saturdays

Station		10	11	12	13	14	15	16	17
		am ③	am ③	am	pm	am	am	am	am
PADDINGTON	dep	9L10	9L10	9 45		9d15	9d15	9 45	
High Wycombe		9 58	9 58						
Princes Risborough		1017	1017						
Ilmer Halt		1023	1023						
Haddenham (Bucks)		1029	1029						
Dorton Halt		1038	1038						
Brill and Ludgershall		1044	1044						
Bicester North AA	arr	1055	1055						
	dep	11 0	1114						
Ardley		1110	1123						
Aynho Park Platform		1119	1132						
63 Bournemouth Central	dep			7 30				7 30	8 40
63 Portsmouth and Southsea				7 29				7 29	8 50
63 Southampton Central				8 25		7T32		8 25	9 15
63 Basingstoke				9 40				9 40	1030
61 Reading General				1023		10 4	10 8	1033	
61 Bristol (Temple Meads) 169									
62 Weymouth Town									
61 Swindon							10b8		
Didcot	dep					1038	1047		
Appleford Halt						1044	1053		
Culham						1047	1057		
Radley						1053	11 4		
Oxford	arr			1057		11 2	1113	1115	
	dep						1118		
Kidlington, for Blenheim									
Bletchington									
Tackley Halt									
Heyford									
Fritwell and Somerton									
Aynho, for Deddington									
King's Sutton		1124	1137						
Banbury General	arr	1131	1144				1150		12 2
	dep						1152		12 5
Cropredy			Stop						
Fenny Compton									
Southam Road and Harbury									
Leamington Spa General	arr						1218		1229
	dep						1221		1232
179 Stratford-upon-Avon	arr								
	dep								
Birmingham (Snow Hill)	arr						1 0		1 5
	dep				1230				
Wolverhampton (Low Level)	arr				1 4				
	dep				1 12				
Dunstall Park					1 15				
Birches and Bilbrook Halt					1 20				
Codsall					1 23				
Albrighton					1 29				
Cosford					1 33				
Shifnal					1 39				
Oakengates West					1 48				
New Hadley Halt			pm		1 50				
Wellington			1 45		1 56				
159 Crewe	arr								
159 Manchester (London Rd.)									
Notes		Saturdays only	Except Saturdays	Except Saturdays. RC Paddington to Oxford	Saturdays only	Saturdays only. RC Paddington to Didcot	Except Saturdays. RC Paddington to Didcot	Saturdays only. RC Paddington to Oxford	TC Portsmouth & S. to Birmingham. Saturdays only. Runs 23rd July to 20th Aug. incl.

Station		18	19	20	21	22	23	24	25
		am	am	am	am	am	pm	am	am
PADDINGTON	dep	11 10	10 50	10 0		1110		9z45	
High Wycombe									
Princes Risborough									
Ilmer Halt									
Haddenham (Bucks)									
Dorton Halt									
Brill and Ludgershall									
Bicester North AA	arr								
	dep								
Ardley									
Aynho Park Platform									
63 Bournemouth Central	dep							7 30	8 40
63 Portsmouth and Southsea								7 29	9 15
63 Southampton Central								8 25	9 15
63 Basingstoke								9 40	1045
61 Reading General				1050				1040	
61 Bristol (Temple Meads) 169					9 35			9 35	
62 Weymouth Town									
61 Swindon				1020	11 5			1045	
Didcot	dep			1122				1125	
Appleford Halt								1130	
Culham								1134	
Radley								1140	
Oxford	arr			1140	1150			1150	12 0
	dep			1145	1153				12 5
Kidlington, for Blenheim									
Bletchington									
Tackley Halt									
Heyford				12 4					
Fritwell and Somerton									
Aynho, for Deddington									
King's Sutton									
Banbury General	arr		12 11	1219	1225	1232			1240
	dep		12 14	1221	1229	1235			1244
Cropredy									
Fenny Compton									
Southam Road and Harbury									
Leamington Spa General	arr	12 40	12 39	1248		1 0			1 10
	dep	12 42	12 42	1250		1 3			1 14
179 Stratford-upon-Avon	arr	1 38							
	dep	11 55							
Birmingham (Snow Hill)	arr	1 10	1 16	1 24		1 37			1 48
	dep	1 14	1 19	1 28		1 42	1E30		1 54
Wolverhampton (Low Level)	arr	1 34	1 39	1 49		2 2	2E 4		2 28
	dep	1 40	1 45			2 7	2 15		
Dunstall Park							2 18		
Birches and Bilbrook Halt							2 23		
Codsall							2 26		
Albrighton							2 31		
Cosford							2 35		
Shifnal							2 41		
Oakengates West					Stop		2 50		
New Hadley Halt							2 53		
Wellington		2 7				2 35	2 58		
159 Crewe	arr	3k38				4 6			
159 Manchester (London Rd.)		4k35				5 30			
Notes		Except Saturdays Via Bicester North. RC and TC Paddington to Birkenhead	Saturdays only Via Bicester North. CAMBRIAN COAST EXPRESS. RC Paddington to Aberystwyth	Sats. only TC Paddington to Wolverhampton	Saturdays only. Runs 9th July to 27th August inclusive. TC Swindon to Sheffield (Vic.) arr 3 25 pm (Table 38)	Saturdays only Via Bicester North. RC and TC Paddington to Birkenhead		Except Saturdays. RC Paddington to Reading General	Saturdays only Commences 2nd July. TC from Portsmouth H. dep. 9 11 am (Table 40)

Station		26	27	28	29	30	31	32	33	34
		am	pm	am	am	pm	pm	pm	am	pm
PADDINGTON	dep	10d 0							10 25	
High Wycombe				1052						
Princes Risborough				1120						
Ilmer Halt										
Haddenham (Bucks)										
Dorton Halt										
Brill and Ludgershall										
Bicester North AA	arr									
	dep									
Ardley										
Aynho Park Platform										
63 Bournemouth Central	dep	7 30								
63 Portsmouth and Southsea		7 29								
63 Southampton Central		8 25								
63 Basingstoke		9 40								
61 Reading General		11 5							11 33	
61 Bristol (Temple Meads) 169		9 35								
62 Weymouth Town					9 25					
61 Swindon		10 50	11a20							
Didcot	dep	11 46							12p 5	
Appleford Halt		11 53							12 9	
Culham		11 57							12 13	
Radley		12 3							12 20	
Oxford	arr	12 12	12‡15	1222					12 30	
	dep		12‡20					1225		
Kidlington, for Blenheim				Stop				1234		
Bletchington								1239		
Tackley Halt								1243		
Heyford								1249		
Fritwell and Somerton								1255		
Aynho, for Deddington								1 0		
King's Sutton								1 6		
Banbury General	arr		12 51		1 2	1 9		1 12		
	dep		12 58		1 4	1 11				
Cropredy										
Fenny Compton										
Southam Road and Harbury										
Leamington Spa General	arr				1 30	1 39				
	dep			pm	1 33	1 41	1N47			
179 Stratford-upon-Avon	arr			1 27			2N20			
	dep			1 30						
Birmingham (Snow Hill)	arr			2 9	2 3	2 15				
	dep				2 8					
Wolverhampton (Low Level)	arr				2 34					
	dep									
Dunstall Park										
Birches and Bilbrook Halt										
Codsall										
Albrighton										
Cosford										
Shifnal										
Oakengates West										
New Hadley Halt										
Wellington										
159 Crewe	arr									
159 Manchester (London Rd.)										
Notes		Saturdays only	Mondays, Fridays and Saturdays only. To Newcastle on Fridays. TC Swansea to York (Table 38) RC on Fridays and Saturdays	Via Thame (Table 60). TC Swansea (dep 9 35 am) to Birmingham (Table 169)	Saturdays only Runs 25th June to 3rd Sept. incl. TC Weymouth Town to Wolverhampton	TC Margate dep 8 55 am to Birmingham (Table 41). Saturdays only. Runs 2nd July to 27th August incl.	Saturdays only	Except Saturdays	Except Saturdays	Saturdays only. Runs 2nd July to 10th September inclusive. TC Cardiff dep 12 38 pm to Manchester (Ex.) (Tables 164 and 168)

By the mid-1950s, the traditional two-hour expresses to Birmingham often continued to Wolverhampton or beyond. This page is from the Western Region public timetable for summer 1955 and, as far as Wolverhampton, the Kings and Castles shared the duties.

Ironically, it was only just over a year before Swindon's revision of plans for the future that No 6000 had performed yet another special duty: on 28 January 1957, the locomotive was in charge of the inaugural Royal Duchy express.

By 1960, diesels had started to commandeer West of England services and some of the displaced Kings were transferred to duties through the big hole under the Severn to Cardiff. In October 1960, No 6019 *King Henry V* became the first of the class ever to be allocated to Canton shed and, by the end of the following year, five more Kings were resident at Canton with their star turn being the Red Dragon. One of the Canton contingent was No 6018 *King Henry VI* and, in tandem with *King George V*, it worked the royal train to the opening of the Spencer steel works at Newport on 26 March 1962. By then, No 6006 *King George I* had already been withdrawn and the massacre of the other twenty-nine Kings was started in July 1962 and completed five months later.

In their final months, the Kings became sought-after engines for a countless number of enthusiasts specials and were always willing to prove that they were far from ready for the torch. No 6002 *King William IV* spent early September 1962 as an exhibit at Snow Hill station in Birmingham but, when a diesel failed en route to Wolverhampton, No 6002 stepped into the breach without a grumble. After four months in Swindon's scrap siding, No 6018 *King Henry VI* was steamed again on 28 April 1963 for use on a Stephenson Locomotive Society special and, despite its lay-off, the engine clocked up speeds in excess of 90mph on the run. The trip was from Birmingham to Southall, on to Swindon and then back to Birmingham — all for a fare of 30s6d (£1.52½)!

When the Kings were withdrawn, ten had come within 100,000 miles of the magic two million mark. They were Nos 6000/01/03/04/09/10/12/13 15/19 and, of these, No 6013 *King Henry VIII* claimed the record with a grand total of 1,950,462 miles on the clock. Three of the Kings escaped cutting up and, predictably, the first to be saved

A heavy loading seemed to make no difference to No 6010 *King Charles I* as it cruises effortlessly with an express working near Reading on 2 July 1952.

Photo: D. K. Jones Collection

TABLE 6.3: SHED ALLOCATIONS OF KING CLASS LOCOMOTIVES

LOCO	FIRST	1/32	1/36	1/40	1/44	1/48	1/52	1/56	1/60	1/62	LAST
6000	OOC	OOC	OOC	SDN	PLY	PLY	BRS	OOC	OOC	OOC	OOC
6001	OOC	OOC	OOC	OOC	OOC	OOC	OOC	WOL	WOL	WOL	WOL
6002	PLY	PLY	PLY	EXE	PLY	PLY	OOC	OOC	OOC	PLY	WOL
6003	OOC	OOC	OOC	OOC	OOC	OOC	OOC	OOC	OOC	CDF	CDF
6004	PLY	PLY	PLY	PLY	PLY	PLY	WOL	PLY	OOC	OOC	OOC
6005	OOC	WOL	WOL	WOL	WOL	WOL	WOL	WOL	WOL	WOL	OOC
6006	PLY	WOL	WOL	WOL	WOL	WOL	WOL	WOL	WOL	WOL	WOL
6007	OOC	OOC	OOC	OOC	OOC	OOC	OOC	OOC	WOL	WOL	WOL
6008	PLY	WOL	WOL	WOL	WOL	WOL	WOL	PLY	WOL	WOL	WOL
6009	OOC	OOC	OOC	OOC	OOC	OOC	OOC	OOC	OOC	OOC	OOC
6010	PLY	OOC	PLY	PLY	PLY	PLY	PLY	PLY	OOC	CDF	CDF
6011	OOC	OOC	OOC	BRS	PLY	WOL	WOL	WOL	WOL	WOL	OOC
6012	NTA	PLY	PLY	PLY	PLY	PLY	PLY	OOC	OOC	OOC	WOL
6013	OOC	OOC	OOC	OOC	OOC	OOC	OOC	OOC	PLY	WOL	WOL
6014	NTA	WOL	OOC	OOC	OOC	OOC	OOC	WOL	WOL	WOL	WOL
6015	OOC	OOC	OOC	OOC	OOC	OOC	OOC	OOC	OOC	OOC	WOL
6016	PLY	PLY	PLY	PLY	PLY	PLY	PLY	OOC	PLY	PLY	WOL
6017	OOC	WOL	WOL	BRS	PLY	PLY	OOC	OOC	WOL	WOL	WOL
6018	PLY	NTA	NTA	NTA	NTA	NTA	OOC	OOC	OOC	CDF	CDF
6019	WOL	WOL	PLY	PLY	PLY	PLY	OOC	OOC	OOC	CDF	WOL
6020	PLY	PLY	PLY	PLY	PLY	PLY	WOL	WOL	WOL	WOL	WOL
6021	OOC	OOC	OOC	OOC	OOC	OOC	OOC	OOC	OOC	OOC	OOC
6022	PLY	PLY	PLY	PLY	PLY	PLY	PLY	OOC	WOL	WOL	WOL
6023	NTA	NTA	NTA	NTA	NTA	NTA	PLY	PLY	OOC	OOC	OOC
6024	PLY	PLY	NTA	NTA	NTA	PLY	PLY	OOC	OOC	CDF	CDF
6025	OOC	OOC	OOC	OOC	OOC	PLY	PLY	PLY	OOC	OOC	OOC
6026	OOC	OOC	WOL	BRS	PLY	PLY	PLY	PLY	PLY	OOC	OOC
6027	OOC	OOC	OOC	OOC	OOC	NTA	PLY	PLY	OOC	WOL	WOL
6028	OOC	OOC	OOC	OOC	OOC	OOC	OOC	OOC	OOC	CDF	CDF
6029	OOC	OOC	OOC	PLY	PLY	PLY	PLY	PLY	OOC	OOC	OOC

ABBREVIATIONS:
BRS: Bristol (Bath Rd); CDF: Cardiff (Canton); EXE: Exeter;
NTA: Newton Abbot; OOC: Old Oak Common; PLY: Plymouth (Laira);
SDN: Swindon; WOL: Wolverhampton (Stafford Rd);

OTHER SHEDS TO WHICH KINGS WERE ALLOCATED:
AYLESBURY: No 6015 from 5/1947 to 7/1947.
READING: No 6026 from 8/1930 to 10/1930.
TAUNTON: No 6013 during 5/1930 only.

was No 6000 *King George V*. After Swindon Railway Museum had rejected No 6000 due to reasons of space, Messrs. H.P. Bulmer Ltd. of Hereford bought the engine and a rake of five Pullman coaches in 1968 with the intention of using the ensemble as a mobile promotional department. No 6000 was

The commendably tidy way in which the destination code has been chalked on the smokebox of No 6002 *King William IV* is quite in keeping with the locomotive's lofty status. This picture shows the engine passing Plymouth Laira with an up express on 16 July 1953.

Photo: E. R. Morten

restored to main-line standards by Messrs. A.R. Adams of Newport and arrived at Hereford on 30 October 1968. Three years later, it was given the go-ahead by British Rail for work on the main line, so inaugurating an era of main-line steam working which continues to this day. The other two members of the class which survive are No 6023 *King Edward II* and No 6024 *King Edward I*, both of which are based at Didcot. The latter is currently the only one of the preserved Kings which has main-line authorisation from British Rail. No 6023 is in the early stages of a long-term restoration, while No 6000 is in store at Swindon awaiting the funding to allow an overhaul to commence.

The Kings represented the final stage in the development of the GWR's express passenger locomotives and were, undoubtedly, the best engines of their type ever to emerge from Swindon works. Their lives were not, however, quite as long as some of their contemporaries, but this is in no way a reflection of their capabilities as even locomotives of this calibre could not outwit British Railway's insistence on total conversion to diesel traction.

Bibliography

Several publications have been consulted during the preparation of this book and they include:

An Outline of Great Western Locomotive Practice 1837–1947. Holcroft. Ian Allan.

British Locomotive Catalogue 1825–1923. Baxter. Moorland Publishing.

Great Locomotives of the GWR. Nock. PSL.

Great Western Railway Locomotive Allocations. Harrison/Pocock. Wild Swan.

Great Western Saint Class 4-6-0. Nock. PSL.

History of the Great Western Railway. MacDermot/Clinker/Nock. Ian Allan.

Kings of the Great Western Railway. Coffin. 6000 Locomotive Association.

Locomotives of the Great Western Railway. RCTS.

Locomotives of the LNER. RCTS.

Pictorial Record of Great Western Engines. Russell. OPC.

Preserved Locomotives of British Railways. Fox/Webster. Platform Five.

The British Steam Railway Locomotive 1825–1925. Ahrons. LPC.

The British Steam Railway Locomotive 1925–1965. Nock. Ian Allan.

Assorted Public and Working Timetables.

A wealth of information has been gleaned from a collection of railway periodicals, both old and new. These include:

Steam Classic, Great Western Echo, Railways, Railway World, Railway Magazine, Trains Illustrated, Mole Husbandry for Engine Drivers.